SPOONING WITH
ROSIE

SPOONING WITH ROSIE

FOOD, FRIENDSHIP & KITCHEN LOVING

Rosie Lovell

FOURTH ESTATE • *London*

First published in Great Britain by
Fourth Estate
A division of HarperCollinsPublishers
77–85 Fulham Palace Road
London W6 8JB

www.4thestate.co.uk
Love this book? www.bookarmy.com

10 9 8 7 6 5 4 3 2 1

A catalogue record for this book is available from the British Library

ISBN 13 978-0-00-728517-4

Map reproduced on page x copyright © www.collinsbartholomew.com
Recipes for Puff Pastry Pie on page 98, Chicken Pieces with Oranges & Honey and Chicken Pieces with Creamy Lemon
on pages 100–101 inspired by Nigel Slater

Design by Ed Grace
www.edgrace.co.uk
Typeset in Avenir and Minion by Envy Design Ltd
Printed and bound in Great Britain by Butler Tanner and Dennis Ltd, Frome, Somerset

Rosie Lovell is the fresh new face of city cooking. Five years ago Rosie opened her deli, Rosie's Deli Café, in the heart of Brixton market. It has become an intimate place where food, music and people from all over the world tumble into one place on Electric Avenue.

Spooning with Rosie teems with favourite recipes and stories from Rosie's life: meals encountered on her travels, in the deli and at home. Food that depends on who you are with, how you are feeling and what's in the fridge.

There are recipes for the dawn chorus: food for the first wave of a hangover, or just to start the day with a bang. Simple suppers from warm roasted chicken with lemons to squid ink spaghetti, finished off with affogato. Or individual dishes of soulful grub to comfort and soothe; menus for clandestine dates to fall in love over; balmy bites for the sunshine and feasting fiestas for flocks of hungry friends.

Feisty and fresh, *Spooning with Rosie* is a book about food, friendship and the joy of good food shared together.

To Raf – the harshest critic and the hungriest companion

CONTENTS

INTRODUCTION

Another late night in Soho at the New Evaristo Club. Now, as usual, my alarm is pounding at me, calling me to the deli. Showered and squeezed into trusty jeans, I dash out of the door of my damp 1930s flat. Round on the main road I pass Simon, one of the more amenable local down-and-outs. 'All right, Ma'am.' He'll be in later for his hot chocolate with five sugars. I nip into the Portuguese deli to pick up fresh rocket for the shop, and then into the Iraqi supermarket to buy free-range eggs for the scrambling rush later. Electric Avenue is particularly alive at this time of the morning, with sex workers, red snappers, pig's tails and pulsing beats coming from every crevice. The fishmongers holler at me and, laden with my shopping, I nod my good-mornings to market traders and road sweeps.

Arriving at the deli, I fling the door wide open, turn the fans on and get The View playing, to beat out my tired head. Pastry out of the fridge for rolling, cakes onto the stands, tables and chairs outside, oven on, flick lights. The daily cheese and bread deliveries arrive – Sardinian Pecorino, Taleggio, Mrs Kirkham's Lancashire, Hereford Hop, sourdough, rye, ciabatta – just as I'm making myself a double-shot cappuccino to drink in the last bit of peace on my doorstep.

Brixtonians rush past on their way to the tube, with cheery waves. My moment is broken by the first telephone call of the morning – Alice. 'What shall I cook for my date tonight?' (She's excited, so I'm thinking risotto with black pudding and ice cream drowned in espresso.) By this point I'm juggling, squeezing lemons for the daily batch of houmous with the phone wedged between my shoulder and cheek. My first early customers, the loyal Bharat and superwoman Kylie Morris, arrive, armed with newspapers and requesting their morning soya lattes.

As I steam their milk, I'm mulling over what salad to make this morning. Vietnamese carrot and peanuts, nutty brown rice with seeds, or couscous with mint and feta? And as they eat their toast with mackerel pâté, I'm wondering what will soothe my weariness tonight. Baked polenta, beans on toast or boquerones? Mum is calling. Have I got time to pick up the phone before the next customers descend? 'Oh darling, you'll never guess what we had for supper last night …' Asparagus from her garden. The day is truly in swing now. I'm navigating cooking, serving breakfasts and all the usual flurry of telephone calls, Daddy's usual herbal tea and the ordering, when I drop my ciabatta … a curly-haired boy has just ambled in … And how shall I woo you with my wares?

GENERAL ADMISSION

SECTION   ROW/BOX   SEAT
10 JUL 2006   6.00

MON

G-LOVE
SPECIAL
SAUCE

Marmalade Muffins

for   breka

HOT
PEPPE
COND

DAWN CHORUS

Foods for the first wave of a hangover, or just to start the day with a bang, when you need some morning loving or have a dawn appetite. These breakfast recipes hail from the deli, my travels and a frugal upbringing. Favourite morning foods. Starting the day with an egg is surely one of life's best treats. But sometimes we crave something more wholesome, to kick-start the morning and give sustained energy, like porridge or muesli. I often make a vat of muesli, which keeps me going for a few months and is a good economy drive when I'm a bit stumped for cash.

It all rather depends on who you're with and how you're feeling, and what's actually in the fridge: hangovers usually demand fried foods like Rupert's eggy bread, but friends for breakfast could prompt some steaming sweet muffins. My mum says breakfast is the best meal of the day, which it certainly is at her big oak table, with her homemade yoghurt, popovers, marmalade and bread and fragrant coffees.

Each country has its own take on breakfast too, often revolving around the glorious egg. I never tire of the magical egg. Egg-fried noodles on the Khao San Road in Bangkok, eggs Benedict in London, oeufs en cocotte in France. An omelette is one of my favourite ways to use up leftover vegetables.

Some of the recipes, however, like soda bread and muesli, require some pre-planning to stand you in good economical stead during the week. Other breakfast recipes will be more for that weekend drawn-out brunch affair, like the ultimate sausage sandwich along with a big cafetière. Many of these recipes are just as good for a last-minute supper or a lovers' midnight feast. And of course the bread (on page 12) is fantastic as an addition to every meal of the day.

Menu

Breakfasts

Muesli *in storecupboard quantities with coconut & currants*	4
Pancetta & Quail's Egg Tart *a classy fry-up*	7
Cinnamon Toast *inspired by Pooh*	9
Creamy Scrambled Eggs with Chilli Jam	10
Mum's Seedy Soda Bread	12
Rupert's New York Eggy Bread with Bacon & Maple Syrup	15
Omelette with Potatoes, Peperoncino, Tomatoes & Cheese *(I love leftovers)*	17
Fried Bread with Sweet Chilli Sauce *An Anna Green-Armytage special for a pyjama-sofa start*	19
Hangover Cures	20
Mum's Piping Popovers	22
Australian Marmalade Muffins	24
Porridge with Golden Currants & Muscovado Sugar	26
Gazpacho for a Barcelona Morning	27
Raspberry Risen Pancakes with Clotted Cream	29

Muesli

Makes about enough for 30 breakfast sittings

Muesli is such a great breakfast hero. You will start the day with health and happiness. It's wholesome, and I like it with lots of wheat flakes. My mum used to add cream to every cereal we ate, but I'm managing to restrain myself here, in favour of cutting up crunchy apple and sweet banana and spooning tart yoghurt on top. If you make a vat of this, you can keep it jarred up in the cupboard and it works out so much cheaper than buying packets of the stuff. And it can last up to six months – well, that's if you still have any left after that long.

You will need a really serious piece of Tupperware to store this.

First of all heat the oven to 200°C/Gas 6. Lay out the coconut flakes on a large baking tray and scatter over the caster sugar. Place in the oven for 10 minutes, or until the flakes are toasty and golden – keep checking them, as they are easily burnt. Set aside to cool. Meanwhile, measure out the oats, currants and wheat flakes and pour into your big container. Give them a thorough mix around. This is best done by sealing the container and jiggling it around, like a barman with a cocktail shaker. When the coconut is cool, add it to the muesli and give it another good shake to distribute.

250g coconut flakes
3 tablespoons golden caster sugar
1kg jumbo oats
700g golden currants
1kg wheat flakes

For 1 Bulky Breakfast Sitting

Measure out the muesli into a bowl. Core the apple and slice it into 8 pieces, which you then again cut into little bits over the muesli. Then slice over the banana and pile on the yoghurt, honey and milk. I eat this in bed, with mint tea.

1 cup of your homemade muesli
1 small Braeburn apple
1 banana
1 tablespoon natural yoghurt
1 dessertspoon runny honey
2 tablespoons full-fat milk

Pancetta & Quail's Egg Tart

Makes 6 squares

I think I snitched this from a magazine, because it looks so beautiful and clever and is actually very simple to make on a Saturday morning in the deli. There are two ways my trusty customers devour this: either they grab a slice on the run, as if from a pizza stand, or they eat a square with a spinach and olive salad, more as a brunch. It's a versatile tart. I've also made it for a light supper, along with a good Sunday night film, because it's easy-peasy.

The quail's eggs are just so lovable for their dinkiness. Being made of pancetta and these mini eggs means that the tart needs a little pre-planning. Chinese supermarkets sell quail's eggs, as do good butchers and niche delis. Smoked pancetta is also sold at good delis, preserved along with herbs and peppercorns. So it's the kind of thing to cook if you know in advance that you are having a sleepover or want to impress a guest. Slice it into squares, if you are all on the run first thing, as I do in the deli. Regarding the puff pastry, I prefer the ready-rolled kind, but the thicker slabs are more widely available. It depends what you can get your hands on.

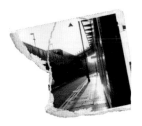

250g puff pastry
  (defrosting bought
  ready-rolled puff
  pastry will take
  1½ hours)
some plain flour for
  rolling
10 thin slices of smoked
  pancetta
6 cherry tomatoes
a little full-fat milk for
  glazing
6 quail's eggs

Preheat your oven to 160°C/Gas 2. Ideally, you will have bought ready-rolled pastry. If not, roll out the pastry slab on a floured surface so that it is big enough to cover a baking tray that measures about 20 x 30cm. Spread the pastry out over the baking tray so that it comes right up to the edges. Lay the pancetta on the pastry, leaving a couple of centimetres clear all the way round which you should then incise with a sharp knife so that the pastry can rise around the pancetta to form a crust. Slice the cherry tomatoes in half and lay them on top of the pancetta, cut side up. Using your fingers (or a pastry brush if you have one), wipe a little milk around the pastry edge to help it brown. Place the tart in the oven for 10 minutes, or until the edges are puffing up around the pancetta and browning just a little. (You may need to further incise the pastry to release so that it can puff, after it's been in the oven for 5 minutes.)

Remove the tart from the oven and carefully crack the quail's eggs evenly over the pancetta layer (the shells have much more give than our more familiar brittle chicken shells). Return to the oven for just long enough for the eggs to solidify, which will be 4 or 5 minutes. The pancetta should now be getting crisp and dark too. It is a matter of a few minutes, though, so keep a close eye on the oven.

When the tart is ready, slice it into 6 pieces with a sharp knife. It is at its best when the yolks are still soft in the middle, and ooze out over the pancetta in your hands.

Cinnamon Toast

Makes 6 slices

My brother Olly and I loved *The Pooh Cook Book* when we were little. The wording was great; all about 'Smackerels, Elevenses and Teas'. I love those weird made-up words. Alice (my beautiful partner in crime) and I use 'melge', which really means to mix, and mush and marinade, but it's our own more onomatopoeic version.

Mum amazingly let us make a mess and get enthusiastic about cooking even at this level. I hope I do the same with my children, as we definitely had a good time beating butter, licking bowls and watching cakes rise through tinted oven glass. This cinnamon toast is a classic. All you need to do is make a flavoured butter and lather it over what you have to hand, bagels, buns, toast, whatever. The butter keeps for ages in the fridge, so if you make a big batch, you have midnight feasts covered too.

Leave the butter out for a few hours at room temperature, to soften in a large mixing bowl. Then gradually cream in the sugar and cinnamon with a sturdy fork until it is a homogeneous paste. Alternatively, you can whiz it all up by using the pulse mode of a blender, if you have one. Decant the butter into a small pudding basin, toast your toast, and lather on the sweet, flavoured butter.

150g unsalted butter
100g golden caster sugar
35g ground cinnamon
brown bread for toasting

Creamy Scrambled Eggs with Chilli Jam

For 2

This comes originally from the little deli I first worked in, in Rotherhithe. It was set right by the Thames, and was a dream world of fun with fellow delistress Lulu, fantastic evenings of cooking and dancing. She taught me how to woo in an apron. These creamy eggs were a best-seller there, and are in my shop too. It's so cherished that on a Saturday morning it's pretty much all we make. The chilli jam surprises everyone, as the sweet spiciness works just right with the velvety eggs. I use Tracklements, but if pushed, sweet chilli sauce would do. It's the ultimate hangover cure according to my oldest girlfriend, Doctor Helen, combined with a feisty Fentiman's ginger beer, a macchiato, and a sparkling water, all consumed in unison by those in the know. Sometimes I make it mid-afternoon for a snack too.

Crack the eggs into a microwaveable bowl. Lightly beat them with the cream and salt, so that there are still some defined yellow and white bits. Slice the ciabatta and place under a low grill, dough side up, in order to crisp up and lightly brown. Place the eggs in the microwave for 1 minute. With a fork, scrape around the edges of the bowl and break up any firmer bits. Return it to the microwave for another minute and repeat the process. It may need a further 20 seconds. Be careful not to overcook the eggs. They should be creamy and delicious and lightly risen, which, remarkably, the microwave is perfect for. They continue cooking once they are removed from the bowl, so if in doubt, do slightly undercook them.

If you do not own or prefer not to use a microwave, making them old-school style is great too. For this, melt a little extra butter in a medium pan. Beat together the eggs, cream and salt while the butter is slowly warming. Add this to the pan, and continually stir with a flat-ended wooden spoon to keep pulling up the cooked layers of egg that are created at the bottom of the pan. When the eggs are still pretty liquid but forming enticing sunny lumps, remove from the heat to sit for a few minutes. Just as with the microwave method, the eggs will continue cooking even when removed from the heat. And so, by removing them early, this is how to get them perfectly creamy and not overdone.

Once removed from the grill, lather the ciabatta with butter, arrange on two plates with the prosciutto and chilli jam, and divide the eggs between the plates. Scrunch over a hefty dose of ground black pepper for seriously perfect eggs.

6 medium free-range
  eggs
200ml single cream
a generous pinch of
  Maldon sea salt
1 ciabatta loaf
butter for the ciabatta
4 fine slices of prosciutto
2 tablespoons chilli jam
freshly ground black
  pepper

Mum's Seedy Soda Bread

Makes 2 loaves

Soda bread is a wonderful cheat's bread. It makes for an encouraging initiation into the world of baking, so get cracking. My mother skilfully leavened abundant firm loaves practically daily, decorated with beautiful wheatears and laden with seeds. But for me, it felt like a whole other level of kitchen excellence, slightly out of my reach. By its very nature, soda bread does not require all the leavening and kneading of a normal yeast loaf, so don't be shy. And once you can see the texture that it needs to be, sloppy but nutty, like a moist porridge, you can be free to throw in whatever you want: poppy seeds, dried herbs, sesame seeds, olives, pumpkin seeds. And you can substitute the sugar here with good honey, for a deeper flavour. Making two loaves, you can put one in the freezer for a rainy day, but if you just want to bake one loaf, divide the quantities below in half.

Of course there's something deeply impressive about baking your own bread, so I frequently find myself making Mum's soda bread when I've got people over for dinner. It's so easy: make the bread first (as soon as you get in the door), and while it's in the oven you'll have time to prepare some other knick-knacks for dinner. It's particularly delicious with my favourite salmon and fennel pâté (see page 95) and a crunchy salad. And incidentally, it's slightly lower in gluten due to the spelt flour.

Preheat the oven to 200°C/Gas 6. Butter two traditional 900g bread tins (about 19 x 11cm) and then lightly flour each one, banging it around so that the base and sides are lightly dusted. Set these aside. Measure out the flours, bran, wheat germ, baking powder, salt, sugar and seeds into a big mixing bowl. With a fork toss around to evenly distribute the flours and seeds. Then measure out the milk and gradually mix it in with the fork. It should look sloppy, so don't worry if it doesn't look how you imagine bread dough to be. The reason it is so wet is so that it makes for a really deep flavour, once everything has been dehydrated by the baking process.

Turn this mix out evenly between the two bread tins, which will require you to use a spatula to get all the liquidy cakey mix out. Place in the oven for 25 minutes. It should have risen by this point and be crisp and cracking on the top. Then turn the oven down to 170°C/Gas 3 and continue baking for a further hour and 10 minutes.

Once removed from the oven, turn out the loaves on to a cooling rack for an hour. If they are baked right, they should make a hollow sound when tapped on the bottom. These loaves are best when they have been cooled for a few hours or overnight. Eat for breakfast, lunch and dinner with unsalted butter.

a small knob of butter
200g wholemeal flour, plus a little more for dusting the bread tins
300g spelt flour
4 tablespoons bran
2 tablespoons wheat germ
2 heaped teaspoons baking powder
Maldon sea salt
1 tablespoon muscovado sugar
4 tablespoons sesame seeds
1 tablespoon caraway seeds
2 teaspoons coriander seeds
100g linseeds
565ml semi-skimmed milk (milk on the turn is even better)

Soda Bread with Tomato & Oregano

Makes 1 loaf

100g white flour
150g wholemeal flour
1½ tablespoons bran
1 tablespoon wheat germ
1 teaspoon baking powder
2 handfuls of sesame seeds
1 dessertspoon honey
1 tablespoon tomato purée
150ml full-fat milk
1 tablespoon dried oregano

Follow the directions above, adding the tomato purée to the milk to dissolve it. Then mix the milk into all the dry ingredients as normal and bake for an extra 20 minutes to dry out any excess moisture.

Rupert's New York Eggy Bread with Bacon & Maple Syrup

For 2

In New York for a decadent long weekend, I gorged on those famed diner breakfasts and my good friend Rupert immediately leapt to the forefront of my mind. When we lived together in Edinburgh, he'd emerge from his cupboard-like room at 1 p.m., saunter down to the shop and buy his essential breakfast ingredients, and offer up this fantastic creation to whoever was disclosing their woes at our kitchen table.

This early morning dish has all the abundance of a New York start, with the thick sweetness of syrup and saltiness of bacon. (There's something really great about sweet things like maple syrup with bacon. Actually almost anything sweet with pork is a winner: honey, apples, plum sauce, a sugar glaze with cloves …) According to heroic food writer Jake Tilson, 'For a Breakfast lover, visiting New York is like finding the source of the Nile.' That amazing American abundance: never-ending weak coffee, and sticky jugs of maple syrup at every table. This breakfast combines both Rupert's loving moniker, and that distinctive New York flavour.

4 large free-range eggs
1 coffee-sized cup of
   full-fat milk
freshly ground black
   pepper
Maldon sea salt
2 tablespoons vegetable
   oil
4 slices of really soft
   fresh white bloomer
4 rashers of smoked
   streaky bacon
maple syrup

Find a wide flat-bottomed bowl or serving dish, and in it beat together the eggs, milk, pepper and salt. You will need to get two frying pans hot and at the ready. If possible, a bigger one for the bread, and a smaller one for the bacon. Divide the vegetable oil between these pans. Allow 2 of the slices of bread to soak in the egg bowl and drink up a quarter of the beaten egg. When the oil is quivering, begin by frying the rashers in the small pan. Turn the slices of bread over and coat again to absorb a further quarter of the egg mix. Add the 2 slices to the bigger of the pans, and get the other 2 slices of bread soaking in the same way so that all the egg is equally absorbed. Now add these to the larger bread pan. Sizzle each side of the bread slices, while keeping an eye on the bacon. The bacon should be beginning to brown and crisp at the edges. When the bread slices are browned as well, and slightly swollen and risen, remove to a plate and top with the crisp bacon and lots of maple syrup. Have it with strong tea, and a good gas.

Omelette with Potatoes, Peperoncino, Tomatoes & Cheese

For 3 hungry friends or 4 abstemious ones

Mostly because we were never flush, but also because he rightly hates waste, my father had the habit of frying up leftovers. This did lead to some serious disasters along the way. My brother Olly and I still giggle over his duck skin stew! However, leftovers can be a great addition to a morning omelette: a little remaining tomato sauce? Peppers on the turn? Slightly dry Cheddar? Daddy's old schoolfriend Giles even recently wrote to him about the merits of leftover angelfish curry in an omelette.

Here I use cooked potatoes. They could be little new ones, cold mashed or just boiled from the night before. They would all work. The dried chilli flakes are a great storecupboard essential, and, added here, will really wake you up. I bought a few jars of peperoncino when I was in Italy, but you can get little bags of these chilli flakes in good old-fashioned continental delis too. I most recently made this spiced omelette with Raf for our super-cool adopted DJ son, Toddla T, after a night out at the Grecoroman Sonic Wrestling party. The chilli flakes were our tonic. It hardly needs to be mentioned that an omelette is also an excellent last-minute dinner. When I'm back a little late, it's what I cook up. You too will be sated in a matter of minutes.

2 tablespoons olive oil
1 medium onion
200g cherry tomatoes or
about 3 ripe plum
tomatoes
400g cooked potato,
either boiled or
mashed
1 teaspoon peperoncino
(chilli flakes)
6 medium free-range
eggs
100g Gouda or any
really melty cheese
freshly ground black
pepper
Maldon sea salt
a healthy handful of
rocket or spinach

Find a large heavy-bottomed frying pan and begin warming the olive oil on a low heat. Meanwhile get all the vegetables prepared: peel and finely chop the onion, cut the tomatoes in half, and if need be further slice the potatoes so that they are in about 2cm cubes. Add the onions to the pan and let them sweat until they are turning transparent. Now add the tomatoes and sweat for a further few minutes along with the peperoncino, stirring all the while. When the tomato skins are beginning to split, add the cooked potatoes.

In a bowl, beat the eggs thoroughly and then grate in half the cheese. When the potatoes are hot through, pour in the egg mixture and season well. Tumble the rocket over the top of the omelette, followed by the remaining cheese. Keep heating the omelette on the hob until it is drying out at the edges, which should take a few minutes.

Meanwhile turn the grill on to a low setting. Place the omelette under the grill so that it is just sealed on top, which will take about 2 minutes. You still want some soft creamy egg in the middle. Slice into 3 or 4 pieces and dish up with some Dijon mustard.

Fried Bread with Sweet Chilli Sauce

For 2

When we lived together at university, Anna and I frequently felt …
a little tender. We'd set ourselves up good and proper for a day of
vegging. Still in our pyjamas, we would go down to the shop to buy
bumper amounts of juice, cheap bread and sweet chilli sauce, to
accompany an array of high-school movies and a day's hilarity. Really,
we were making our own fun, because we were just too broke to
order a takeaway. This became our substitute for sesame prawn toast
and those exciting hot tinfoil boxes of Chinese delights. They really
hit the spot in a gross and junky way, which is sometimes exactly
what we needed to indulge ourselves.

Carefully slice the crusts off the slices of bread. Heat the vegetable oil
in a big frying pan on a medium flame. When the oil is rippling, dip a
corner of the bread into it to check that it sizzles. Providing it does,
add the 4 pieces of trimmed bread and fry until golden and crisp.
Turn them over to do the same on the other side. Pour out the sweet
chilli sauce into a ramekin and set aside ready for the dipping. When
the bread has absorbed the oil and is stiff and golden on both sides,
remove from the pan and, on a wooden chopping board, slice each
piece into soldiers. Scoop these into the sweet chilli sauce, and munch
immediately. There you have our fakery. For best results repeat this
dish a few times throughout a long and lazy day.

4 slices of corner-shop
   bread
3 tablespoons vegetable
   oil
2 tablespoons sweet
   chilli sauce

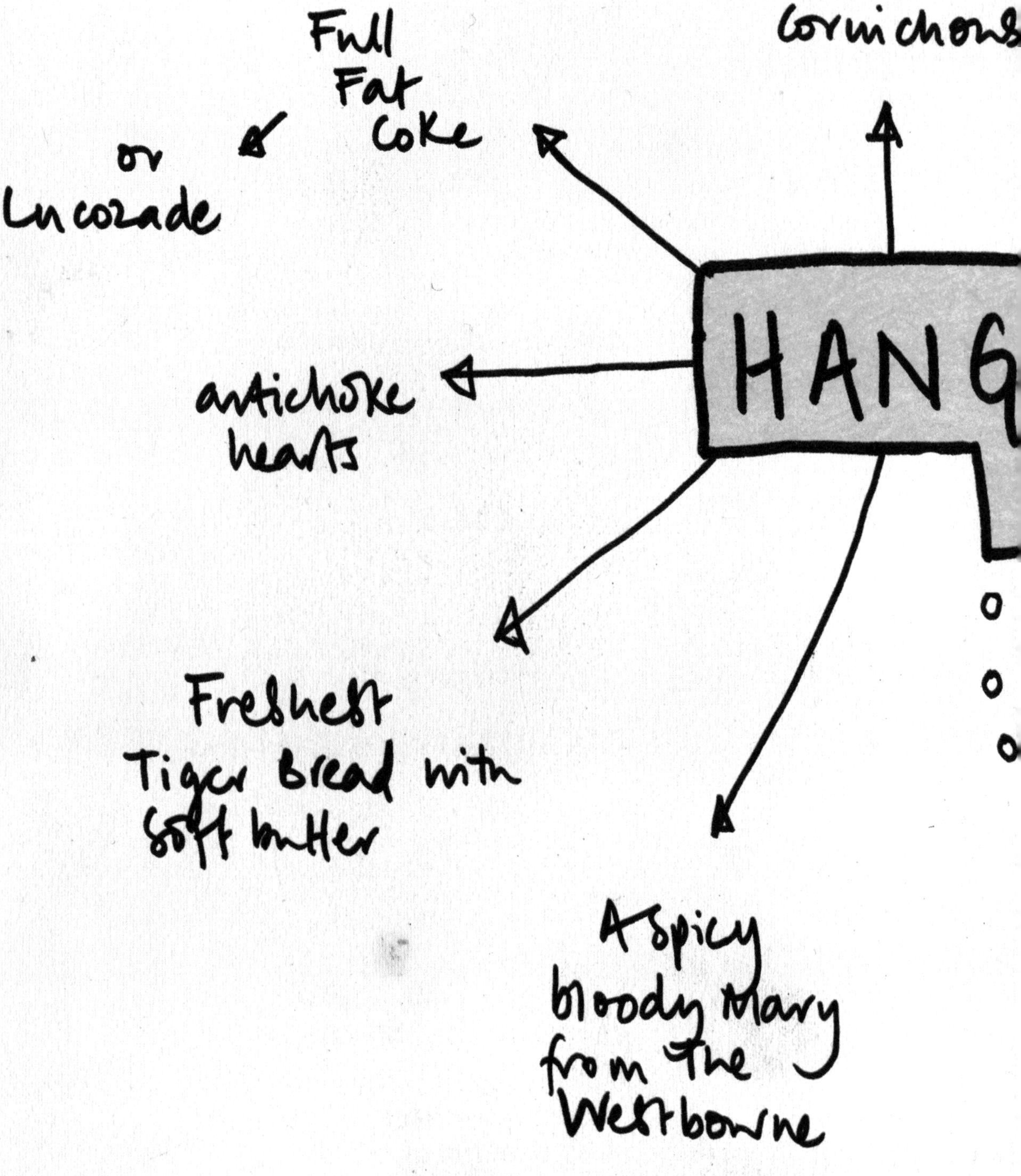

Cornichons

Full
Fat
Coke

or
Lucozade

HANG

antichoke
hearts

Freshest
Tiger bread with
soft butter

A spicy
bloody Mary
from the
Westbourne

VER CURES

→ Roll mops on toast

→ Boquerones, straight from tub to mouth

→ pickled onions

→ or better still, a ploughman's on the sea front

Rat's lettuce soup

A HOLIDAY

Mum's Piping Popovers

Makes 6 to 8 popovers

Popovers are another of my mother's great brekka additions. She caught her obsession for these sweet Yorkshire puddings at her sister Judith's house, and has made them ever since. If we found out that they were on the breakfast menu, my brother and I were up early and eager and at the table, armed with knives and forks. The hole in the centre of the popover is filled with a knob of butter and a generous splash of maple syrup. The most exciting bit is when you pull them open, and the unctuous saccharine river oozes out from them.

115g plain flour
a pinch of salt
a little freshly grated
    nutmeg
2 medium free-range
    eggs
215ml full-fat milk
3 tablespoons vegetable
    oil
butter and maple syrup,
    to serve

Preheat the oven to 220°C/Gas 7 and place a deep muffin tray in the oven to warm right up. If you are using a liquidiser, put the flour, salt, nutmeg, eggs and milk into the bowl or jug, and give it a good whiz, so that it is a smooth batter. If you are using a whisk, start by beating the eggs in a big jug or mixing bowl. Then add a little of the milk before adding the flour, salt and nutmeg. Loosen it again with the rest of the milk.

Take out the piping hot tray, pour a little oil into each hole, and return to really hot up in the oven. This will take about 5 minutes. Then pour the batter into each hole, about halfway up because they will rise. They will sizzle and start to cook the minute they hit the oily hole. Return the tray straight away to the oven, turning the temperature down to 170°C/Gas 3, and bake for 20 minutes, by which time they will look like little Yorkshire puddings. They should be, according to my mum, 'puffy, crisp and hollow inside'. To serve, place a little knob of butter into each sunken centre, along with a glug of maple syrup.

Australian Marmalade Muffins

Makes 8 muffins

Marmalade and muffins are both time-honoured components of a breakfast, and are happily joined under the same umbrella in this clever recipe. Whilst in Australia I learnt a lot about a decent breakfast: muffins and cupcakes, savoury pastries and delectable coffees. I picked up this winner too. While we are on the subject of Australia, I swear by the *Australian Woman's Weekly* books. They are not only reasonably priced magazine-style books, but really comprehensive and much more adventurous than you may think at first. They span national to mood foods, and are never too expensive if you fancy getting your head around a new issue in the kitchen.

These are magnificent breakfast treats packed with marmalade and are best straight out of the oven, first thing. So when I make them in the deli, they don't last long on the cake-stand. They are particularly good with a well-brewed pot of tea. And the trick with muffins, for that lovely risen and cracking top, is not to over-combine the mixture in the final stages. This means that they are best made, really, in a slapdash fashion, which is lucky.

Preheat the oven to 160°C/Gas 2. Using a pastry brush or some oiled kitchen towel, grease each hole in a muffin tray with a little vegetable oil. Measure the butter, flour and baking powder into a big mixing bowl. Quickly rub them together, as you would when making pastry, lightly with the tips of your fingers. Now grate the zest of the orange into this. Beat the eggs together in a cup, and roughly add to the flour mix with a knife. Then roughly stir in the sugar, marmalade and milk with speed. Do not over-mix, or it will become too homogenised.

Turn the mix out equally into the muffin tray, but do not overload the holes, as they really do rise. Place in the oven for 20 minutes or until just firm and steaming. You can also check them by plunging a toothpick into the middle of one. If the toothpick comes out clean, they are ready, but if there is any liquid or cake mix clinging to it, they need a few more minutes. Remove to a cooling rack by releasing each muffin with a fruit knife, and cool for a few minutes before dishing them up with a big pot of tea.

1 tablespoon vegetable oil
125g softened butter
300g self-raising flour
½ teaspoon baking powder
1 orange
2 medium free-range eggs
150g caster sugar
2 tablespoons thick-cut marmalade (preferably my mum's dark one)
125ml full-fat milk

Porridge with Golden Currants & Muscovado Sugar

For 2

Word has it that oats are a superfood (which means, for me, merely that it keeps the wolf from the door). And porridge is one of those delicious breakfasts that not only keeps your energy up but in winter keeps you warm on the inside too, rather like a hot bath. This is very useful if you start the day at the bus stop in the cold. When customers come into Rosie's looking a little sorry for themselves, I usually suggest a big bowl of steaming porridge, to ward off the morning misery.

The golden currants are a sweet addition, and the muscovado sugar gives it that treacle-like rich depth. The timing of porridge rather depends on the oats. If you use the coarse nutty kind, it will take longer to homogenise. If you use finer, flourier packaged supermarket oats, it should take a little less time to achieve this comforting and maternal dish.

100g wholegrain rolled
    oats
500ml full-fat milk
a pinch of table salt
100g golden currants
2 dessertspoons
    muscovado sugar

Measure out the oats into a small pan along with the milk. Add a pinch of salt and put the pan on the smallest ring on the hob. Rapidly heat for 5 minutes, stirring with a wooden spoon until it looks deliciously nutty and gluey. Take it off the heat for a moment to settle, before dishing out into bowls and topping with the light currants and dark sugar. You may want to wash the porridge down with a little extra cold milk.

Gazpacho for a Barcelona Morning

Makes a big bowl or about 8 mugs

The first time I tasted gazpacho was at Laurie Castelli's house. He was one of the first to discover my little deli in Brixton, and so then we were new friends. He now lives in Colombia with his beautiful son and wife, but at the time he lived on crack alley, Rushcroft Road. He lured me over to his stylishly minimal flat to try his brother Gian Castelli's impeccable cold tomato soup. I left with the offer of a ride on his Moto Guzzi, a cinema date at the ICA, and a delicious taste for this perfect Spanish pick-me-up. As it's a soup, it's an unusual choice for breakfast, but trust me, this will wake you up, and cleanse you too. Because the vegetables are all raw, it feels incredibly medicinal.

The next time I came across gazpacho was in Barcelona. My friend Lovely Linda, who was heavily pregnant with Leo at the time, downed a carton of this each morning. And when I tried it too, it made perfect sense. But feel free to drink it at any time of day: in little glasses as a summer starter; in thimbles accompanying a light supper; or as a mid-afternoon reviver. And the trick with Gian's gazpacho is the use of ground cumin, giving it a Moorish edge. Beware, though, I've bust a few blenders masticating this soup. It's pretty hard to pulverise.

1kg ripe red tomatoes
1 red pepper
1 medium cucumber
1 medium onion
2 garlic cloves
120ml extra virgin olive oil (for posterity's sake, Spanish, if you can find it), plus a little more for drizzling over at the end
2½ tablespoons sherry vinegar
2 teaspoons ground cumin
2 teaspoons caster sugar
1 teaspoon Maldon sea salt
freshly ground black pepper

Find a really big mixing bowl to decant each of the ingredients into once they have been prepared: roughly chop the tomatoes into eighths; deseed the pepper and slice into strips; peel and roughly chop the cucumber, complete with seeds; peel and dice the onion and peel and chop the garlic cloves. Pour the extra virgin olive oil, sherry vinegar and cumin into the bowl and mix everything up with your hands. If you have a strong hand-held blender, give it a really good purée, but it's better still if you have a Magimix, which you can decant the lot into and pulse away on.

When it is a smooth thick soup, you are ready for the next stage. Find a large sieve, place it over another large mixing bowl and pour the gazpacho into it (though Raf recently picked me up an amazing mouli-légumes in Barcelona, which is the real deal in blending a perfect gazpacho). With a metal spoon or a spatula work the soup through the sieve so that it becomes ultimately smooth. You will need to scrape the bottom of the sieve from time to time, to remove the thicker bits. By the end, you will be left with just the woody parts of the vegetables and seeds in the sieve, which you can then discard. Now give the silky gazpacho a thorough mix with a whisk, and season according to your taste, with a little sugar to bring out the flavour of the tomatoes, and also pepper and salt. Serve with a few ice cubes in each mug and a drizzle of excellent Spanish extra virgin olive oil.

Raspberry Risen Pancakes with Clotted Cream

Makes 10 pancakes

These should really be cooked on a griddle pan, like my mum has, but I'm still fruitlessly trying to prise it away from her. A griddle pan is one of those entirely flat iron pans that has a handle running up and over and round to the other side, almost looking like one half of a weight and measure. And because I don't have this wonderful tool, and you probably won't either, I just cook them in a big flat frying pan. The warm raspberries are absolutely delicious with thick clotted cream, and are reminiscent of a good old-fashioned cream tea. I'd just as easily cook these for pudding, with some delicious vanilla ice cream to serve.

British raspberries are in season during July and August, so this is naturally a summer brekka. If you stumble upon a good supply during these months, buy a fair few punnets and freeze whatever is surplus to your requirements. Raspberries lend themselves very well to freezing, and your conscience will be clear too. At other times of the year, you may choose to vary the topping. In deepest winter, try finely sliced ripe pears as a substitute.

Preheat the oven to 100°C/Gas ¼. Line an ovenproof serving dish with a clean drying-up cloth, and place in the oven to warm gently. You will decant each batch of pancakes on to this to keep warm. Thoroughly beat the egg in a mixing bowl. I use my lipped batter bowl, but a wide jug would also do. Add half the flour, the sugar, salt and baking powder, beating with a whisk. This will form a thick elastic batter. Then add the milk, making sure there are no lumps but that the batter is now light and smooth. Now add the remaining flour. It may need a little water to loosen it further. The consistency should be thick but creamy and entirely lumpless. Set aside for an hour if you can stand the temptation, as this makes for a better pancake in the end.

Heat 1 tablespoon of the butter, or some vegetable oil, in a large flat-bottomed frying pan, so that it is silky with fat but not verging into deep-frying territory. Allow the fat to become melted and hot and slippy when the pan is tilted, and then pour out some batter, or add a spoonful of the batter if you are using a bowl, and drop over this 6 or 8 raspberries. The pancakes should be about the diameter of a wine bottle. You will get 2 or 3 in the pan. Allow them to really brown and go golden on the bottom. They are ready to turn when the top side is bubbling and beginning to firm up around the berries. Flip each one over with a heatproof spatula or palette knife, and colour the other side. They should rise a little and firm up, and each side should take just over a minute. Remove to the warm dish before going on to the next batch. They are best after 10 minutes drying out in the warm oven. Finally dust the pancakes generously with some icing sugar if you like. Serve with a smudge of clotted cream on each.

1 medium free-range egg
130g self-raising flour
50g caster sugar
a pinch of salt
1 teaspoon baking powder
150ml full-fat milk
2 tablespoons butter
170g raspberries
a dusting of icing sugar
clotted cream

Colombian Scrambled Eggs with Frills

For 2

There's a great bona fide Colombian restaurant in Brixton market called Como y Punto, and they do an epic breakfast. Their proud kitchen is reassuringly evident from the café, and little pots of salsa sit at every table for you to help yourself to. The last time I ate there, we entirely demolished the salsa, because it's so jolly delicious.

Luckily there are wonderful shops in Brixton where you can buy and even see corn bread being made. Though in case you haven't any Central or South American shops near you, I've added a cornmeal pancake recipe too, from Raf's mum, Maggie, and her epic cookery book collection. This colourful and tangy breakfast is all about finely chopping everything. It is best with milky Colombian-style coffees.

The Salsa

1 big juicy tomato
a few stalks of fresh
   coriander
1 spring onion
1 big red chilli
2 teaspoons white sugar
3 dessertspoons white
   wine vinegar
½ teaspoon table salt

First prepare the salsa by seriously chopping the tomato, coriander, spring onion and chilli finely with a large sharp knife. For best effects, you want to get a swinging rhythm going by holding down the pointed end of the knife and chopping all over the vegetables. However, if you have a little hand-held blender it would be helpful here to make this a thin and fine salsa. Then add the sugar, vinegar and salt. Decant this into a ramekin for the table.

The Corn Cakes

Measure out the cornmeal, flour, salt and bicarbonate of soda, and thoroughly mix together. Then beat together the egg and soured milk, and gradually whisk this into the dry ingredients. It should be a sloppy cake-mixture type of batter. Heat a teaspoon of oil in a medium frying pan on a high heat to bring the heat of the pan right up. When the oil is rippling and ready, turn the heat right down to low and wait a moment before pouring in enough batter to form a 12cm round. Fry for a few minutes, so that the edges are quite brown and crinkled and the surface is smattered with rising bubbles and is nearly dry. Release the cake around the edges with a palette knife or flat frying flipper, and turn it over. You will only need to fry the second side for a moment, to seal it. The cake should be speckled brown and a little risen if fried correctly.

Remove from the pan to a kitchen towel, to absorb any excess oil. Repeat this process with another teaspoon of oil until all the batter is gone.

100g coarse or medium cornmeal
40g plain white flour
½ teaspoon salt
½ teaspoon bicarbonate of soda
1 large free-range egg
200ml soured milk (soured by squeezing ½ lemon into the milk, and leaving to rest for 5 minutes)
4 teaspoons vegetable oil

The Eggs

1 green chilli
1 tablespoon vegetable
  oil
1 small onion
1 small fresh tomato
4 large free-range eggs
a pinch of table salt

Remove the seeds from the chilli and finely chop so that it is almost shredded. Heat the oil on a medium heat in a big frying pan. When it is rippling, add the fine pieces of chilli. While they're sizzling, peel and dice the onion really small and add to the pan. Deseed the tomato, and again finely chop this before adding to the pan. Leave to sweat for a minute. Then crack the eggs into the frying pan. With a heatproof spatula, break the yolks and stir everything together, but so that the white and yolk colours are still quite defined. Turn the heat down and continue to fold the eggs over with the spatula. When they are quite firm and integrated with the vegetables, remove everything from the pan and lay it out on two plates with the corn cakes. Heap the salsa on top, and season with table salt if necessary.

Buckwheat & Banana Pancakes with Runny Honey

Makes 4 pancakes

I love making pancakes: so easy a child can make them, and super fun because of the theatrical flipping. I spent a good deal of my formative years making pancakes, so I have happy flipping memories, but I must admit I don't always get it quite right. I loved making them so much that in my early teens my dad bought me a beautifully thrown pottery batter bowl with a perfectly sculpted lip for pouring. The best pancakes are made with a little patience, as the batter should really sit for an hour at least before it is used. And for some reason, the first one to hit the oil is always a bit dud. My grandmother calls the first the dog's pancake, for that very reason.

Buckwheat has a really distinctive flavour and texture. It is almost sour but in a really good tangy way, and gives a much more delicate body to the pancake, as it seems more finely ground than regular flours. It is also dark with a malty aftertaste, which really suits the combination of the banana and honey. By whisking the egg white in these pancakes, you will achieve a wonderful lightness that perfectly contrasts the dense banana and sticky honey.

1 medium free-range
egg
80g buckwheat flour
100ml full-fat milk
a pinch of salt
1 tablespoon golden
caster sugar
4 bananas that are just
about to turn
3 tablespoons vegetable
oil
4 dessertspoons runny
honey

Separate the egg, placing the yolk in a lipped jug or bowl, and the white in a really clean metal mixing bowl. Add the buckwheat flour, milk, salt and sugar to the egg yolk, and whisk thoroughly to integrate into a smooth thick paste. There shouldn't be a single lump. Set this aside for an hour and then vigorously whisk the egg white so that it forms quite firm peaks. Fold this into the thick batter mix, being careful not to lose the air you have laboriously made.

Peel the bananas and set aside, ready to be rolled in the pancakes. Heat a little oil in a good hard-bottomed frying pan. Get it consistently hot before pouring in about a cup or ladle of batter. You should have to really work it around the pan to cover it, as the foamy batter is not loose like a regular batter. By working it, though, it will be a light and crisp affair (rather than a stodgy mattress of a pancake). When the first side is cooked, the pancake will begin to brown at the edges. At this point quickly flip it (or turn with a flat bendy knife, carefully releasing it from the edges) and quickly cook the other side by merely sealing it. The pancake should look slightly decorated with golden spots. Now place a banana off centre on the pancake and fold the pancake around it, pressing down a little to seal. After a few minutes, remove from the pan to a waiting plate and hungry face before starting the whole process again with a little more oil if necessary. Pour over a little runny honey before serving.

The Ultimate Sausage Sandwich

Makes 2 sandwiches

I'm so lucky that there's a great butcher round the corner from my shop. They make their own sausages in all the colours of the rainbow … with herbs, lamb, leek, even chicken. If you can build up a relationship with your butcher, meat-buying will be a rewarding and pleasurable part of the shop, so give it a go. And you'll be supporting your local community, which will make it a better place for you to live.

The ultimate sausage sandwich is subtle in perfection. Sometimes the simple things are the most challenging to get right, like a roast or a fry-up. Here, it's all about the scrumptious balance of husky sausage, tart mustard, sweet tomato, peppery rocket and buttery warm bread. These are fast catching up with scrambled eggs and chilli jam as the Saturday morning favourite at Rosie's.

3 good pork sausages
1 small ciabatta loaf or
  2 ciabattini
2 large tomatoes
unsalted butter (French,
  if you can find it)
2 teaspoons smooth
  Dijon mustard
2 handfuls of fresh
  rocket
freshly ground black
  pepper

Preheat the oven to 200°C/Gas 6. Divide the sausages, but do not prick them (that way you will keep hostage all the wetness and flavour that is waiting inside for you). Line a baking tray with greased paper and lay the sausages on top. Place in the oven on the top shelf for 20 minutes, turning once. Remove the sausages from the oven but leave the oven on. Cut the ciabatta into 2 square hunks, and slice each again in half. Place these back on the top shelf of the oven, dough side up, to warm and crisp and colour.

Meanwhile, slice the tomatoes into roundels, and the sausages in half. These will be divided between the two sandwiches, giving each one 1½ sausages. When the bread is beginning to colour, which will take 3 or 4 minutes, remove from the oven, generously butter, and add a teaspoon of Dijon mustard to 2 of the slices. Add 3 sausage slabs to the Dijon-decorated sides and split the tomatoes between each sandwich. Finally grab a handful of rocket, shower with freshly ground pepper and seal with the singularly buttered top layer of ciabatta. Tuck in.

Economical Oeufs en Cocotte

For 2

This is a great way of using up a leftover tomato pasta sauce. It is basically an egg poached and baked at the same time, in a tomato nest. Many countries have a version of it. I recently found a Turkish variation called *menemen*. This nestles in a vegetable ragout and is on offer as a quick snack in train stations and ports, which goes to show that it's another one of these breakfast recipes that's just as good, any time of day.

Anyway, Alice and I first ordered eggs en cocotte without really knowing what we were getting, in a brilliant little café in Camden Passage, giggling our morning heads off. Needless to say, I ate both hers and mine, as she had, as always, lost her hangover appetite, and because I thought it so tasty and clever. I wanted it over and over.

They will be most successful if you have those lovely shallow terracotta ramekins, but a small oven dish will do. If you just fancy this for breakfast, but don't have the necessary leftovers, you can quickly rustle up a simple sauce for the eggs' bed. I eat it for a light supper when it looks like there's nothing in my very occasionally unloved cupboards.

The Sauce

450ml leftover tomato
    sauce, or
1 tablespoon olive oil
½ medium onion
1 garlic clove
5 large tomatoes
1 teaspoon tomato
    purée
1 teaspoon sugar
Maldon sea salt
freshly ground black
    pepper

Preheat the oven to 160°C/Gas 2. If you are making the tomato sauce from scratch, first warm the olive oil in a frying pan on a medium heat. Peel and finely dice the onion and add to the hot oil. Sweat for a minute, then peel and crush the garlic and add this to the pan. Chop the tomatoes into about 12 pieces each, and add these too. Simmer for 15 minutes, or until the sauce is reduced and quite smooth. Finally dissolve the tomato purée in the sauce, with some sugar and seasoning.

The Eggs

2 large free-range eggs
smoked paprika

Decant the sauce into either two big ramekins or one smaller oven dish. Make two deep holes in the bed of sauce for the eggs, and crack them in, pinching a little paprika over each yolk. Place in the oven for 10 to 15 minutes, or until the egg is just firm on the top and the sauce is sizzling with a deep redness at the sides. Serve with some good buttered bread. One of my favourites is sourdough.

Red Pepper & Mint from
Brixton Market...
ASPERGES
45
R.P.M.
HOT STUFF

LOVESOME TONIGHT

Food and love are hopelessly entangled in my mind. I for one have a hungry heart. Feeling giddy with excitement, eating oysters at Borough Market, while my boy held my hand. Slipping out of bed on a Sunday morning, to the Portuguese for *café con leche* and *pastéis de nata*. Preparing a big winter hotpot together for our friends, listening to Radio 4. And the simple stuff, like shelling beans, while the heart goes boom. It's all to do with the senses.

Here is a gathering of recipes, all successfully tried and tested, for seduction in the kitchen. Whether it's an emergency date, or one of those evenings planned long in advance, full of anticipation and palpitation, my advice is to crank up the music, and let the juices flow. It's one of the finest things to do for the one you love. You should really enjoy working your magic, and casting some culinary spells.

Generally I like to eat quite simple foods when I'm in for seduction. Simple but really impressive, like for instance duck breasts, or really good steak. Your meal should be full of impact and thought, without appearing fussy or over-zealous. And don't forget, if you are cooking for men, the demands are altogether different: Raf's face frequently falls when I realise I've not incorporated massive potatoes, pans of rice and wedges of plantain into every meal!

I once shared a Bramley sorbet with verbena jelly in a dark and seducing booth in Black's. It's in the depths of sultry Soho and is one of my favourite places to go for simple food and uncomplicated dining. It was subtle, refreshing and lip-tinglingly good. Inspired by this, I have kept these puddings simple but suggestive, because hopefully you'll be too enthralled by your date to want to be clattering around in the kitchen blow-torching a brûlée.

Menu

Meals

A Hispanic South
London Affair

Puddings

Risotto Milanese with Morcilla & Rocket & Asparagus Salad

For 2

I first made this for a clandestine, last-minute dinner date. Alice and I had been drinking rosé in Brixton when he called ('Oh God, Al, what am I to wear? Crap, the flat's a tip!'). I rushed round the corner, a little tipsy, to get express advice from Manuel in the Portuguese deli and butcher, O Talho. He recommended this simple risotto, with the rich addition of morcilla (Spanish black pudding). The greenery and risotto are a perfect contrast of crunchy and fresh with wet and warm, and the Parmesan brings all the flavours together. So there is a happy relationship on the table already. It turned into a whole weekend of delirious fun together. Eureka.

Rocket & Asparagus Salad

This is a simple salad but rather depends on the seasons. Asparagus is in season from April through to June. When shopping for vegetables I try and bear this in mind, especially on the rare occasions that I'm in a supermarket. In these larger shops there always tends to be a choice – you just need to look closely at the label. As everything tastes much better if rightly in season, it's in your interests to make that little extra effort.

To make the salad, bend the asparagus spears until they snap. This will have them breaking at just the point of tenderness, and eliminate any woody stumps. Heat some olive oil in a griddle pan, and when it is really hot, and just beginning to smoke, add the spears. Sear until they are tattooed with black lines, then remove from the heat and allow to cool a little. This will only take a few minutes. On a flat serving plate, lay out the rocket leaves and scatter the asparagus over them. Simply season with the lemon juice, the oil from the griddle pan, and lots of pepper and salt, before piling on the shavings of Parmesan.

a bundle of asparagus
lots of olive oil
3 generous handfuls of
    fresh rocket
juice of 1 lemon
freshly ground black
    pepper
Maldon sea salt
50g Parmesan shavings

Risotto Milanese with Morcilla

Although risotto is easy to cook, it is a challenge getting perfect results. This dish should not be a sloppy rice pudding, neither should it look like an oily paella. It is somewhere in the middle. Sophisticated but soothing.

Regarding the stock, it's preferable to have made a good chicken one. However, few have the time to labour over bones. I mostly use a good European powdered stock. If you are feeling lavish, however, you could buy a fresh jarred stock. These are available in some delis and better supermarkets. The John Lusty brand is pretty trusty.

a big knob of butter
1 large onion
150g Arborio rice
500ml hot Marigold Swiss vegetable bouillon powder stock
1 large glass of wine (about 200ml)
1 tablespoon olive oil
6 roundels of morcilla or black pudding
lots of freshly grated Parmesan

When it comes to cooking the risotto, remember that all the additions to a risotto are salty, so beware of seasoning until the end. While half the butter is melting in a wide flat pan on a very low heat, peel and very finely dice the onion and add to the pan. The onion will gradually appear soft and translucent, but not browned (about 5 minutes or so). Add the rice and mix in, then cook for about a minute, to seal it. When it is just beginning to brown, add a ladleful of hot stock and stir until the rice has absorbed it. Keep adding stock, bit by bit, stirring all the time and giving it lots of love and affection. Add the wine, again gradually, allowing the alcohol to bubble off and evaporate.

Once the rice has absorbed most of the stock, and tastes almost cooked, heat some oil in another frying pan, so that it is really hot. Add the roundels of morcilla and crisp them up. This will take a minute or so on each side. The risotto takes about 20 minutes of nurturing before it is nutty but cooked. Like al dente pasta. When you feel that the texture is both shiny and creamy, turn the heat off and melt in the final bit of butter, and the Parmesan, almost beating it. This, according to Locatelli's bible, is the *mantecatura*, where it all comes together. Place the lid on the risotto pan and let it sit for a few moments. Heap the risotto on to a plate, with the morcilla pieces balancing on top.

Tomato & Pont l'Evêque Proposal Tart

For 2 with leftovers

The quick rubbing and drawing together. The rolling, chilling, blind baking and goldening of pastry. It's a tactile thing. And finally, filling the case and seeing the results prosper. As a child I couldn't bear the feeling of melting butter between my fingers, rather like sand between my toes. I'm a little more worldly now, and love getting my hands stuck in. Nothing beats homemade pastry (though I have been known to cheat and buy shop-bought, if really short of time). This tart prompted a proposal from an old boyfriend of mine, Pat, so it must be good, surely?

Once you have mastered the basics, your tart options are endless. Broccoli and Saint-Agur; Mrs Kirkham's Lancashire and apple; fennel and Pecorino; pea, mint and feta; spinach, black olive and anchovy; wild porcini and Gruyère and so on. All you need to know is what marries well, which comes with practice and confidence.

Serve this tart with a well-dressed green salad, and homemade soda bread (or a good shop-bought one, if you haven't the time). A simple but perfectly sating meal for two, which would be especially ideal if you've got a vegetarian on board too. The tart is a generous one: I use a 25cm diameter fluted flan tin that feeds four. That way you'll have something tasty for leftovers.

The Pastry

200g plain flour, plus a little more for rolling
110g unsalted butter
Maldon sea salt

You can make the pastry separately from the tart, even a day before. Fill a generous mixing bowl with the flour, diced butter and a pinch of salt. With cold hands quickly rub it between your fingers. The lighter your touch, the more delicate your pastry will be. If done with finesse you will have superb results. When the butter is consistently combined with the flour, drizzle small amounts of cold water over it, bit by bit, and with a knife draw the breadcrumb-like mound together into a moist ball. On a floured surface, roll out the pastry to fit your tin. Push it in all directions, so that it makes a circle a little bigger than the tin. Roll this up on to the rolling pin, and then unravel it gently over the tin, tucking the pastry into the edges and pressing firmly into the crinkles. Finally roll the rolling pin over the top of the tin to perfectly trim the sides to the correct height. Turn the oven to 250°C/Gas 9 or as high as it will go, but put the pastry-filled flan tin into the freezer. After 20 minutes, remove the flan tin, line it with greaseproof paper, and fill with baking beans, or dried chickpeas. Blind bake for 10 minutes. For the best pastry, remove the paper and beans and return to the oven for a further few minutes to dry out the base of the case. No one likes soggy pastry.

The Tomato & Pont l'Evêque Filling

750g cherry tomatoes
2 tablespoons balsamic
    vinegar
1 teaspoon caster sugar
a little olive oil
4 medium free-range
    eggs
284ml double cream
freshly ground black
    pepper
Maldon sea salt
1 x Petit Pont l'Evêque
    or 250g Pont
    l'Evêque
2 teaspoons dried or
    fresh thyme

To make the tart, preheat the oven to 180°C/Gas 4. Slice the cherry tomatoes in half and place cut side upwards in a roasting tin lined with greaseproof paper. Drizzle over the balsamic vinegar and sprinkle with sugar and a little olive oil too. Place them in the oven and allow them to dry out – they'll take on a rich, sweet flavour. They should take about an hour. Meanwhile, whisk up the eggs and cream in a measuring jug, with seasoning. Turn the tomatoes out into the baked pastry case and pat them down to make a dense rich red layer. Pour the eggy custard on top of the tomato and place in the oven for 10 minutes. Take out of the oven. Slice the Pont l'Evêque into strips and place on top of the nearly set and firming custard. Shred over the thyme, and return to the oven. Bake for a further half an hour, or until the cheese is blistering and turning golden and the tart is entirely set.

Garlic Fried King Prawns, Hot Spanish Squid & Balsamic Onion Tortilla

For 2

Sometimes a girl's got to give. A few years ago I was forced to go to extreme lengths to steal an evening with my then boyfriend. It was near impossible to find time when he wasn't DJ-ing, going to a gig, or sorting out his sock drawer. So I lovingly took this whole meal on the P4 bus, with each individual bit prepared in little pots so that I could create it *in situ*. That's love, or is it dementia?

Saucy and juicy, the seafood flavours are wonderful mopped up with the yolky yellow tortilla. I like sucking the sweet garlicky coating off the prawns, then shelling them and devouring the tender meaty chunks within. The chilli will have your mouth wonderfully tingling too. And the squid has good smoky paprika as the resounding Moorish ingredient. This is something I only discovered when I opened my little shop in Brixton market. There are many varieties of this magic dust, and it usually comes in beautiful little tins. I use a hot Santo Domingo, which is imported by Brindisa and will bring a smouldering heat to almost any meal. These smells remind me of Marrakesh and Barcelona all in one, full of mystery and hot reds.

The way you manage this meal is up to you: the prawns could be served as a starter or all together with the squid and tortilla. And if you don't want to do both the squid and the prawn dishes, double up the quantities of one and serve it with a simple green salad. Though if you are using this for wooing, you might just check that your lover doesn't have an aversion to seafood. It is a bit like Marmite: you either love it, or you hate it.

Balsamic Onion Tortilla

1 medium free-range egg
3 medium free-range egg yolks
500g new potatoes
lots of olive oil or butter
100g balsamic onions (or pancetta)
Maldon sea salt
freshly ground black pepper

The essence of a tortilla is patience. First, whisk up the egg and yolks in a mixing jug and set this aside. With the fine flat blade of a mandolin, finely slice the potatoes. Heat lots of olive oil or butter on a low heat in a good non-stick frying pan. This is so that the potatoes (with their high starch content) don't stick to the bottom of the pan. Add the potatoes and attentively turn them, while also allowing them to become golden in parts. When they are beginning to look transparent, after about 20 minutes, use a flat-ended wooden spoon to slightly mash them up. In doing so, the potato pieces will be able to lie side by side to make a compact cake like a jigsaw puzzle.

Chop the balsamic onions (or pancetta) and scatter over the potatoes. Season with lots of pepper and salt, and then pour in the egg mix. This should be just enough to bind the tortilla, which is much lighter on the egg front than an omelette. Continue to cook on a very low heat until it begins to come away from the edge of the pan. Using a flat plate, turn out the tortilla so that it can then be returned to the pan to brown the top side. This will take 5 minutes, much less time than the first side. When you are happy with the golden colour, remove from the pan, and slice like a cake.

Hot Spanish Squid

For the squid dish, deseed the pepper and cut into hunks. Whiz them up with the peeled garlic and the chillies to make a purée, using a hand-held blender or Magimix. Warm some olive oil in a pan and fry the paprika, cumin and caraway seeds. This is the best way to release the aromas of spices. After a few minutes' frying, add the pepper purée. Cook at a very low heat for about half an hour, or until the juices are a little reduced. If it begins to dry out, add a tablespoon of water at a time to loosen and continue breaking down the flavours. During this time, rinse the squid under a cold running tap and chop into rings 1cm wide (you may need to remove the cartilage, which lies inside the white squid sac. See Feasting Fiestas, page 121). Add this to the pan at the last minute, along with the sugar, lemon juice and parsley, which should be roughly chopped. It will need a minute or two to combine all the flavours and cook the squid, which will go from milky clear to white, but not rubbery please. You may need to add another teaspoon of sugar to balance the flavours, so taste to check.

1 red pepper
4 garlic cloves
2 chillies
lots of olive oil
1 teaspoon smoked paprika
1 teaspoon ground cumin
1 teaspoon caraway seeds
3 tubes of squid
1 teaspoon golden caster sugar
juice of 1 lemon
½ bunch of fresh parsley

Garlic Fried Prawns

To cook the prawns, heat the butter in a pan, peel and finely chop the garlic and chilli and throw them into the pan. Allow them to fry long enough to smell but not turn brown; a few minutes. Add the prawns and then the wine, so that they have just enough time to turn from translucent to pinky-white, and the alcohol from the wine has had time to evaporate. You will need to turn over the large prawns so that each side gets well cooked. It will take 3 to 5 minutes. Then take off the heat. Roll up your sleeves, and enjoy the mess.

6 garlic cloves
1 fresh chilli
a big knob of butter
12 large king prawns
1 glass of white wine or rosé

Vietnamese Salad with Steak

For 2

This salad will always remind me of a summer date, in the early throes of romance. We'd been to a private view at my friend Piero's gallery, and when we finally hailed a taxi back to Brixton it was much later than expected. Luckily for my date, I'd thought ahead: the fresh, crunchy flavours of the Vietnamese salad had been marinating all afternoon, and so we were at the table in minutes, devouring this awesome Asian feast.

I mix and match the salad ingredients according to my mood: sometimes heavy on the carrots, sometimes lighter on the coriander. With noodles. With poached chicken pieces. It's an endlessly evolving prototype, so feel free to experiment. Whatever you decide on, this dish is full of colour and texture and abundance and is really impressive.

I cannot stress enough how much I love my mandolin slicer. It makes everything that comes under its knife look seriously svelte. And where a grater releases a lot of the juices, a mandolin is sharp enough to leave the vegetables unbruised. There are few things that are imperative in a kitchen, but I would say that the mandolin is one. So …

The Salad

With a mandolin slicer on the fine setting, slice the peeled carrots over a nice big salad bowl. Slice the peppers and spring onions lengthways into matching shards. If you have a Magimix, pulse the peanuts to crumbs, but not dust. I usually put them into a plastic bag and attack them with a rolling pin, which can look a little crazed if someone unexpected finds their way into the kitchen. Finely chop the herbs and then mix everything together in the bowl with your hands. Finally mix up the remaining ingredients with a fork and pour over your salad.

4 medium carrots

1 red pepper

1 yellow pepper

3 spring onions

3 tablespoons slightly salted peanuts

a big handful of fresh coriander

a big handful of fresh mint

juice of 1 lime

2 teaspoons fish sauce

2 tablespoons peanut oil

2½ tablespoons rice vinegar

1 dessertspoon soy sauce

1 teaspoon sugar

The Steak

2 fillet steaks, weighing about 180g each
5 tablespoons soy sauce
freshly ground black pepper
1 tablespoon soya paste (which can be bought at Korean and Japanese supermarkets: see My Favourite Places to Eat, Drink & Shop, page 338)
2 tablespoons peanut oil

Now for the steak: first, don't hold back on the price, especially if you like it rare, because if it is not good quality it will be tough. Although I don't advocate big spending, it really is worth it here. Marinate the steaks in 3 tablespoons of the soy sauce and lots of black pepper for an hour at the least. Meanwhile, thoroughly mix the remaining soy sauce with the soya paste. This will be the accompanying dipping sauce for rare steaks.

In a heavy-bottomed pan, heat the oil so that it is piping hot. Add the steaks and turn down to a medium heat. Fry them for just long enough so that they are sealed and browning in parts, which will be about 4 minutes on the first side. Flip and do the same on the other side, adding any leftover soy sauce to the pan. For rare steak, when you press it, it should feel like the flesh between your thumb and index finger, when spanned and relaxed. Remove quickly from the pan, and serve up with the salad as a vibrant feast.

Pyrenean Duck with Champ

For 2

The fattiness of a duck breast is amazing, and anyone who removes it is insane. The best duck I have ever eaten was with Pat, in the heart of the Gers. We were staying at his parents' beautiful home, in the shadow of the Pyrenees. They fried it on their open fire and we all huddled around to ward off the January frosts. It was a rare and wonderful moment. The skin of the bird became sweet and crisp, but the flesh was still rare and tender. Sheer indulgence, and possibly the best way to eat this game.

In this recipe, the aim is to have really crisp skin on top and tender, rare flesh underneath. When you carve the breasts, a fair amount of juice will run out. Catch this, and pour over the champ after plating it all up. This meal is great for real meat lovers, with wonderfully conventional tastes. I tested the recipe out on the lovely Miranda and Mr Smiley, and even converted him to the merits of fruit with meat, so was very satisfied indeed. The fruit against the tangy champ is yet another great dynamic on the plate. Serve with a little broccoli or wilted spinach leaves or green beans.

The Champ

Peel the potatoes and cut them into quarters. Place in a large saucepan of water and bring to the boil. Put a lid on top, and simmer on a medium heat until they slip off a sharp knife (up to half an hour). In the meantime, finely chop the spring onions, using as much of the green parts as you can. Drain the potatoes and return them to the pan. Add the butter and the cream. Mash thoroughly, until creamy and smooth, then season with pepper and salt. Champ is much more velvety than its English brother mash, so really put some elbow grease into it. You could even use a hand-held whisk. Finally, add the spring onions.

500g King Edward potatoes, or any other British floury variety
6 spring onions
50g butter
100ml double cream
freshly ground black pepper
Maldon sea salt

The Duck

Now for the breasts: score the skins so that you go almost as deep as the flesh. Using a griddle pan, if you have one, heat the butter on a medium to high heat so that it is near to smoking. Attentively place the duck in the pan, skin side down. This will create some serious spitting. Fry for 10 minutes, or until the skin is beginning to brown and become crispy, then turn the breasts over. Continue to cook, allowing all the fat to melt out of the bird, while finely slicing the nectarine. Once the breasts have had another 5 minutes and they are to your taste (like steak, it is up to you how rare you want them – for me, the bloodier the better), remove and let them relax on a chopping board. Add the sliced nectarine to the pan, so it cooks in the duck juices. Quickly pan-fry for a few minutes, then with a heavy fork mash it a little so that it is almost like a chutney. Carve the duck into morsels and pile the champ on to the plate, with the nectarine alongside.

2 duck breasts
50g butter
1 nectarine

A Ceviche Fish-off with Corona & Guacamole & Tomato Salsa

For 2

I'm planning a fish-off with Raf. He's going to cook tuna marinated in grapefruit juice and soy sauce, and I'm seducing him with ceviche and Corona. Do eat it with beer, though: I've made the mistake of eating this with red wine, and spent a good few minutes hopping around trying to assuage the heat of the chillies.

Most famously from Peru, ceviche is seafood marinated in lime juice. You can use any white fish or shellfish: scallops, prawns, squid, sea bass, cod and so on. Partially cooked by the lime, it's just a small step from sushi, and therefore exceedingly enticing for fish fanatics. The chilli heat is tempered by the tender fish that will melt in your sizzling mouth. The first time I made this dish, it really did blow my mind.

The flavours in the fish are fresh and zesty and chilli hot, and suit equally fresh vegetables like this salsa and guacamole. You'll need to buy a sack of limes. You have been warned! The ceviche and salsa can be served with fried plantain, pitta, crispy tortilla chips or with the corn cakes in Dawn Chorus (on page 33). I like the pic'n'mix style – an array of little bowls to get entangled over. But of course, guacamole is one of those favourite foods that everyone loves, especially if there's a big bowl of it in the middle of a table of waiting and drinking friends. I often make this to whet everyone's appetite, whether having an Americas meal or not.

The Ceviche

Start with the ceviche, as it needs time to marinate. You need to prepare your fish carefully, so with a very sharp knife, cut down the back of the prawns and remove the black string. Strip them of their legs and shells, carefully removing the head. Take the skin off the fish and cut into slivers about 1cm wide. Place the seafood and fish in a freezer bag. Finely chop the chilli and coriander, and add this to the bag. Squeeze in the limes and give it all a really good mix around. Tie up the bag and leave to marinate in the fridge, sitting in a bowl, for a couple of hours.

12 tiger prawns
200g sea bass or sea bream
1 fleshy index-finger-sized chilli
2 generous handfuls of fresh coriander
6 limes

The Guacamole

Now for the guacamole. If you have a hand-held blender this would come in very handy. (If not, a pestle and mortar is fine.) Peel the garlic and place in a tall-sided bowl or jug. Now stone the avocados (I do this by halving the fruit then flailing a large knife into the stone, which will twist the whole thing out – precarious but effective) and scoop the bright green flesh into the bowl. Chuck in the tomatoes, and squeeze in the lime juice. Then add the chopped chilli, peeled and diced onion and roughly chopped coriander, and give it a good pulsing with the blender. Season after tasting.

2 garlic cloves
2 really ripe avocados
3 cherry tomatoes
juice of 3 limes
1 fleshy index-finger-sized chilli, with seeds
½ red onion
a small handful of fresh coriander
Maldon sea salt
freshly ground black pepper

The Tomato Salsa

Lastly the salsa. Partly peel the cucumber, halve it lengthways and then deseed by incising either side of the seeds and scooping them out with a teaspoon. Deseed the tomatoes. Chop both finely into little cubes, peel and finely chop the garlic, and put everything into a bowl. Dress with the olive oil and season.

½ cucumber
4 big tomatoes
3 garlic cloves
2 tablespoons extra virgin olive oil
freshly ground black pepper
Maldon sea salt

Partners in Crime

Parmesan

pine nuts

spinach

nutmeg

cheese

onion

MINT

PEA

4 EVA

tomatoes

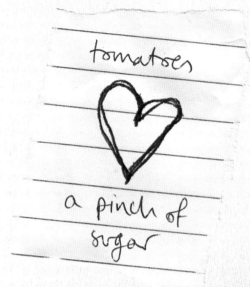

a pinch of
sugar

COURGETTE

PECORINO

AUBERGINE

SALAMI

lentils

saffron

Frozen Berries & Grapes

For 2

This was Doctor Helen's idea. It's brilliant, and perfect for sharing, cuddled up on the sofa with your sweetheart. It is exactly as it says, and so couldn't be easier. The frozen fruits come out like little bullets of sorbet, perfect for grappling over after a good feed.

berries of your choice

Choose your berries (I would suggest green grapes and blueberries, and raspberries are great too, all in season during the summer) and rinse them under a running tap. Dry them with some kitchen towel or a clean linen drying-up cloth. Leave them in a Tupperware box for at least 2 hours in the freezer, and there waiting, with no effort, are your mini sorbet jewels.

Sweet Pastry Swirls

Makes about 15 sweets

Using up off-cuts of pastry is something I end up doing a lot. It's my family thriftiness, where all wastage was rehashed into the next meal, fed to the chickens or dogs, or put in the compost. It is a natural reflex. So if you have some leftover pastry, after making a tart, you are already halfway there. I'm cheating by calling it pudding, because it is really just something to munch on with coffee that will look effortless. In the shop I make these with cinnamon, to treat my special customers, a surprise nestling in the saucer of their cappuccino. You could also try spreading with a film of chocolate or jam – fig or quince is delicious. It is not that far from a fig roll, after all. You can really experiment.

Preheat the oven to 180°C/Gas 4 and line a baking tray with grease-proof paper. Roll out the pastry on a floured surface so that it forms a long but not too wide sheet, about 10cm in width, and as long as you can make it. Create a paste by mixing the olive oil with the sugar and ground cinnamon. Add 1 tablespoon of milk to the paste to loosen it. With a palette knife, spread this evenly over the pastry. Using a pastry brush, dab some of the remaining milk along one side of the pastry sheet. Now roll it from the opposite side to create a long thin sausage. It should seal where you have dabbed it with milk when pressed. Paint the top of the sausage with the rest of the milk. Slice into 2.5cm pieces, and bake on the lined baking tray for 10 minutes, or until the pastry colours. Remove from the tray to cool, and serve with good coffee.

off-cuts of pastry, about a handful
some plain flour for rolling
1 teaspoon olive oil
1 tablespoon granulated sugar
3 tablespoons ground cinnamon
2 tablespoons warm full-fat milk

Affogato

For 2

This is a great way of doing something super stylish with zero effort. Perfect, therefore, for a date. It is, quite simply, ice cream drowned in espresso. There is something amazing about the contrasts of hot and bitter with ice cold and sweet. It throws your tastebuds into confusion. The added brilliance is that you can really experiment with the ice cream flavours here, though I would avoid fruit ice creams. Anything nutty works really well with the espresso. My favourite is Amaretto, but Jude's (www.judes.co.uk) do an awesome butterscotch one too that is delicious here and perfectly sweetens the coffee.

2 small strong cups of espresso coffee (I use Molinari because it's what I serve up at Rosie's)

4 balls of good-quality ice cream

Boil the kettle to make a strong pot of coffee, like espresso, pouring over the water and letting the mountain of coffee settle until it can be easily plunged. You can leave it to sit for 10 minutes or more. The stronger the better, as it will get the heart racing. Meanwhile, bring the ice cream out of the freezer so it has time to soften enough for you to scoop it out. I sometimes serve this in my little Pyrex coffee cups, which I bought in France at a *brocante*. Put a couple of scoops in each coffee cup and bring to the table with the cafetière. Pour over an espresso-sized amount of coffee, or one part coffee to one part ice cream. Eat sooner than immediately.

Lemon Tart

For 2 with leftovers

My first experience with a serious lemon tart was in Toulouse on a mini-break. The boy in question and I had just shared a sturdy cassoulet by the cathedral, and were walking through the back streets when we stumbled on a beautiful teashop. This idyll was a heavenly Alice in Wonderland boudoir, with cakes piled high on tiered stands, and chic, sleek, gossiping French women. My eyes were on stalks and we shared the most delicious lemon tart. So delicious that it famously caused a stir in his trousers and it has been our joke ever since.

Here is my re-creation. It's something to do with the contrast of the sweet pastry and sharp custard that does it, making your jaw ache with longing for more and more citrus custard. And it being a classic pudding means that pretty much anyone you are entertaining will fancy a slice. This sunny tart goes down a treat at Rosie's because it's just so perfectly tangy.

The Pastry

For the pastry, sift the flour and sugar together into a large bowl, and chop the butter into this. Quickly and with cold dry hands, rub in the fat until it looks like damp breadcrumbs. Separate the egg and throw the yolk into the pastry mix. With a knife, cut through the mixture to combine into a dough ball. You may need a little extra cold water to fully draw it together.

On a floured surface, roll out the pastry to fit a loose-bottomed rectangular flan tin measuring about 8 x 23cm. Sweet pastry, or pâte sucrée, is stickier than the average shortcrust, so make sure you have plenty of flour to hand. Then roll it over the tin and push in the edges, being careful not to split the pastry. Roll the pin over the tart tin to cut off any excess pastry (which you can keep aside for pastry swirls, see 69), and place in the freezer for half an hour.

Meanwhile, heat the oven to 200°C/Gas 6. When the oven is piping hot, and the pastry is really cold, you are ready to blind bake. Line the pastry tin with greased paper or tinfoil, and scatter with baking beans or dried chickpeas. Place in the oven for 10 minutes, or until the edges are beginning to brown. Keep a close eye on it. Remove the baking beans and lining paper and bake for a further couple of minutes to dry out the base. Remove from the oven to cool while you make the lemon custard filling. Keep the oven on, but reduce the temperature to 180°C/Gas 4.

100g plain flour, plus extra for rolling
25g caster sugar
50g fridge-cold unsalted butter
1 medium free-range egg yolk (keep the white for meringues)

The Lemon Filling

2 lemons
2 medium free-range
    egg yolks
2 medium free-range
    eggs
90g sugar (caster or
    icing sugar)
150ml double cream,
    plus a little extra for
    serving if you like

For the lemon custard, grate the lemon zest and combine with the egg yolks and eggs. Sift in the sugar and then add the cream. Lastly mix in the juice of the lemons. Return the pastry case to the oven shelf, and pour the filling in now. That way you can't spill it over the edge of the pastry case in transit. Bake for about half an hour, or until the top has just stopped wobbling.

Bunty's Brandy & Oranges

For 2

My grandmother Bunty is a great cook too. When people knew little of Mediterranean food in the 1950s and 1960s, she was churning out moussaka and pasta for her large and extended family. This dish is her moniker. Though perhaps it's brandy that is her signature really. Brought up in France, she has a tipple in her coffee every morning to jump-start her day. The brandy is a good way to inject a little life into your lover, as it has a tendency to make the heart rather palpitate.

The key to this simple dish, apart from being utterly delicious and full of kick, is in the presentation: either laying the slivers of orange out flat on a pretty, decorated serving plate, or piling them up in coloured glasses or flutes with a brandy and juice pool enticing you at the bottom.

With a very sharp serrated knife, peel the oranges, removing all the pith. Slice them finely into roundels and arrange, as you will serve them, either in a beautiful bowl or a couple of flutes, catching the orange juice.

In a small saucepan, make a caramel syrup with the sugar, water and excess orange juice. Warm this on a low heat to reduce. It should begin to darken and thicken. When this has just turned a golden brown colour, but before it burns, pour the brandy over the oranges, and then this syrup. You can do all of this in advance. Resist serving with cream, as it curdles with the juice of the fruit. In winter, adding a cinnamon stick to the syrup will add warmth, while in summer you could add a sprig of mint.

4 oranges (I sometimes use blood oranges)
2 tablespoons granulated sugar
6 tablespoons water
8 tablespoons brandy

view from Cafe del Epices

FEASTING FIESTAS

I love dinner parties. Plotting, inviting, shopping, scrubbing, cooking … and devising the menu to fit my hatching plan: are we having a drawn-out dinner with red wine and kitchen dancing, and lots of courses, or are we having an impressive but light meal before going out like an army of ravers? And then, have we got enough chairs? I usually over-invite and end up with a ram of people around a small table. And then there is the mixing of friends, old and new. I love the melting pot.

My parents were always feeding people, beautifully, on a shoestring. Flowers crept in from the garden, chard and borage picked from the vegetable patch. My dad polished candlesticks, with Jimmy Cliff records playing in the background. As they sat down to eat, I'd sit in the dark at the top of the stairs and eavesdrop on all the family secrets. And when we were a little older, my brother Olly and I were included in these feasts of gratin, salmon and hollandaise.

My dinners are a little more informal than my parents'. I expect people to help themselves and clear the plates and really get stuck in. I probably cook more laid-back food, and things are always a bit makeshift, and quite often I forget some ingredients and have to improvise. When Alice and I lived together in a tiny little flat above a fishmonger, with no natural light, we managed to feed a stream of friends, and all around our glass-topped desk. And we were constantly broke too, so it was a thrifty but consistently exuberant business.

Menu

Meals

Esme's Hot Wings, Daddy's Jamaican Ackee & Saltfish, Fried Plantain & Coconut Coleslaw — 80

Moroccan Honey Chicken, Pomegranate Couscous & Chickpea Purée — 85

Lots of Houmous, Halloumi with Red Onion, Stav's Babaghanoush, Daddy's Meatballs & Carrot Purée — 89 *an Eastern type dinner party*

Roasted Salmon & Fennel Pâté & Puff Pastry Pie — 94

Chicken Pieces Two Ways, Potato Gratin, Carrot & Celeriac — 99 *birthday banquets from Edinburgh*

Hot Chips & Tips — 104

Rice Cubes, Tofu with Mangetouts, Mango, Cucumber & Mint Salad, Sweetcorn & Carrot Fritters — 108

Apricot-stuffed Belly of Pork, Spring Cabbage with Caraway Seeds, Spinach in White Sauce — 114 *saturday afternoon with Daisy, Sam & Simon*

Indian Stuffed Squid, Jeera Rice, Turmeric Cabbage — 120

Puddings

Esme's Hot Wings, Daddy's Jamaican Ackee & Saltfish, Fried Plantain & Coconut Coleslaw

For 8

My dad had a few Jamaican girlfriends in his youth, before he met my mum. He picked up this dish too, ackee and saltfish. It's one of my all-time far-out favourites. When I moved to London with him, aged eighteen, I'd beg him to make this, whenever we were having Peckham dinner parties. Ackee is a delicate yellow fruit that feels a little like a tender egg yolk, and looks brainy. The fish is salted to preserve it, like the Spanish *bacalao*, and is the perfect wedding to the ackee. And of course, the ingredients are everywhere in abundance in Brixton market.

Esme, of Esme's hot wings, is the wonderful Jamaican lady who runs an organic vegetable shop opposite mine in the market. She's a real mum, and has always looked after me. This is her spicy marinade. The reason I started making hot wings is that I'm a horror, and love the odd late-night takeaway. My glamorous funny friend Zezi and I have been known to devour more than a box each, after a night out. So I figured it was better for me to learn to make them for myself than to gorge in such a rotten way. These hot wings are good for a summer picnic too.

Esme's Hot Wings

Preheat the oven to 150°C/Gas 2. If you have a blender this will come in really handy now. If you don't, then you are going to have to finely chop the ingredients thoroughly to form a blended marinade and possibly use a potato masher to really pulverise them. Back to the blender though: roughly chop the tomatoes, peel the onion and place in a blender along with the chillies and lime juice. Use the pulse to blend the vegetables, and then add the curry powder, cayenne pepper, soy sauce, sugar and cloves. Pulse again so that it is a watery paste, and no one thing is visible. It should be a pale red. Now add the self-raising flour and salt and pulse again.

Pour this marinade over the chicken wings and give it a thorough mix around so that the pieces are entirely coated. Decant the hot wings to a non-stick baking tray and place in the oven for 1½ hours, turning about three times during this period. When you turn the wings, make sure you really coat and scoop them round in the marinade. Inevitably, some of this marinade will have stuck to the pan. So when you remove the chicken from the pan, make sure you are fastidious in getting all of it out. Lather any of this remaining sauce over the chicken pieces. You can eat these either warm or cold. And they are great to munch on when you get home and in need of a little salt; just remember to wash your face before you go to bed.

3 fresh plump tomatoes
1 medium onion
2 large chillies
juice of 1 lime
1 teaspoon mild curry powder
2 teaspoons cayenne pepper
1 tablespoon soy sauce
3 teaspoons caster sugar
1 teaspoon ground cloves
2 tablespoons self-raising flour
2 teaspoons table salt
16 medium chicken wings, organic if you can find them

Ackee & Saltfish

I recently had an excellent ackee and saltfish with Raf. He took me, and the famous poet Derek Meins, to Lundies in Brockley. They make the best jerk pork I've ever tasted. It is succulent and amazingly slow-cooked. And the ackee and saltfish was deliciously made, full of soft onions and strips of green pepper. So I've incorporated some of their style into my dad's recipe, and also the fine advice of my gigantic Jamaican hustler friend Larry, who recommends adding either tomatoes or tomato ketchup. This is the endearing way in which recipes grow and evolve.

800g skinless and boneless saltfish pieces
2 tablespoons coconut oil
1 teaspoon ground cinnamon
1 teaspoon freshly ground nutmeg
4 medium onions
2 green peppers
6 rashers of unsmoked bacon
2 teaspoons cayenne pepper
1 x 400g tin of chopped tomatoes
4 teaspoons fresh thyme
a pinch of granulated sugar
2 x 540g tins of ackee in salt water

You need to soak the saltfish for at least 12 hours. This is very important, as it will clean off all the preserving salt. If you don't, you will have a seriously parching dinner. Once it has thoroughly soaked, rinse the fish under a running tap and set aside. Heat the coconut oil in a large saucepan on a low flame and fry the cinnamon and nutmeg briefly to release the flavours. Meanwhile, peel and slice the onions into thin strips, and deseed and finely slice the peppers. Add these to the pan, and gently fry for a few minutes to soften. Now cut the bacon into finger-width strips and add to the pan. Sweat for a further few minutes before adding the cayenne pepper, tinned tomatoes, thyme and sugar. Place a lid on the pan and simmer for half an hour, so that the onions are as soft and sweet as they are at Lundies. Now add the rinsed saltfish and simmer for another 5 minutes. Finally, drain and rinse the ackee very carefully, as they break up easily. Add to the saucepan for just long enough for them to warm through, stirring as little as possible.

Coconut Coleslaw

Peel the carrots and slice into little strips, preferably using a mandolin slicer. Put them into a large salad bowl. Now also slice the cabbage into fine strips and, using your hands, mix with the carrots. Dress with some groundnut oil, and a squeeze of lemon or lime. Scatter the coconut over, and give it all a good tossing so that the salad is flecked with the shredded coconut.

4 large carrots
the same amount of
    white cabbage as
    carrots
2 tablespoons
    groundnut oil
1 lemon or lime
2 tablespoons
    desiccated coconut

Fried Plantain

Peel each plantain and slice into 3 chunks. Now slice these chunks lengthways into strips and set aside. For the coating, peel the garlic and crush into a light mixing bowl (light enough for you to toss the plantain and generally throw around). Deseed and very finely chop the chilli, and also add to the bowl. Mix in the thyme, cinnamon and nutmeg. Heat the oil in a frying pan, and when it's really hot, add the plantain in batches. Fry until they are browning and becoming a deep tan colour. Turn to fry both sides, and then remove to the bowl with all the flavours waiting. Toss the batches of plantain around, swirling the bowl, so that the chips are well coated in the aromatics. Serve these along with the ackee and saltfish, hot.

6 large plantains, green
    and darkened
4 garlic cloves
1 chilli
2 teaspoons fresh thyme
1 teaspoon cinnamon
1 teaspoon freshly
    grated nutmeg
6 tablespoons coconut
    oil

Moroccan Honey Chicken, Pomegranate Couscous & Chickpea Purée

Feeds a flock of friends (a meal that can stretch and stretch, but could be for 10)

I fell in love with Moroccan food whilst on holiday in Marrakesh with my flatmate Tom Punch and our good friends the Golding girls. We all really needed this holiday from the Smoke. Returned, refreshed and invigorated, I was fixed on recreating the same exotic and vibrant flavours that had revived us all: pyramids of eggs, oranges, almonds, prunes and apricots reign over the bustling crowds of these speedy alleyways. It is a heady almost hallucinogenic atmosphere: streetfood sizzling everywhere, rich colours, thick smells and overwhelming noise. The magnetic mystery of Morocco is hopefully transported in this meal. I always recommend bringing a little holiday home with you.

It's a great one to fall back on too: I've cooked it in Brixton for the waifs and strays for our alternative Christmas. And I've also transported it up to Islington for Alice's New Year's Eve party and fed more mouths than I could count: like feeding the five thousand. The simple flavours of honey and cloves and clean chicken are great. In fact, this is great to gorge on at Christmas, and I prefer it to any turkey. With this meal, I would serve a simple cheat's pudding: go and buy dates, apricots, nuts, baklava even, or any sweet treats to go with strong coffee.

The chickpea mash belongs to Raf. I first ate it on a Sunday afternoon not having been to bed, still in my glad – but slightly grubby – rags. He took one sorry look at me and started concocting the necessary comfort food. The balance of sweet onions and floury peas is perfect.

Moroccan Chicken

2 French hens, weighing
  1.5kg each
3 bay leaves
4 teaspoons whole
  cloves
2 teaspoons
  peppercorns
2 tablespoons olive oil
4 medium onions
2 teaspoons ground
  cloves
2 sticks of cinnamon
2 bird's-eye chillies
6 garlic cloves
1.2kg fresh plum
  tomatoes
5 tablespoons runny
  honey
freshly ground black
  pepper
Maldon sea salt

Immerse the chickens in a really big pot full of water, with the bay leaves, cloves and peppercorns. I use one of those awesomely deep saucepans. Simmer for an hour and a half, or until the birds are fully poached (and no blood runs from the flesh when pressed into with a sharp knife). This poaching makes for wonderfully moist succulent meat. Allow the chicken to cool right down, otherwise you will have blistered fingers from the stripping. This cooling will take a few hours. During this time you can get on with the other two dishes. Stripping is really satisfying if you get your sleeves rolled up and get down and dirty. It took me a long time to get the guts to really go for it. Keep the stock aside from the poaching pan, and use for loosening the tomato sauce and hydrating the couscous. You can also freeze any surplus stock for a rainy risotto day.

For the tomato sauce, warm the olive oil on a low heat, in a really big pan. Peel and finely chop the onions into 5mm pieces or smaller. Add to the pan and gently fry, along with all the ground cloves, cinnamon and finely chopped chillies. After a few minutes peel, crush and add the garlic. While this is sweating away (but not browning), roughly chop the tomatoes and add to the pan. You are aiming for this to be a very clean and smooth sauce, so it will require long slow cooking for around an hour. It may need a little stock (from the chicken) to loosen the sauce. When you are satisfied with the texture, add the honey and the stripped chicken pieces, pepper and salt.

Pomegranate Couscous

This kind of a couscous is great: full of colour, texture and surprise, adorned like a Hatton Garden jewellers. The pomegranate seeds really make it. I buy whole pomegranates in Brixton market, but the seeds are also available in tubs in some supermarkets.

Scatter the almond flakes in a large dry frying pan. Continually toss them on a low heat until they are toasted a warm peachy gold. The turning happens quickly, so keep an eye on them. It will take just a few minutes. Remove the almonds from the pan and set aside to cool on a plate (if you leave them in the pan they will continue to toast and may still burn yet).

Heat the chicken stock to simmering point in a pan. Next pour the couscous grains into a big bowl, much bigger than the dry volume, as the grains will expand greatly. Pour the hot fresh chicken stock over the couscous to cover, plus an extra 5cm. Immediately cover the bowl with clingfilm and let it steam itself in this sealed environment. Leave for at least 20 minutes before uncovering and fluffing with a fork (not a spoon) to get air into it. If it is still a little crunchy in the centre of the grain, drizzle over a little more hot stock. Beware though. It is really easy to overdo the amount of liquid and end up with a sodden schmaltz. Season with lots of pepper and salt. While it is cooling, pull apart the pomegranate and take out the seeds, being careful to remove the pith from around these jewels. Scatter these and the toasted almonds over the couscous.

400g flaked almonds
1.5 litres stock from the chicken pot (or vegetable bouillon if you are making the couscous dish separately from this meal)
5 coffee cups of couscous (1 cup per 2 people)
freshly ground black pepper
Maldon sea salt
1 pomegranate

Chickpea Purée

This is the smudge to accompany the rest of the meal, the anointing extra.

3 x 400g tins of
    chickpeas
1 large onion
3 tablespoons olive oil
1 teaspoon ground
    cumin
juice of 1 lemon
fresh coriander leaves
freshly ground black
    pepper
Maldon sea salt

The chickpea purée will take no time. Drain the chickpeas and rinse in a colander. Peel and finely chop the onion. Warm the olive oil in a medium pan on a low heat, add the onion, and sweat until transparent and deliciously sweet, then add the cumin. This will take about 5 minutes. Add the chickpeas and let them warm through, adding a little water, lemon juice and more olive oil if necessary (as the spices can make the situation a little sticky). When the ingredients are hot throughout, blend, or mash if your arms are feeling more robust. Turn out into a good serving dish and scatter the top of the purée with chopped fresh coriander and lots of pepper and salt.

Lots of Houmous, Halloumi with Red Onion, Stav's Babaghanoush, Daddy's Meatballs & Carrot Purée

For 4 to 6

I love all things Eastern, and especially Turkish. I fell in love with the Yesil Irmak shop in Peckham and it was one of my first food onslaughts when I moved to London, all naïve and too friendly at eighteen. I would pop in there on my way home each night and wonder at the foreign delights: baklava and aniseed bread, pots of fresh cheese and curious dark sausages. This encouraged my girlfriends Zahra and Flora and me to head off for a holiday to Istanbul. We laughed our way through a lot of grilled sardines and the warm and spiced streets. So these dishes conjure up a hash of wonderful memories, people and places.

For entertaining I really like interactive little piles of food. Having lots of plates of food is a good way of everyone getting stuck in, encouraging sharing and reaching over each other. It's the same at Rosie's: people have to borrow sugar bowls from one another, and reach over the small space to find a corner of sanctuary: it's not polite, but it's much more fun, and if your friends don't all know each other, it breaks the ice.

I'm pretty excited, looking at the potential of an abundant table, tumbling with mismatching plates of delicate morsels and colours and lots of candles and open bottles. And these dishes are super simple and really tasty. I had some lovely girls and Raf and his friend Kris round for dinner for this banquet. Kris is a local Brixtonian, and works at Soul Jazz records in Soho. They were all well sated by the end of these exotic flavours, so you'll be flying.

Lots of Houmous

Houmous is a great thing to master, and once you see how easy and cheap it is, you'll never buy the shop stuff again. I make it daily at Rosie's to go in granary sandwiches with black salty olives and ripe tomatoes. And at home it often provides the padding when I've got a few too many guests and stomachs need filling. My friend Matt Slop is obsessed with it, and adds all sorts of delights: coriander, sunblushed tomatoes, olives. He likes an economical packed lunch in the office and saves loads of money like this. You can also toast cumin seeds and sprinkle them on top. Below is the basic structure from which to work.

2 x 400g tins of
    chickpeas
6 garlic cloves
2 tablespoons tahini
juice of 2 lemons
4 tablespoons extra
    virgin olive oil
2 teaspoons Maldon sea
    salt

Drain the chickpeas and rinse thoroughly. Place all the ingredients in a jug and whiz up with a hand-held blender. Do taste, as getting the balance of houmous right is a satisfying calculation and can take a little playing around.

Halloumi with Red Onion

Finely chop the chilli. Warm the olive oil in a frying pan on a low heat and when it is hot, add the chilli. After a minute or so turn the pan up to a moderate flame. Slice the cheese into thin slivers, less than 1cm, and add to the pan. Turn with tongs once each side is golden and decorated (if you don't have tongs, use a fork). Then peel and very finely chop the red onion and scatter half on a flat serving plate. Remove the halloumi from the pan when golden and wilting and add to the serving plate. Scatter over the rest of the onion, along with a little chopped mint. Cut this salad with the acidity of a juiced lemon and some pepper.

1 fleshy index-finger-sized chilli
2 tablespoons olive oil
2 packs of halloumi
1 large red onion
a handful of chopped fresh mint
1 lemon
freshly ground black pepper

Stav's Babaghanoush

Stav and I have worked together for a few years and we party together too. She's vegan, which is a real test on my culinary skills, but I'm beginning to satisfy her demands. This is a great recipe of hers, which is of course vegan. And smoky, and velvet-textured and really delicious. It's as easy to make as houmous too, only requiring an initial roasting followed by some good blitzing.

Preheat the oven to 180°C/Gas 4. Slice the aubergines once length-ways, and place, cut side up, on a non-stick baking tray. Bake in the oven until they are really soft, which may take an hour or more. They should scrape easily out of their skins once released around the edges with a sharp knife. Pile this flesh, along with the paprika, lemon juice, olive oil, peeled garlic cloves and seasoning, into a bowl and thoroughly blend with a hand-held blender. Taste and add more seasoning if necessary. Cool before serving.

2 medium aubergines
½ teaspoon smoked sweet paprika
juice of 1 lemon
1 tablespoon extra virgin olive oil
3 or 4 garlic cloves
Maldon sea salt
freshly ground black pepper

Daddy's Meatballs

My dad makes these regularly, and they are one of his *pièce de résistance* dishes, linking him with his Sufi philosophy, a big love of Turkey, and his continually growing collection of Islamic arts. He's a bit of a prophet, so you should feel some magic in these balls.

800g lamb mince
2 handfuls of rolled oats
2 medium carrots
2 medium free-range eggs
1 teaspoon ground cumin
2 garlic cloves
freshly ground black pepper
Maldon sea salt
150g medium-ground polenta
3 tablespoons olive oil

It's great if you can overcome any squeamishness and really clothe your hands in this dish. Pile the lamb into a bowl with the oats, and loosen it first with your fists. Peel and grate in the carrot. Beat 1 of the eggs and add, really squelching the meat around between your fingers. Add the cumin, and crush the garlic and add this too, along with some seasoning. Let it sit for a few hours so that it can really melge (if you have time, overnight).

After a few hours, make little balls in your palms about 5cm wide. Beat the second egg and pour on to a plate. On another plate, lay out the polenta. Roll each meatball in the egg mix and then in the polenta. When all the meatballs are ready, heat a tablespoon of the oil in a frying pan and warm the oven to 100°C/Gas ¼. When the frying pan is really hot, add a few of the prepared balls and brown them all over. When they are coloured, remove from the pan to an ovenproof dish and place in the oven. Fry the next lot of meatballs, adding more oil where necessary. Let them sit in the oven for half an hour to just cook them through tenderly.

Carrot Purée

This originally came from a recipe by Ghillie Basan that I've tweaked to fit my Turkish memories. The purée acts as a sauce for the meatballs and cuts the rich aromatic meat with a sweet and spiced freshness. I've done it many times, with different meals. It works well as a dip with pitta bread, or slathered on to a forkful of barbecued kebab, and it looks like a wicked inside-out egg.

Peel and chop the carrots. Place them in a pan with water and bring to the boil. Simmer until they are tender and slip off a knife, near the point of overcooking. Drain away the water and return to the heat, now low. Add the olive oil and the caraway seeds and sweat for a moment to release the flavours. Cool before blending with half the lemon juice, and then the mint leaves. Add more olive oil if it needs some give. Turn this out into a big bowl to cool. In another bowl, beat up the yoghurt, pepper and salt and remaining lemon juice. Peel and crush the garlic and add this to the yoghurt too. Make a well in the middle of the carrot purée and dollop the yoghurt mix into this.

4 large carrots
1 tablespoon olive oil
1 teaspoon caraway seeds
juice of ½ lemon
a few sprigs of fresh mint
4 tablespoons natural yoghurt
freshly ground black pepper
Maldon sea salt
2 garlic cloves

Roasted Salmon & Fennel Pâté & Puff Pastry Pie

A dinner party for 4

If you are trying to create an impression, then this is a great meal – none of the elements are actually complicated, but it all appears dead dextrous.

I worked out the pâté recipe really because fennel, in season July to October, is my favourite vegetable. It is delicately aniseedy and of a light texture too, which when combined with the fine-textured salmon makes a smooth chemistry. And making it with organic salmon is undoubtedly a cut above: the fillet will be pale and velvety, and much more subtle in flavour than its fishier bright coral counterpart. However, when I'm strapped for cash, I do go for mainstream non-organic salmon.

You could serve this as a starter salad by dressing some sweet lamb's lettuce leaves and dolloping big spoonfuls of the pâté in the middle of each plate. It is very adaptable and super easy. If you decant the mix into little ramekins and seal it as described, with a lid of melted butter, it keeps for almost a week and can then be spread on pitta or toast. So if you make a little too much, you will have a midnight feast or breakfast morsel sorted too.

The pillow pie is an old favourite and all it needs is a salad for company. There is something fantastically exciting about plunging a big sharp knife into this pillow of light pastry and revealing the self-steamed contents. First drawn to my attention by Nigel Slater, I have cooked this formula time and time again: birthday parties, Sunday lunches, last-minute gatherings (the joy of keeping some puff pastry in the freezer), with many different combinations inside. All you have to do is roll out the pastry and fill it at your whim. Easy. Courgette, ham and pecorino? Pea and Taleggio? Pea, mint and goat's cheese? Mushrooms, crème fraîche and Parmesan? Onion, leek and parsley? There are endless choices. Like a risotto, once you have mastered the format the rest is plain sailing. And while it is in the oven you will get a chance to straighten out your flat and have a quiet drink, before your friends arrive.

Salmon & Fennel Pâté

Preheat the oven to 180°C/Gas 4. Cut the fennel bulb into about 6 slices, working from leaf to root. Place on a baking tray, pour the olive oil over and put into the oven for 30 minutes, or until it is soft in the centre and browning at the edges. Remove to a bowl and cool.

Meanwhile, cut the fish into 12 chunks and place it on the same tray in the oven for 10 minutes or until it is just cooked. While the salmon is roasting, combine the fennel with the crème fraîche, lime juice and parsley. Using a blender, pulse this to form a light smooth paste. Now add the slightly cooled salmon, forking it into the creamy mix. Melt half the butter and add this too. Now taste and season. Spoon and firmly pack into four ramekins or one big shallow dish and allow the pâté to cool. Melt the rest of the butter, pour over the pâté to create a lid (and therefore a perfect preserving seal) and place in the fridge. When it is nice and firm, serve. This is best made the night before, if you have the time.

1 fennel bulb
1 tablespoon olive oil
350g good salmon fillets
1 tablespoon crème
    fraîche
juice of 1 lime
a handful of fresh
    parsley leaves or
    some fresh dill
100g butter
Maldon sea salt
freshly ground black
    pepper

Puff Pastry Pie

a knob of butter or 1 tablespoon vegetable oil

500g puff pastry (defrosting bought ready-rolled puff pastry will take 1½ hours)

a little plain flour for rolling

150g ham (I am currently using a free-range Sussex ham)

½ bag/100g spinach

80g pecorino (or any other melty cheese you can find: raclette, Emmental, Fontina)

200g crème fraîche

100g frozen garden peas

1 teaspoon dried thyme

1 teaspoon dried oregano (which can be substituted with parsley, marjoram or basil)

freshly ground black pepper

Maldon sea salt

1 medium free-range egg for glazing

Preheat the oven to 170°C/Gas 3. You will need a flat baking tray, preferably non-stick. Grease this with a knob of butter or some vegetable oil. I like ready-rolled pastry in this instance, because it cuts down your workload. However, if you have got those slabs of frozen puff pastry that's fine too. And if you do, then roll out these two sheets of pastry on a lightly floured surface to fit the tray, right up to the edges. Place one of the pastry leaves on the tray, ready, and set aside.

For the filling, you need to prepare each ingredient and pile it into a large mixing bowl: roughly chop the ham and spinach into 2.5cm pieces. Grate the pecorino, and measure out the crème fraîche and peas. Finally add the thyme and oregano and seasoning. Work these ingredients together in the mixing bowl. Leaving a couple of centimetres around the edge, heap this mixture onto the pie base. Beat the egg and paint around the edges of the base. Now roll the top sheet of pastry over the pie, and marry to the bottom, sealing it. You may want to use a fork to really bind the crusts together. Make a couple of holes in the pastry lid so that some steam can release when the pie is baking. You can incise the top with a knife to create a decoration, if you fancy a harvest festival/village fête look. Brush the lid with the rest of the egg and place in the oven. The pastry should puff up and become a rich gold. That is when you know it is done, but it should take just over half an hour.

Chicken Pieces Two Ways, Potato Gratin, Carrot & Celeriac

For 6

My birthday dinners at university were always bountiful. I cooked for at least twenty each year, and always for next to nothing. Anyone can do it with a little enthusiasm. Suddenly, pulling out those family favourites for the first time as a semi-adult, I realised how lucky my childhood had been after all. My four very different university kitchens became drop-in centres for hungover and hungry boys. Alice made the tea, and I did the cooking.

The gratin here and also the very simple carrot and celeriac with lots of lemon juice are two of my mum's staple dishes. Simple flavours and easy to recreate. The two chicken recipes are inspired by Nigel Slater, my food hero. I spent much more time poring over his books than I ever did over my lecture notes. Using chicken pieces rather than breasts in this recipe is much more flavoursome, because of the juice-enhancing bone marrow. And they are cheaper too, if you are on a short string.

Chicken Pieces with Oranges & Honey

2 tablespoons runny
    honey
2 oranges
2 tablespoons sweet
    chilli sauce
1 tablespoon soy sauce
2 teaspoons
    peperoncino (which
    are chilli flakes; they
    can be found in good
    old continental delis
    and are the same as
    what gets sprinkled
    on a pizza)
12 pieces of free-range
    chicken
lots of olive oil
freshly ground black
    pepper
Maldon sea salt
a handful of fresh
    coriander leaves

In a bowl, make the marinade by beating up the honey, orange juice (keeping the skins aside), sweet chilli and soy sauces and peperoncino chilli flakes. Place the chicken in a baking dish, pour over the marinade, and let it sit for a few hours at room temperature.

Preheat the oven to 200°C/Gas 6. Finely chop half the orange skins, and roughly chop the other half. Scatter all these around the chicken pieces, wedging where you can. Drizzle with olive oil, pepper and salt, and put in the oven for 50 minutes or more. The chicken skin should be crisp and becoming bubbled and golden. Roughly chop the coriander and scatter over the dish to serve.

Chicken Pieces with Creamy Lemon

Heat the oven to 200°C/Gas 6. Place the chicken in a non-stick baking tray. Peel the garlic and chop the lemons into 6 wedges per fruit. Jam them, and the thyme, around the chicken. Drizzle with olive oil and lots of pepper and salt. Bake for 50 minutes, or until the chicken pieces are crispy and cooked. Check by piercing them with a small knife. The liquid that runs should be clear. Remove the chicken pieces from the tray to an ovenproof dish and return to the oven, turning the oven off, so that it is just keeping them warm with the residual heat. Meanwhile, shred the little leaves off the thyme, discarding the woody stalks, and return them to the baking tray juices. Squeeze the lemon juices in too, discarding the skins. On the hob, on a very low heat, warm the baking tray and gradually add the crème fraîche, using a whisk to fully combine with the flavoursome gravy. Season with a little more pepper and salt if you need to. Pour this creamy sauce over the chicken pieces and serve up.

12 pieces of free-range chicken
6 garlic cloves
2 lemons
a bunch of fresh thyme or tarragon
2 tablespoons olive oil
freshly ground black pepper
Maldon sea salt
200g crème fraîche

Potato Gratin

You can substitute the Gruyère here with any melty cheese, like Edam, Gouda, raclette or Emmental; it depends on your budget. And for the potatoes, anything comfortingly floury is great: Maris Piper, King Edwards, or even Desiree, which are a little tighter but lovely too.

1.5kg good fresh potatoes, like Maris Piper (whatever you get hold of, it makes sense to get English ones)
50g butter
400ml full-fat milk
400ml single cream
4 garlic cloves
freshly ground black pepper
Maldon sea salt
120g Gruyère

Preheat the oven to 180°C/Gas 4. Peel the potatoes and exceedingly finely slice them (preferably with a mandolin slicer) into a big saucepan with the butter, milk, cream, peeled and finely chopped garlic, and lots of pepper and salt. The liquid should come halfway up the potatoes. Simmer on a very low heat turning from time to time (as the dairy element burns easily). When nearly cooked, decant the entire contents of the pan into an ovenproof dish and grate the cheese over. Bake in the oven for 20 minutes, or until firm, golden and bursting with creamy bubbles at the sides. This can even be prepared the night before, leaving the final baking for the night.

Carrot & Celeriac

Peel the carrots. Prepare the celeriac by meticulously cutting away all the knobbly bits, to leave you with a firm white heart. (However, don't overdo it. You don't want to end up with just a mini nub.) Using a mandolin slicer, set to the finer shredding blade, finely slice the carrot and celeriac into a medium saucepan. Add the butter, lemon juice, salt and pepper to this and place on a low heat. With the lid on, sweat the vegetables for 10 minutes, or until they are sweet and fresh but still quite firm. Serve this straight from the pan or decant to a warmed serving dish.

4 medium carrots
400g celeriac
a big knob of butter
juice of 1 lemon
Maldon sea salt
freshly ground black
pepper

Hot Chips & Tips

China

Instead of buying expensive homeware, scour your local junk and charity shops. And pound shops too. I'm a particular fan of Barnado's and the New Covent Garden Sunday market. Of course, nothing beats a car boot sale.

Jars

Decant your ambient ingredients into old jars and those big rubber-sealed Le Parfait jars. It will keep out the weevils.

Shopping Bags

Buy a big basket to take shopping with you, instead of using countless plastic bags. You'll feel regal too.

Snivelling Colds

Pour hot water over fresh ginger, lemon, honey and a real chilli. It'll knock your socks off. I make the last one of the day with a shot of whiskey too: a medicinal nightcap.

Miso soup is what I yearn for when I'm feeling really sorry for myself. I think it must replace all the salts.

Washing Up

Doctor Helen says if you rinse your wooden chopping boards first with cool water it's better. Otherwise they keep the taste of garlic and onions, as it's cooked into the wood by hot water.

When I'm doing a big wash up after a party I always try to do the glasses first, as these need to look the most sparkling.

Fishy Hands

Gervase, Helen's brother, maintains that if you've been handling fish you should wash your hands with cold water first, as hot water will open your pores and let the fish oil seep in.

Tea Stains

Mix bicarbonate of soda and juice of half a lemon in the bottom of a stained teapot or mug, and leave for half an hour to fizz and clean.

Best Pot of Tea

This is made using 1 bag of Earl Grey and 1 bag of PG Tips, which should be brewed for about 5 minutes before pouring the milk into the cup first. Trust me.

Olive Oils

Keep olive oil for cooking and extra virgin olive oil for fresh use and dressings. That way you won't waste the flavour that releases with heat.

Egg Whites

Use a super clean bowl for egg whites, as any oil or fat will prevent them forming peaks when you beat them.

Flavoured Sugar

Use some deseeded vanilla pods in your sugar jar, and you'll have delicately flavoured vanilla sugar.

Over-salting

This is genius advice from my friends Robyn and Lucy. All you need to do is sit a potato in the over-salted dish for 5 minutes, and this porous vegetable will absorb the excess salt.

Blocked Drains

Lelah recommends pouring really short strong coffee down the drain, and watching the blockage bubble up and slip down.

Relaxation

Pat swears by a can of Guinness after a day's labour.

Clothes Pegs

These double up as food storing clips.

Souring Milk

To make sour milk for baking, add 4 tablespoons of lemon juice to 500ml milk and let it sit for 5 minutes.

Fruit Bowls

Leave bananas with your unripe fruit and they will speed up the process. However, bananas with ripe fruit will turn them, so in this case, keep them separate.

Rice Cubes, Tofu with Mangetouts, Mango, Cucumber & Mint Salad, Sweetcorn & Carrot Fritters

For 4 or 5

My conversion to all things Asian, like any personal discovery, was amazingly exciting when it happened and is now almost religious, my passion is so strong. My first memorable foray was sushi with Jasper Swallow, to cleanse a Notting Hill-imposed hangover. And it does do exactly that. I'm now in love with Thai noodles, the stickiness of rice and Chinese supermarkets, the strong-smelling bottles of mysterious fishy sauce and, well, all of it. Attempting to master these far-off flavours is a feat and an exciting challenge.

My following Asian education came through many guises. Tom Punch and I cooking together with ginger and garlic, mastering our favourite pak choi recipe. Being taken by Raf for the best sushi of my life, on Kingly Street, the finale being a mad giblet omelette! And the Chinese supermarkets in Peckham and Brixton, reminding me of travels to Thailand and Singapore. I get a rush of excitement going to shops where I don't recognise the foods on the shelf, and just take a lottery. As my mum always says, 'Suck it and see, darling.' These dishes are a mix and match. All the flavours are fresh and light, and not complicated either. Your friends will get dead excited at such delicate opulence and colour too.

Rice Cubes & Sharp Dipping Sauce

1½ cups of fragrant Thai rice
1 bird's-eye chilli
8 tablespoons rice vinegar
2 tablespoons water
1 tablespoon sugar
1 sprig of fresh mint
1 teaspoon fish sauce
1 teaspoon soy sauce

Overcook the rice, simmering it in a medium pan for about 5 minutes longer than it says on the packet. Taste to test that it is pulpy and sticky. With a potato masher, beat the rice up to break at least half of it down. Line a small shallow tin or bread tin with clingfilm and meticulously press the rice down into the mould, right into the corners, so that it is a dense little brick. Cool to room temperature before chilling for 8 hours in the fridge. Bring out to return the rice to room temperature again and then slice into 1cm cubes with a sharp wet knife (so it doesn't stick to the mould). Mound these up on a nice plate to serve.

Finely chop the chilli into roundels, and place in a pan with the vinegar, water, the sugar, mint and two magic sauces. Simmer for 15 minutes on a low flame to reduce and infuse. Decant into a dipping bowl and leave to cool. Quickly dunk the rice cubes into the dipping sauce and enjoy.

Tofu with Mangetouts & Enoki Mushrooms

I get little bags of ready-fried tofu from my Chinese supermarket in Brixton. They can be found in China Town too, and are delicious and porous, and wonderfully absorb the sweet honey and sharp lime here. This is one of my all-time favourite dishes and I'm always wowed by the beauty of these mad little mushroom bundles that appear so alien and underworld. They become soft, tender and almost meaty once they are cooked, like a good noodle.

Slice each piece of ready-fried tofu into 4 pieces and set aside. Heat the groundnut oil in a medium pan, on a high flame. When it is beginning to form small bubbles, add the tofu, and turn down to a medium flame. Sizzle for a few minutes and then sprinkle in the ginger followed by the mangetouts. Split up the mushrooms into finger-width clumps, as they will come in a big fused bundle. Now add these to the pan as well. Mix this all around a bit, then add the soy sauce and honey and squeeze in the juice of the lime. Let it spit away for a few minutes. When the mangetouts are shiny and a little darker than when they started, the dish is cooked. The greens should be only just cooked and still succulent and crunchy. Spoon the warm salad out on to a serving dish to share around.

400g fried tofu
2 tablespoons groundnut oil
2 teaspoons ground ginger or 1 teaspoon freshly grated ginger
200g mangetouts
120g enoki mushrooms
2 tablespoons dark soy sauce
1 dessertspoon honey
1 lime

Mango, Cucumber & Mint Salad

I really love this salad. It is the coolest, freshest, most revitalising salad ever. I first made it for Tom Punch, and really wanted him to be proud of my advance in the Asian kitchen, as he had taught me so much. And it will take you all of three minutes to prepare, so is ideal if you are busy bubbling other pots.

2 mangoes
1 cucumber
2 handfuls of fresh mint
2 tablespoons toasted
   sesame oil
1½ tablespoons rice wine
   vinegar

Slice the mangoes into little pieces. I do this by chopping off discs of the fruit, scoring it like a chessboard, and then slicing the skin away (as you won't be wanting this, or the furry stone). Try to get as much of the honey flesh off the stone as you can. Pile it into a salad bowl. Peel the cucumber with a potato peeler, then slice lengthways in half. You need to remove the seeds, by using a teaspoon and scraping away. Then slice the two halves again lengthways, and chop into little cubes. Add the cucumber to the mangoes. Now take the mint leaves off their stalks, finely chop, and sprinkle over the salad. Pour the sesame oil and rice wine vinegar over and give it all a good toss around before serving.

Sweetcorn & Carrot Fritters

Makes about 10 little cakes

These fritters are deliciously sweet and crisp. I've made them many times to pick me up. They are just as good when there's little in your cupboard as they are for a feast. You can either dunk them in the rice-cube dipping sauce (and therefore make double the amount suggested on page 110) or serve them up with shop-bought sweet chilli sauce.

Crack the eggs into a nice medium bowl and beat thoroughly with a whisk. Add the cornflour and baking powder to make a smooth paste. Finely chop the spring onion, peeled garlic and coriander and fold into the mix along with the drained sweetcorn. Finally, peel and grate the carrot and add this to the mix. Heat the oil in a frying pan so that it is really hot and quivering, before dolloping these Asian patties in the pan and allowing them to spread, become golden and crisp up. They should be about 5cm in diameter. Remove from the heat to a kitchen towel to get rid of some of the oil. They are best still warm, so if you are doing them in batches it's best to keep them in a warm oven.

2 medium free-range eggs
3 tablespoons cornflour
½ teaspoon baking powder
1 spring onion
1 garlic clove
a small handful of fresh coriander
1 x 285g tin of sweetcorn, drained
1 carrot
3 tablespoons peanut (or vegetable) oil

Apricot-stuffed Belly of Pork, Spring Cabbage with Caraway Seeds, Spinach in White Sauce

Feeds 4

I got a call from Oliver Danger at midnight on Friday, having just got into bed. I adore him so much that when he said he was on his way to Brixton, I got dressed again, reapplied my face, and headed out in the drizzle to repaint the town red at the Dogstar with my best-looking boy friend. We ended up back at mine before not too long, and I didn't make it to sleep until six in the morning, for all of our loony chatting.

But, knowing I'd organised a Saturday afternoon roast with friends (Daisy Bird, Simon Diamond and Sam Michell), and with pretty shaking hands, I got cracking. Reassuring proof, then, that it can't be a hard meal to re-create, and that good times and lack of sleep shouldn't get in the way of some more sophisticated amusements. Having my friends around on the weekend feels like family too: all pitching in to help and working out our love lives via ridiculous horoscopes. This time everyone had such a relaxed afternoon that they were still lolling around on my sofa at two in the morning, with telltale red-stained lips.

Apricot-stuffed Belly of Pork

Preheat the oven to 180°C/Gas 4. Finely chop the apricots and peeled garlic. In a mixing bowl combine the sausagemeat, thyme, apricots and garlic. Season with pepper and salt. I like really squelching everything between my fingers to mix it up. Unwrap the belly of pork on a chopping board. Make sure the skin is well scored, either by you or the butcher. Pack the stuffing on to the meaty side, leaving space along one of the long sides of the slab, where the two will meet. Do your best, when rolling up the belly, to keep the stuffing on board. With some string, tie the mega sausage together like a roasting joint. Place on a baking tray, seam side down. If the butcher has given you the spare ribs as well, place these under the belly on the baking tray. Drizzle the scored skin with olive oil and add more salt, so that it crisps up. Roast for 1½ hours. Allow the pork to rest for 10 minutes or so, covered with some foil, so that it is tender. This relaxes the meat, making it easier to carve. Serve each roundel with a few of the juicy spare ribs.

200g dried apricots
4 garlic cloves
200g sausagemeat
1 teaspoon dried thyme
freshly ground black
    pepper
Maldon sea salt
a slab of belly of pork
    weighing 1–1½kg (you
    can always ask your
    butcher for advice;
    that's what I do)
string
olive oil

Spring Cabbage with Caraway Seeds

Cabbage and pork work really well together, as do all aniseedy flavours: cabbage and sausage hotpot, red cabbage with caraway seeds, fennel salami, which I serve at Rosie's and makes a delicious salad with antipasti. So it is quite fitting to serve belly of pork with this crunchy and verdant scented cabbage.

2 small pointy spring cabbages
1 tablespoon olive oil
2 teaspoon caraway seeds
1 tablespoon white wine vinegar
1 teaspoon sugar

Cut the cabbage into 2.5cm pieces. Warm the oil in a medium pan on a medium flame. Add the caraway seeds and let them sizzle for a few minutes. Add the chopped cabbage and toss for a few minutes to seal. Lastly add the vinegar and sugar, and put a lid on the pan before turning the flame down to low. Sweat it away until the cabbage is tender. This should take about 20 minutes and you may need to add a little water if it starts sticking. You want it to be nicely al dente.

Spinach in White Sauce

Spinach in white sauce is one of Bunty's favourites. It is really comforting nursery food. In fact, most things at my grandmother's house come in a gooey béchamel sauce. Making a really good and well-flavoured one is a useful and adaptable skill for the kitchen. I've made many that are too floury, too wet, too thick, and the rest. The trick is to sweat the roux, and in doing so, to cook the flour. Also, in this instance, the nutmeg works perfectly with the spinach, bringing out all its rich dark irony flavours. Although bagged baby spinach is fine, if you can get hold of proper woody-stalked spinach that would be even better. Try a farmers' market, as it will taste much more substantial and lush. I've listed vegetable stock because most of you will have this. However, if you are a dynamite and you've made some chicken stock with a leftover carcass that would be even better.

In a medium pan on a medium flame, warm the butter until it is melted. Meanwhile, measure out the flour. With a whisk, gradually add this to the butter so that it is well combined. Continue to mix, and let this sweat for a few minutes so that the flour cooks. It will look like lumpy breadcrumbs. Then gradually add the milk, followed by the stock, also continuously and vigorously whisking so that the lumps are smoothed out. It may take some elbow grease to get a silky texture. Now, season with the pepper, nutmeg and mustard. Turn down the heat and let it warm like this for a few minutes. In this time, you can wash the spinach and then begin adding it in thirds. It will look like a lot of greenery, but don't worry, it will all wilt down, and then you can add the rest. Finally, when the spinach has softened into green strands, add salt accordingly. You may not need much, as spinach is salty anyway.

25g butter
30g plain flour
200ml full-fat milk
200ml vegetable stock
freshly ground black
    pepper
a good grate of a whole
    nutmeg
1 teaspoon smooth
    Dijon mustard
1 bag/225g spinach
Maldon sea salt

Indian Stuffed Squid, Jeera Rice, Turmeric Cabbage

For 4

These are some of the favourite dishes I tasted in south India. Every mouthful I eagerly demolished was deliciously simple and delicately infused, and not at all like the British Indian takeaway. Goa is full of light garlicky fish dishes, and mustard seeds abound. Sweet puri, hot dosas, crisp samosas. It makes me warm just to think of it. We ate like kings, sunned ourselves like cats, and slept like babies.

This meal is cheap as chips, and the rice and cabbage are pretty simple. The only thing that really needs attention is stuffing the squid, which can be a little fiddly. But don't be put off. The results are really satisfying. I strongly recommend hunting down coconut oil (not olive oil, please). Although it can be hard to find, it gives everything that sweet beach edge, without being thickly sweet like coconut milk.

Indian Stuffed Squid

First of all, muster a little pluck and prepare the squid: grip the body in one hand and firmly tug from below the eyes with the other, to remove the head from the body. Keep the detached heads aside. Then find the cartilage and carefully release it. It looks strangely like clear plastic. You will know when you find it. Under a running cold tap give each squid a good clean. Stick your finger right inside to make sure it is a clean empty pouch. Now, remove the tentacles from the heads you set aside, as these will make part of the stuffing. Discard the body innards, leaving you with a plate of clean deboned squid, and a plate of clean tentacles.

Preheat the oven to 160°C/Gas 2. Heat the oil in a frying pan so that it melts. Peel and finely chop the onion and garlic and add to the pan. Then add the cumin seeds and curry powder and fry until everything in the pan is turning golden. Now finely chop the tomato and add, followed by the purée. Let this sweat for 10 minutes before finally adding the squid tentacles. Remove from the heat and cool a little before stuffing the little beasts, and sealing with a toothpick. A teaspoon may be too big an implement for the stuffing. I use the handle of a knife, and if need be, make a little slit in the body so that you can get right in there with the stuffing. Place in a baking dish in the oven for half an hour.

500g little squids, all intact (I get them frozen from L.S. Mash & Son)
1 tablespoon coconut oil
1 small onion
2 garlic cloves
1 teaspoon cumin seeds
1 teaspoon mild curry powder
1 tomato
1 tablespoon tomato purée
toothpicks

Jeera Rice

Jeera, or cumin, rice is an Indian staple. The cumin transforms what could be bland, and is one of my favourite spices.

1 tablespoon coconut oil
2 teaspoons whole
    cumin (jeera) seeds
300g basmati rice
500ml water
Maldon sea salt

Heat the oil in a big pan (with a matching lid) on a medium flame. Add the cumin seeds and fry until they begin to smoke. This will be a lot less than a minute. Then add the rice, followed by the water. Bring to the boil before fitting on a lid, and turning down the heat. Simmer like this for 10 minutes. When all the water on the surface is absorbed, and little chimneys of bubbles have emerged, turn the heat off, but put the lid back on. Leave the rice to sit for at least 20 minutes. This is the final cooking phase. Grind salt over before serving.

Turmeric Cabbage

600g white cabbage
1 tablespoon coconut oil
1 teaspoon cumin seeds
2 teaspoons turmeric
2 teaspoons mustard
    seeds
285ml water
sugar
table salt

Very finely chop the cabbage so that it is almost shredded, and set aside. Heat the oil in a big pan on a medium heat. Throw in the cumin seeds, turmeric and mustard seeds and fry until they begin to smoke. Add the cabbage and seal with the spices, giving it a good mix around. Then add the water and bring it to a simmer before covering. Continue to heat like this for 40 minutes before adding a good pinch of sugar and salt.

Ice Cream with Chocolate & Honey Sauce

For 4

Olly and I used to go crazy out for this. Pooh Bear wrote one of the best cookbooks ever. Well, I think it probably wasn't written by Pooh, but my brother Olly and I thought it was at the time. The sauce is super sweet because of the honey, which is probably why our childish sweet teeth loved it so much. But the honey also means that the sauce becomes stringy, like mozzarella, when it hits the chilling ice cream. You may end up with a mucky chin, but it'll be worth it. If you've been labouring over a hot stove all afternoon with your banquet, and are tired of ferrying plates back and forth, then this is the pudding, because it's so easy. All you need is some superior vanilla ice cream.

First of all remove your ice cream from the freezer so it has a moment to soften. Now place the three sauce ingredients into a medium pan on a very low flame. Gradually whisk and fully combine the honey, chocolate and butter. As it begins to bubble up like lava, it's taking shape. When the dark sauce starts to rise about an inch further off the bottom of the pan, remove the pan from the heat and let it sit for a minute. Scoop out the softened ice cream into 4 bowls, and pour over the chocolate sauce. It should firm as it hits the cold ices and become stringy and sticky. Tuck in quickly.

good-quality vanilla ice
    cream
100g runny honey
60g drinking chocolate
a generous knob of
    butter

Yoghurt, Saffron & Cinnamon Sorbet

For 4

This is a recently concocted pudding, and it goes very well with anything Moroccan or Turkish or Moorish, being that scented kind of a sorbet. However, without an ice cream maker, it can be a bit of a peril on the arm, requiring frequent beating, in and out of the freezer each hour. It is a lovely thing to nurture of an afternoon, however, while doing other potterings at home, so long as you are up to the task. Serve this sorbet either just as it is, or with a drizzle of runny honey.

100g soft brown sugar
a little water
a good pinch of saffron
    threads
1 stick of cinnamon
500g Greek yoghurt
100ml crème fraîche

Using a small saucepan, make a syrup with the sugar, a little water, the saffron and cinnamon stick. Do so by warming this slowly so that all the flavours infuse and it begins to turn golden. Beat the yoghurt and crème fraîche together in a metal bowl. Discard the cinnamon and add the syrup to the yoghurt mixture. Whisk thoroughly, and taste. It should be tangy and sweet and have a dry aftertaste. Place the metal bowl in the freezer. Return to it every half hour for 4 hours, to give it a good beating with a whisk. It will gradually begin to set throughout, at which point you should turn it into a nice china bowl and let it finish setting in the freezer. However, don't leave it so long that it gets rock solid, as it will then be hard to carve out. It's best pulpy and just setting.

Carrageen with Nutmeg, Cream & Maple Syrup

For 4

Carrageen is an Irish set milk pudding made with seaweed that is incredibly light and jelly-like. Combined with the aromas of masculine nutmeg, good cream and thick maple syrup, it is a sophisticated glutton's treat with many sensory layers to the experience. And it is quite unlike anything else you will ever have come across. The light hint of seaweed throughout is honestly awesome in its difference and elegance. It's dead easy too.

I was reminded of it a couple of years ago when shopping in Brixton Market. As soon as I saw it, the excited memories of this delicately textured and at the same time rich pudding of my mother's came flooding back to me. Seaweed is everywhere here, as it is used in Jamaican foods as a gelling agent, sometimes substituting for eggs too. And in Jamaica this summer I was also told that seaweed has powerful qualities for men … and their prowess.

2 little pickings of dried seaweed
1.3 litres full-cream Jersey milk
single cream
maple syrup
freshly grated nutmeg

Soak the seaweed in a little water for 10 minutes to rehydrate. Add the fragile weeds to the milk, in a medium pan, and carefully simmer on a low heat for 30 minutes. Be careful not to burn this. With a sieve, pour out the milk into a serving dish, and catch the seaweed. Using a good wooden spoon, press the seaweed through so that you purée it all to a fine pap. Scrape it off the sieve and add to the milk mixture. You may need to give it a good whisk to combine the seaweed thoroughly with the milk. Leave to cool in this serving dish or decant into individual glasses and then chill in the fridge until set, which may take a few hours. Serve with generous portions of top-notch single cream and maple syrup, and a grating of fresh nutmeg.

Poached Pumpkin with Crème Fraîche

For 4

This is another Turk-like recipe. I cooked it first for Bharat, a loyal customer and friend and a bit of an oracle too. The texture of pumpkin is quite like potato, which initially seemed incongruous in a pudding, but soaked in the sweet syrup it is wonderfully graceful in flavour and texture, cut with crème fraîche to serve. Before I knew it, Bharat and I had polished off the lot. And the joy of this pudding as part of a banquet is that it requires no skill and little time, freeing you up to concentrate on other stuffing, cutting, simmering, cleaning and beautifying.

900g pumpkin or
  butternut squash
150ml water
300g sugar
2 tablespoons walnuts or
  green pistachios
200ml crème fraîche

Peel the pumpkin, using a large and sharp knife (which is, be warned, a little hard on the hands), and cut it into 2.5cm cubes. Place the pumpkin in a big saucepan, pour in the water and add the sugar. Bring to the boil and poach gently with the lid on. When the pumpkin cubes are done, which will be about 20 minutes, they will slip off a sharp little knife like a boiled potato. Remove the pumpkin from the pan to a serving dish. Reheat the syrup and reduce it down to about 2cm before spooning on top of the pumpkin. Let it soak for a few hours in this delicious syrup before crushing up the nuts and sprinkling on top. Serve with crème fraîche to cut these rich sweet Turkish delights.

Barbara Fitzgerald's Clafoutis

For 8

Clafoutis will forever remind me of Yew Tree Cottage, my childhood home. We had a quince and two plum trees in our garden, which my brother Olly and I would climb (and brave the wasps). And the fruits of the exercise went into this summer pudding, meticulously cooked by my mother. Her good friend Barbara, a brilliant Swiss cook, in turn, handed her the recipe. If you can find Calvados, then that really will be the icing on the cake. If not, a little brandy will do.

Preheat the oven to 180°C/Gas 4. Core or stone and chop the fruit into 2.5cm pieces. If you are using apples, you can peel them as well, though I don't always. It rather depends on my mood. Butter a baking dish and scatter the fruit into this. In a bowl, thoroughly beat the eggs, then add the flour so that it forms a smooth but glutinous paste. Make sure that there are no lumps. Gradually add the cream and milk and finally the sugar so that it becomes a creamy batter. Add 2 tablespoons of the Calvados to this before pouring over the fruit. Place in the oven for 40 minutes, and then, when removed, pour over the remaining Calvados.

900g apples or Victoria plums
25g butter
4 medium free-range eggs
100g plain flour
150ml double cream
300ml full-fat milk
100g caster sugar
4 tablespoons Calvados or, if you can't find this, use brandy

Marmalade Queen of Puddings

For 4

Queen of puddings is my dad's favourite, but this is my friend Caroline Muir's twist. It's one of those wonderfully dated but timelessly fantastic puddings. Raf thinks it's pretty far out. The contrast of bready custard base and light-as-air meringue topping is an old school triumph. And the fact that breadcrumbs are used means that it's economical: you can use up leftovers, which is what makes it so wonderfully wartime. It comes out differently according to how fresh the breadcrumbs are: if they are really stale, you need to add more milk, as they will absorb more liquid. If you have fresh crumbs, stick to the amounts below.

10g butter, and extra for the dish
565ml full-fat milk
100g breadcrumbs
zest of 1 lemon
50g caster sugar
2 medium free-range eggs
2 tablespoons thick-cut marmalade (preferably my mum's dark one)

Heat the oven to 150°C/Gas 2. Butter a medium baking dish or 4 little ramekins. Heat the milk in a saucepan until it just reaches the boil. Remove from the heat and add the butter, breadcrumbs, lemon zest and 25g of the sugar. Thoroughly mix, so that the butter really melts. It should have the consistency of a fine custard. Set this aside for 15 minutes to swell and melge. When a little cooler, separate the eggs and add the yolks to the custard. Mix well again. Pour this mixture into the buttered dish and place in the oven for 20 minutes, or until it is just beginning to swell but is still wobbly as a baby's bottom. Meanwhile melt the marmalade and cautiously spoon over the baked custard base. Beat the egg whites until they form soft peaks. Whisk in the remaining sugar and spoon this on top of the pudding. Return to the oven for a further 10 minutes, or until the soft meringue is beginning to turn golden. Plunge into a zesty dreamland.

Rice Pudding, Indian-style

For 6

The basic un-Indian format of this recipe comes from the (amazing) *Constance Spry Cookery Book*. If you see one in a junk shop, do nab it. Owning this dense book will be like having a mother in the kitchen for advice, constantly at your side. The Indian angle in this recipe came from when Raf and I decided to have a pit-stop in the canteen in Margao train station on our way to Gokana. We chose a thali, which is a divvied-up tray making up a whole set meal, including pudding. You dip and dive between little perfumed piles of goodness. And the pudding was an absolute delight: a cardamom-flavoured fine rice pudding.

It's so easy too. All you do is combine the raw ingredients and bake for a few hours. So if you are cooking this for a feast, make sure it's the first thing you put into the oven, so that it is ready in time. However, don't feel that this pudding is confined to a feast. It could just as easily be the best Sunday comfort food too. The rice I use is Carolina rice, a fat little grain that roasts well, becoming juicy and silky all at once. However, you can also use pudding rice or even American long-grain.

a generous knob of unsalted butter

4 tablespoons Carolina rice

4 tablespoons golden caster sugar

1 big cinnamon stick

10 whole cardamom pods

3 teaspoons ground ginger

1.7 litres full-fat milk or, if you are feeling lavish, Jersey milk

Preheat the oven to 150°C/Gas 2. Into a big baking dish, about 23 x 23cm, measure out the butter, rice, sugar, cinnamon, cardamom, ginger and milk. Give them a little mix around before placing in the oven for 1 hour and 40 minutes. Horrid as this is, it must be broached: before serving, remove the skin.

Sweet Little Coconut Cakes

Makes 16 little cups

These little cakes are gorgeous, and more like sweets really, so are the perfect way to end a feast, along with short coffees, or a digestive. They are vaguely based on a little Brazilian Portuguese dessert that I've had many times at Canela on Newburgh Street, a beautiful wine bar with delicious snacks and great green wine. I often go there for an early drink with girlfriends during the week, and end up eating some of their delicious sweets too. It keeps the wolf from the door if we are planning on heading out afterwards.

This recipe uses cassava flour, a fine flour that reminds me of cornflour. It can be bought in Portuguese and Brazilian shops. Cassava, also called yucca or manioc, is native to South America. You can buy the flour online, but if you have any South American or West Indian shops near you, they are bound to have it too. And of course it means these little cakes are wheat-free. Rose, my sidekick in the shop, fills each cake with a strawberry before baking, which makes for a wonderfully jammy centre.

150g desiccated coconut

1 x 397g tin condensed milk

2 tablespoons cassava flour (may also be labelled as tapioca flour) or plain flour

2 medium free-range eggs

Preheat the oven to 200°C/Gas 6. In a large mixing bowl, cream together the coconut, condensed milk and flour. It will form a really dense sticky paste. Now, in a small bowl, thoroughly beat together the eggs, so that they are only one texture and colour. Gradually beat the egg mix into the coconut mix. Line a cup-cake tray with paper cases, and dollop a generous dessertspoon of the mixture into each case. The cakes will rise a little, so make sure you have enough space for movement. Turn the temperature of the oven down to 160°C/Gas 2 and place the cakes in the oven for 20 minutes. They will be just risen like little mountains. To check that they are cooked, spear one of the cakelets with a toothpick. If it comes back smooth of cake mix, they are ready. Leave to cool in the tray for an hour or so. They will become denser as they cool.

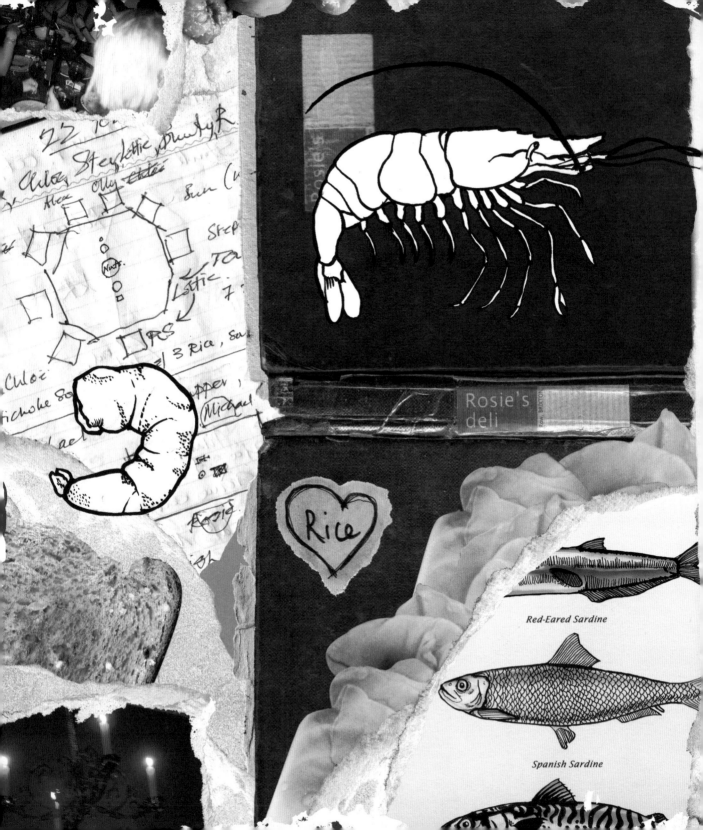

Rosie's deli

Rice

Red-Eared Sardine

Spanish Sardine

JAMMING SUPPERS

Simple supper parties. The kind of meals that are cooked for a few friends, midweek, not entertaining in the formal sense, but nevertheless feeding friends: full of care, but easy to throw together and not too time-consuming. These evenings will be laid-back affairs, where everyone mucks in, but it is a party all the same. I frequently find these evenings turn into an impromptu gaggle of girls putting the world to rights, singing along to Sister Sledge. We usually have a few too many glasses of wine, over a delicious rant, and end up in bed much later than expected, but, and all the better for it, with aching sides from laughing too much.

It might be just one course, but if you're feeling gluttonous there are some simple pudding suggestions too. And because these recipes are pretty uncomplicated entertaining, I've put in some foods that you may want to serve up while your friends are chatting. Amuse-bouche, if you like, but very simple. Most of these would also make a good midnight feast or ravenous afternoon snack.

Menu

Tings on Toast

Mains

for Friday nights in with Doctor Helen, Zahra & Jonathan Ross

Pat's birthday treat

R

Puddings

Tings on Toast

All these little 'tings' on toast can work either as individual starters, or as plates of canapés strategically placed where others might have a bowl of crisps. All the recipes are based, as the name suggests, around toast. So all you are really going to do is heap delicious combinations on good bread. Easy. They'd go down well as a midnight feast too, if you've dragged an unexpected guest home.

If I'm feeding a few friends before going out, I just serve a collection of these little plates along with the bottles my friends have brought. If you do this, you'll be lightly filled and ready for the floor. Eating a kilo of meat before going out on the tiles is always a bad idea. I recently made a collection of these tings on toast before we all headed off to the Horse Meat Disco, glitter balls and all. We were well fed with delicate morsels and able to really strut our stuff.

Pulpo on Toast

Makes 9 soldiers

Pulpo, or octopus, can easily be found tinned in any good continental deli. And it comes marinated in different things, like garlic or spicy tomatoes. These octopussy morsels are meaty and ready-cooked, and a great way of starting off the evening. When Doctor Helen and I were on one of our mini-breaks together in Barcelona, we ate in a fantastic and bustling tapas bar called Cal Pep. I was bowled over by the various and manifold delights that we were offered. Pulpo was just one of them. The chefs found our excitable noises and demonstrative moans hilarious. This little starter reminds me of our gluttons' ham-filled weekend.

Preheat an oven grill on a medium heat. Drain the octopus of the encasing oil but do not rinse it. Tip it out on to a chopping board, and roughly chop the meaty morsels a little smaller, about fingernail size. Decant them to a little bowl. Finely chop the parsley and add this to the bowl of chopped octopus. Now squeeze over the lemon so that it creates a fine marinade with the residual seafood oils. Let this sit and melge, while you place the slices of sourdough bread under the grill. Turn after a few minutes, when the bread is crisping up and becoming golden. Once you have removed the bread, pile on the octopus mix and drizzle with a little really good olive oil.

110g *pulpo al ajillo* (octopus in garlic)
a handful of fresh parsley
1 lemon
3 slices of sourdough bread
a drizzle of extra virgin olive oil

Sardine Pâté on Baguette

Makes about 10 slabs

This is something I never thought I'd actually like, so it was a brilliant surprise. Being proved wrong is consistently refreshing: sardines seemed like the sort of thing you might find at the back of a student cupboard. But then I went on a Sunday-night bike ride with Raf to this lovely Portuguese restaurant. How wrong I was: they serve a homemade sardine spread that comes with bread and olives before your meal. It's totally wicked and revelatory and I ate all of it, and then asked for more. And this recipe couldn't be simpler. All that is required is some tasty tinned sardines really. Make the pâté, spread it over some crusty baguette and taste a sunny Portuguese corner of London.

1 x 115g tin of sardines in tomato sauce
1 tablespoon good mayonnaise
juice of ½ lemon
8 or 10 slices of baguette

Get as much out of the tin of sardines as you can. Decant this into a little bowl, and mash up with a fork. Now spoon in the mayonnaise and lemon juice and thoroughly combine. Slice the baguette up and spread the pâté on top.

Smoked Mackerel Pâté on Toast

Makes 14 small pieces

I love smoked mackerel pâté. We sell it at Rosie's and it's all about the addition of creamed horseradish. For every pot I decant, measure and price, I always lick the spoon. It's super popular among my customers, on toast for breakfast, dolloped over a green salad with sunblushed tomatoes, or taken away with a picnic of antipasti.

As a child, one of our frequent Sunday-night staples was a fillet of peppered smoked mackerel, with a crisp baked potato and a crunchy salad, so it always reminds me of deliciously simple meals. Saving some of the pâté for tomorrow's packed lunch is a good plan too if you are trying to have an economical week.

Peel the skins off the mackerel and break up the flesh into a mixing bowl. With a fork, mash the flesh up so that it looks like a fibrous knitted ball. Now add the horseradish, yoghurt, cream cheese and lemon juice. Give this a thorough beating with the fork to fully integrate all of the ingredients. Now lightly grill roundels of ciabatta under a medium grill until they are crisp, and either spread the pâté on to each piece or just pile the bread into a bowl, add a knife to the pâté, and let people delve in and help themselves. Either way, grind over lots of black pepper.

2 fillets of smoked mackerel, preferably peppered
3 teaspoons creamed horseradish
1 tablespoon natural yoghurt
180g cream cheese
juice of 1 lemon
1 small ciabatta loaf (about 200g)
freshly ground black pepper

Baguette with Boquerones

For 10 or so roundels

I love boquerones. The first time I ate them was on my French exchange, aged eleven. I was jammy enough to have been staying with some serious French gastronomes. Every day delicious salads, these marinated little white fishes and loads of antipasti were prepared, and we would sit around the pool stuffing ourselves in the sunshine. It was bliss.

You can buy boquerones (freshly marinated anchovies) in good delis, either loose in the counter fridge, or in tubs or jars. Brindisa, in Borough Market, do excellent ones in little tubs, and I've also sourced some good Italian ones in jars for Rosie's. They are the sort of thing that can become an expensive addiction. I've been told they make a good hangover cure too.

½ a baguette
about 100g fresh
anchovies marinated
in oil and vinegar

Slice the baguette into thin roundels and place them under a hot grill for a few minutes, turning so that each side gets golden brown. Meanwhile, remove the fresh anchovies from their preserving juices. When the bread is crisp and beginning to colour, remove from the grill to a chopping board. Curl the anchovies on to the bread and serve up, just as they are. The oil and vinegar from these little fishes will soak into the bread and make it even more delicious.

Pan con Tomate

Makes 6 slices

This is a staple Spanish nibble that every tapas bar serves. It is so simple – just garlic and tomato rubbed on to some good crusty bread. Sometimes it is the simple things that are the most effective. And with such simplicity, the quality of the raw ingredients becomes especially important, rather like with the raw fish of sushi. Using good-quality olive oil here, and really ripe dark tomatoes, will make the seemingly ordinary, heavenly.

Preheat the grill to a medium heat. Place the sourdough bread under the grill and brown on both sides, which will take a few minutes. Meanwhile, peel the garlic cloves and slice the tomatoes in half. Press the tomatoes from the outside, turning them inside out. When the bread is golden, rub the bread first with the garlic cloves, and then energetically with the tomatoes, squeezing out the juicy pips. The bread should be coated all over. Finally drizzle over some tasty olive oil, crumble on some good-quality salt, Maldon or Camargue, and hand around.

6 slices of sourdough bread
2 garlic cloves
3 large tomatoes
2 tablespoons extra virgin olive oil
Maldon sea salt

Fontal & Grated Braeburn on Toast

Makes 12 wicked triangles

This isn't a far cry from that 1970s canapé of squidgy cheese and a piece of apple on a cocktail stick. And that is why it tastes so great. Sweet and salty, and perfect with some malty brown bread: deliciously uncool.

3 pieces of brown bread
3 Braeburn or Cox's
  Orange Pippin apples
150g Fontal
Maldon sea salt
freshly ground black
  pepper
1 tablespoon olive oil

First preheat the grill to a pretty high setting. Now lightly toast the brown bread. Grate the apples and Fontal together in to a mixing bowl, and give it a really good stir around with a fork. Season with salt and pepper and, finally, mix in the olive oil. Heap this on to the toasted bread and place under the grill until the cheese is beginning to melt and the apple to brown a little. Remove from the grill to a nice wooden chopping board, and chop up each of the slices of bread diagonally into triangular pieces.

Bruschetta with Cucumber, Basil & Chilli

Makes about 14 slices

I am so excited about this little trick. It came to me, staring out of the window on the train coming back from my mum's house, and I wrote it down straight away, so I could immediately make it on my return. The combination of cool cucumber and hot chilli is a wonder to behold. It's really nice to have something this fresh and light before launching into the rest of your meal. I can't wait to make it again and again.

1 small ciabatta loaf (about 200g)
4 tablespoons extra virgin olive oil
1 large cucumber
a generous handful of fresh basil
1 plump red chilli
juice of ¼ lemon
freshly ground black pepper
Maldon sea salt

Preheat the oven to 170°C/Gas 3. Slice the ciabatta into 8 pieces and rub with half the olive oil. Now place in the oven for a few minutes, so the bread becomes golden and a little crisp. Meanwhile prepare the cucumber by skinning it with a potato peeler. Then use a mandolin slicer to make fine slices. Very finely chop the basil and chilli – the latter you should partly deseed unless you want it really hot. Mix together with the cucumber in a bowl, adding the remaining olive oil and some lemon juice. Season a little. When the bread is ready, remove from the grill and immediately spoon this light fresh mix on top.

Bruschetta with Spinach & Sultanas

Makes 8 pieces

I first had this combination of salty spinach, sweet sultanas and pungent pork at Barrafina, in Soho. It's a great tapas bar run by two brothers with a real knack of combining impeccable style with perfect Spanish fodder. The queue outside this restaurant is always immense. But it's worth the wait. Raf took me there last year for a birthday treat, and because of the long wait, and the exceptional service, we'd already savoured most of a bottle of delicious white wine before we sat down at the bar. This potent little plate sated our excitable mood.

Preheat the oven to 170°C/Gas 3. Slice the ciabatta into 8 pieces and rub with half the olive oil. Now place in the oven for a few minutes, so that the bread becomes golden and a little crisp. Meanwhile, to wilt the spinach, either microwave in the bag, having popped a few holes, for 1½ minutes, or tip the whole bag out into a saucepan on a low heat. Add a couple of tablespoons of water to this, to steam it through, placing the lid on top. This will take a few minutes. Now squeeze the spinach a little to expel any excess water. Heat the rest of the olive oil in a pan, on a low heat. Roughly chop the spinach and add to the pan, along with the sultanas. Cut the serrano ham into this with some kitchen scissors. Season with pepper, and sweat for just long enough to warm everything through, thoroughly mixing. Now remove the golden toasted bread from the oven and heap the spinach on top. Hand around immediately, for your friends to eat, still warm, in their hands.

1 small ciabatta loaf (about 200g)
2 tablespoons olive oil
1 bag/225g baby spinach
40g sultanas
40g serrano ham or, if you can't find this, prosciutto
freshly ground black pepper

Crispy Chicken Pieces, Polenta & Roasted Red Pepper Sauce

For 4

This supper is delicious, variously flavoured and super simple. The chicken is simply boned and then seared to crisp up the delicious skin (where loads of the flavour is) and seal in the juices. It is best as a trinity: morsels of the chicken scooped up on a fork, with the warm wet comfort of polenta, topped with an awakening smudge of the tangy red pepper and caper sauce. And if you are treating some friends, it looks dead pro too because of the three vibrant colours buzzing together on the plate. The first thing to do is get the peppers roasting, as this will take an hour or so, and the polenta and chicken pieces will take about the same small amount of time as each other, so think about cooking them further down the line, in tandem. This would pack a few punches as a good wooing meal too.

Roasted Red Pepper Sauce

This sauce is super vibrant. I've made slightly bigger quantities here so that you can freeze the remainder if you like, or save it for breakfast. It is really adaptable, and can also be heaped on some grilled meaty white fish, like monkfish, lathered in a chunky sandwich with coarse bacon or added to a simple pasta tomato sauce the next day, for extra oomph.

Preheat the oven to 150°C/Gas 2. Slice the peppers in half and deseed, removing also any pithy white bits that line the inside. Place them on a non-stick baking tray in the oven for 1 hour and 10 minutes.

Remove from the oven and cool for a few minutes. In a jug (not a wide bowl, as this may spit when blended – I have the Pollock-decorated T-shirts to prove it), pile in the peppers, basil, anchovies, crème fraîche, olive oil and 2 tablespoons of the capers. Blend until it is a smooth paste. Now fold in the remaining tablespoon of capers, and the juice of the lemon and salt and pepper. You may need to add a little water if it is stiff. It should feel like a fiery red mayonnaise. Leave out on the side to cool (not the fridge), as you want this to be room temperature when you spoon it over the polenta and crispy chicken.

4 plump red peppers
a generous handful of fresh basil
2 anchovies preserved in oil
2 tablespoons crème fraîche
1 tablespoon extra virgin olive oil
3 tablespoons fat capers preserved in vinegar
1 lemon
Maldon sea salt
freshly ground black pepper

Polenta

Polenta is amazing: dead cheap and really filling; creamy and full of flavour; nutty and also homely, it takes on flavours, and still retains its own golden identity. Note, though, that it is the same thing as 'cornmeal', if you are ever baffled in an international shop, as it is used in Portuguese, Brazilian and Jamaican foods. Elizabeth David has a massive array of dishes involving polenta in her guide to Italian foods. It's worth knowing for the future, as she points out, that it also works really well with wild mushrooms, truffles, strong cheeses like Taleggio or a mature hard pecorino, and with a little potent ragù dolloped on top.

700ml water
1 or 2 teaspoons Maldon sea salt
200g fine polenta, but not easy-cook
freshly ground black pepper
50g good Parmesan, or Taleggio, or anything wonderfully strong and salty

Fill a medium pan with the water, salt and polenta. On the smaller ring of the hob, bring this rapidly to the boil. When it forms a thick creamy mixture and the water has combined smoothly with the corn, turn the heat down to low and simmer for a further 10 minutes. It should spit occasionally like a volcano, so watch out. Taste the enticingly sloppy golden mixture to make sure the polenta grains are springy but definitely cooked, and that it is well seasoned. Finally, grate the Parmesan, and beat this into the thick mix. Serve hot, in dollops.

Crispy Chicken Pieces

This is the last leg of the meal and the cooking will take about 15 minutes. Both the process and the flavour of the chicken are reassuringly simple. It only depends on buying some good-quality chicken thighs, so that the natural good taste sings. This is when meat is a real treat. Using thighs here is much better than the inevitably easier breast, as they are full of delicious brown meat and therefore extra juiciness.

To bone the chicken thighs, use a small very sharp knife and carefully cut around the bone. Gently release this from the flesh. Slice the meat out a little if necessary, so that each one forms a good flat slab. This will make it easier and quicker to cook. Now heat the olive oil, preferably in a large frying pan over a medium heat. If you have a hooded hob, or an Expelair, now is the time to get the fan going, as this will create a lot of spitting and sometimes smoke too. There doesn't seem to be a way around this, but it will all be worth it at the end.

When the oil is hot and quivering a little, place the chicken pieces, skin side down, in the pan. Fry for about 7 minutes and then turn over with some tongs. Add the white wine now, and cook the second side for 7 minutes. It should spit and energetically steam. Season at this point, with ground pepper and a little pinch of salt on each piece. To test that the chicken is cooked, incise with a small sharp knife and press the flesh. Any juice that seeps out should run clear, and each side should be a dark and golden colour and really crisp. When you are satisfied, remove the chicken pieces from the pan for a minute, to let the meat rest a little and relax. Now plate up the polenta, pop a chicken piece on the side of this creamy mountain, and dollop some of the pepper sauce on with it.

6 or 8 free-range or organic chicken thighs, depending on what you can afford
3 tablespoons olive oil
2 glasses of white wine
freshly ground black pepper
Maldon sea salt

Squid Ink Spaghetti with Prawns, Chilli & Bacon & Roasted Fennel Salad

For 4

Please take note that if you are making both the pasta and the accompanying salad, the latter will take much longer, so start on the fennel before the swift pasta.

The pasta dish is a hot and yet delicate supper which is very beautiful in the bowl: the lively red of the chillies and prawns, the fine flecks of vibrant green parsley, and the gleaming black spaghetti, which seems enticing and also quite mysterious, like some unheard-of seaweed. Finding this black spaghetti really does tip the balance for this meal, both taste-wise and visually, so it is worth spending a little more time and money to achieve the fullest effect. However, if you can't find it, then linguine, one of my favourite pastas, also works really well here. The shellfish flavours – squid ink and prawn – are full of a sea breeze, which is offset with the bacon and chillies to make a full, steaming and delicious bowl of fodder. It's wicked.

I most recently re-enacted it for my lovely friend Zezi, a big-haired beauty and general girl-about-London-town, before we went off to see The View and The Metros at a funny old flat-roofed pub on Brixton Hill. It was a perfect pre-gig filling, and took no time at all, which was lucky, because she is always fashionably late. The pints of beer that we subsequently drank in true gig style cooled away our chilli-hot mouths, so I would in this case recommend a gig for pudding.

Squid Ink Spaghetti with Prawns, Chilli & Bacon

The ingredients are pretty easy to get hold of, although prawns can be a bit baffling, as there are so many varieties. So in this case, I rather lazily go to a good supermarket and get precooked, frozen, but high-end bags of them. And for the squid ink spaghetti, try any upmarket deli. I highly recommend the Rustichella d'Abruzzo pasta brand. And if you are worried at the lack of Parmesan in this dish, don't fret. It would really be too much with all the other flavours already going on here. You want the delicate prawns to sing for themselves.

Keep the frozen prawns at room temperature for a few hours to defrost a little (check the packet for instructions too, as they will vary). Fill a large saucepan with water, and add a good pinch of salt. Bring this to the boil so that it is ready for the pasta. The prawns themselves will take no time.

For the sauce, trim any rind or excess fat off the bacon and cut it into 1cm pieces with some kitchen scissors. Meanwhile heat 4 tablespoons of the olive oil in a large frying pan on a medium heat. Add the bacon pieces and fry for about 5 minutes, so that the stripes of delicious fat are beginning to crisp up and brown a little. You don't want it to be flabby. Now finely chop the chillies and add to the pan. Sizzle for a few minutes, then add the wine and lemon juice. Trim the roots off the spring onions and cut into thumb-width pieces. Add these to the pan and simmer for a few minutes in the juices. Now add the prawns and heat for just long enough that they are warm all the way through but still delicate and tender, and then turn off the heat. Finely chop the parsley, using a long sharp knife, and fold it into the prawns so that it just wilts and adds another great colour.

400g frozen Greenlandic large cooked prawns
Maldon sea salt
300g streaky British bacon
6 tablespoons olive oil
2 plump chillies
200ml white wine (I use a white burgundy, because I like the rest of the bottle with supper)
juice of 2 lemons
250g spring onions
50g fresh parsley (a few generous handfuls)
400g squid ink spaghetti

Now that the pan of salted water is at a rumbling boil, add the squid ink spaghetti. Simmer for 5 minutes, or follow any packet instructions. Drain when the pasta is al dente, and toss in the remaining 2 tablespoons of olive oil. Share the pasta out between four bowls and pile on the spiced prawn sauce. Tuck in as quickly as you can.

Roasted Fennel Salad

Delicious and super easy, the main things to think about here are …
a slow hot oven for gently roasting the fennel bulbs, and the tang of a
little lemon to dress. Easy.

Preheat the oven to 140°C/Gas 1, and line a baking tray with
greaseproof paper. Slice the fennel bulbs in half lengthways and place
cut side up on the lined tray. Pour the olive oil over and place in the
oven for 2 hours, or until the flesh of the fennel is totally transparent
and really soft. It may take longer, depending on the size of the bulbs.

Remove the fennel to a chopping board with a fork, and slice into
finger-width pieces, widthways, with a large sharp knife. Arrange the
fennel pieces on a plate and squeeze over the lemons. Strip the little
round leaves off the lemon thyme and sprinkle over the salad. Season
with fresh pepper and a little salt. Serve up either as a starter salad or
alongside the seafood pasta. It can be served warm or left to cool,
depending on your fancy.

2 large fennel bulbs
2 tablespoons olive oil
2 lemons
a few sprigs of fresh
   lemon thyme (it's a
   sturdy plant and easy
   to grow, but if you
   can't get it then
   regular thyme is fine)
freshly ground black
   pepper
Maldon sea salt

Fillet of Pork with Mustard & Honey Sauce, Lemon Smashed New Potatoes

An easy feed for 3

I always used to make this when I was little. I obsessively collected those recipe cards by the checkout in supermarkets and this comes from one of those, though it's evolved a fair bit over the years. The creamy sauce has some great tangy simple flavours: honey and mustard and crème fraîche. This whole meal is very light and satisfying. The fillet of pork is sliced up into delicious little lean gems and the lemon with the potatoes is a perfectly light addition too. I made it a while ago for an impromptu midweek visit from Raf and his friend Tomo, who's a brilliant photographer of naughty indie boys. Accompanied by some cool beer it went down a treat. Then we snuck down to a Portuguese bar up the road, Sintra, for a few more. An ideal local get-together.

If you buy some spring greens, or kale or chard, it will be the perfect accompaniment here. I just pile the shredded dark green leaves of whatever is available into a large saucepan, with a knob of butter and the juice of half a lemon. Sweat the vegetables on a very low heat for 5 to 10 minutes, tossing from time to time with a fork.

Fillet of Pork with Mustard & Honey Sauce

Preheat the oven to 100°C/Gas ¼. Warm the butter in a medium pan and, meanwhile, slice the long fillet of pork into two pieces so that they will fit in the pan. When the butter is melted and just spitting, add the pork pieces. Brown them on both sides, which will take a few minutes. Don't worry if the pork sticks a bit, as any leftover bits in the pan will add to the honey and mustard sauce. Scatter the fresh thyme over the bottom of a small baking dish. When the pork is tinted golden, remove from the pan on to this bed of thyme and add half the water. Place in the oven for 2 hours. When the pork is ready, any juices that emerge when it is pierced will be clear. If you want further proof of it being ready, slice the middle of one of the pieces of pork. It should be a pale and inviting pink (not dark pink, which would be undercooked, or grey, which would be overcooked). Fork it out on to a chopping board and leave to sit for a moment while you make the sauce below. Carve into about 18 medallions. I serve the pork straight off the chopping board.

For the sauce – which you should start once you know that the pork is cooked to perfection, and resting for a moment – heat the pan in which the pork was initially sealed, on a low temperature. Scrape loose any scraps of pork that are stuck to the bottom. Now add the mustard, crème fraîche and honey, and melt it all together, using a little vigorous whisking to fully combine. Now add the rest of the water, a bit at a time, to loosen the sauce, and add a generous amount of freshly ground pepper. Decant this into a little milk jug to hand around the table.

a knob of butter
500g fillet of pork (just ask your butcher, as mine sliced it off the carcass right in front of me)
a bunch of fresh thyme
6 tablespoons water
1 tablespoon grainy mustard
2 tablespoons crème fraîche
1 tablespoon runny honey
a generous grind of black pepper

Lemon Smashed New Potatoes

500g baby Maris Peer
new potatoes or any
gem-like new
potatoes
1 lemon
1 tablespoon extra virgin
olive oil
freshly ground black
pepper
a generous pinch of
Maldon sea salt

Place the potatoes in a medium saucepan and completely immerse in salted water. Bring to the boil with the lid on, and simmer for about 15 minutes, or until the largest of the potatoes slips easily off a small sharp knife. Drain into a colander. Return the potatoes to the same saucepan, replace the lid, and give them a really good shaking up. This will smash them up a bit, so that their skins become loose and they are porous to the flavours. So now, squeeze over them the juice of the lemon, and add some good-quality extra virgin olive oil. Give it all another good shaking with the lid on again, and season with pepper and Maldon sea salt.

A Little Roasted Chicken with Lemons & Penne, Tzatziki-style

For 3 or 4

This is a great sunny combination. I love a warm chicken, especially with this bright-tasting pasta. It's a kind of spring-like marriage of light flavours with the minty cool pasta, and it's all very simple too. The chicken goes in the oven, and then the pasta on the hob. All you need to do is get some freshest cucumber and mint chopped and you are away, so it's good for some last-minute week-night amusements. I do this pasta salad all the time: for picnics, in the deli counter, along with a barbecue. It's pretty versatile and one of Doctor Helen's favourites.

A Little Roasted Chicken with Lemons

By stuffing the chicken with lemon butter, the roasted meat will be really wet and succulent and moreish. This simple roasted bird can be the anchor of any great meal: you could also serve it with any substantial salad like a bulgar wheat tabbouleh, or an action-packed cold potato salad, or just with some good bread and a green salad.

100g butter
2 lemons
2 teaspoons fresh or dried thyme
freshly ground black pepper
Maldon sea salt
1 x 1.5kg free-range chicken

Chop up the butter into cubes and leave it for about half an hour at room temperature so that it becomes malleable. Preheat the oven to 180°C/Gas 4. Now, grate the zest of the lemons thoroughly on the finest blade, removing as much as you can and adding it to the butter. Keep the zested lemons aside. Using a flat wooden spoon, thoroughly beat the butter so that it becomes smooth and incorporated with the zest. Now also add the thyme, salt and pepper and give the flavoured butter another beating.

Place the chicken on a large work surface. Make sure there are no untoward innards hiding anywhere. Unwrap the tied legs, and separate the skin from the breasts by delving in with your hands. There may be a membrane that you need to release, which, although it sounds gross, is very easy. Where you have made pockets in the chicken, between the breast and skin, spoon in some of this butter and spread it down the bird with your hands so that it covers the whole of the breast, internally. Now slash a few incisions down the drumsticks, thighs and wings, and rub the remaining butter over these. The lemons you kept aside need to be sliced in half and stuffed inside the chicken cavity so that lemon juice steams up from within as well. Place the chicken in a roasting tin, with 2cm of water, and roast for an hour, or according to weight instructions. When it is well roasted, any flowing juices will run clear.

Penne, Tzatziki-style

Get a medium pan on the hob, filled with lots of salted water. Bring this to the boil and add the penne. Cook it so that it is slippery, a little more than al dente (or according to the packet instructions if they are dramatically different). Meanwhile, to make the dressing, beat together the yoghurt, crème fraîche and half the olive oil in a big salad bowl. Then crush in the peeled garlic cloves, and squeeze in the lemon juice. Now, with a big knife, really finely chop the fresh mint, add this to the dressing and season well. Peel the cucumber with a potato peeler, halve lengthways and cut out the tunnel of seeds, as these are really watery. Then shred the cucumber on a mandolin slicer, or very finely julienne with a sharp knife. Fold into the dressing. Taste and add more garlic and pepper and salt if you need to, as it rather depends on the tartness of the yoghurt. When the pasta is cooked, drain and thoroughly cool under a cold running tap. Now finally fold this into the dressing. Serve up with the warm chicken. Drizzle over the remaining extra virgin olive oil. It will look beautiful.

PS. This is totally the time to make some real stock. Once you have eaten the lemon chicken, add the carcass to a really deep saucepan with a bouquet garni (or some bay leaves, thyme and peppercorns), an onion and a carrot. Totally cover the whole bird with water and very slowly simmer for a few hours with the lid on. It couldn't be easier (though the longer and slower you simmer, the better your juice will be). Then all you need to do is remove the carcass, sieve the stock and decant into Tupperware to cool, then either refrigerate or freeze.

250g penne
3 tablespoons natural yoghurt
2 tablespoons crème fraîche
2 tablespoons extra virgin olive oil
3 garlic cloves
juice of ½ lemon
a generous handful of fresh mint (keep the rest of the bunch for mint teas)
1 cucumber
freshly ground black pepper
Maldon sea salt

Smoked Mackerel & Chard Bake with a Crunchy Top

Serves 3, or 4 if served with a baked potato

I recently rediscovered peppery chard at the Peckham farmers' market. The basic chard season is June to August. My dad used to grow it at home in Suffolk, but it is not in many urban shops. Rediscovering it felt like a homecoming. This market, like most farmers' markets, is great, and the products really varied: venison, buffalo, sweet little celeriacs, duck eggs, grubby Jerusalem artichokes, and lots of verdant kale, to name just a few things that are on offer. So having seen the bushy chard plants, I got to thinking what would go well with them. I bought some broccoli too, and this dish came to pass. It goes to show how spontaneously a good thing may evolve in the kitchen, and also that encountering new or different foods by shopping in quality places gets you thinking beyond your comfort zone.

This dish is delicious: smoky from the fish, and full of green goodness from the lightly cooked vegetables. And the cheese and breadcrumb topping gives extra crunch and punch. One tip is that all the ingredients are potentially quite salty – chard, but also many of the powdered stocks you may use for the white sauce, and any strong cheese that you might grate on the top – so be abstemious when adding additional salt on top of all of these.

Smoked mackerel is a great fish to get your head around too. Cheap, easy to get hold of, and with an excellent oily nature, mackerel is a wonder. It may be psychological, but I always feel more robust after eating mackerel. The oiliness means that it's high in omega 3. There are plenty of ways of eating mackerel too: made into a pâté; with a baked potato and salad on a Sunday night (one of my mum's favourites); laced into a potato gratin, or crumbled into a summer salad with dill and sour cream.

First you need to wash and prepare the vegetables: I chop the root end off the chard, and open out the leaves into a bowl of water. Rub away any mud on the lovely and substantial pinkish stalks and let the leaves swim around for a bit. When the chard is totally clean, remove from the bowl and chop the leaves sideways into inch-wide ribbons. To prepare the broccoli you need to cut the hardened woody tip off the main stump. Slice up the stalk into about 2cm-wide chunks. One by one, remove the florets, and cut them so that they are all about the same size. Fill a large pan with 2cm of water, and place the broccoli in this. Heat on a medium flame, with the lid on, for a few minutes. This will lightly steam the broccoli. Now pile in the wet ribbons of chard and return the lid to the pan. Steam for a further 5 minutes. You don't want to overcook the vegetables at this stage because remember the whole dish is going to go in the oven, further along the line. The chard should be just beginning to wilt and take on a wonderful deeper moss green. When you are satisfied with the vegetables, remove them from the pan with some tongs and scatter them around a large baking dish, about 30 x 23cm, which you should then set aside. Keep the vegetable liquid to use in the white sauce.

400g chard, or better still the beautiful 'bright lights' Swiss chard
400g broccoli
350–400ml chicken or vegetable stock
50g butter
60g plain flour
100ml semi-skimmed milk
½ lemon
1 dessertspoon grainy Dijon mustard
1 teaspoon freshly grated nutmeg
freshly ground black pepper
200g smoked Scottish mackerel
100g breadcrumbs
100g mature Manchego, Parmesan or another strong hard cheese

Now preheat the oven to 150°C/Gas 2. To make the white sauce, boil a kettle and make some stock, so it is at the ready. Now melt the butter in a medium pan on a medium heat. When it is fully melted and beginning to spit a little, add the plain flour. Using a whisk, fully blend these together. It should look like wet sand. Let this sweat for a few minutes to fully cook the flour, mixing frequently. Now gradually add any leftover liquid from the vegetable pan and the stock, whisking all the time, so there are no lumps. It will initially thicken up. Then add the milk, by the same process. It should now be creamy but not glutinous. Turn the heat down to low, and continue to cook for 5 minutes, mixing occasionally. Finally squeeze in the lemon juice and add mustard, nutmeg and pepper to taste. Make sure the sauce is tangy and light.

Peel away the skin of the mackerel, and crumble the oily fish over the vegetables in chunks. Pour the white sauce over this and give everything a really good mix. It should be just enough to loosen the dish, but not saturate it. Now combine the breadcrumbs and grated Manchego, and scatter over the dish. Place in the oven for 35 minutes, or until the broccoli is tender but cooked, and the topping perfectly golden and crispy.

Smoked Haddock & Watercress Risotto with Griddled Courgettes

For 3

I first cooked this risotto for a dinner in Edinburgh. Loads of Alice's and my lovely friends came over, and squished around the table, and then went on to Tom Punch's club night, Absinthe Minded … you work it out! Thank goodness, our stomachs had been lined with this wonderfully pungent warm wet fish supper.

There's something amazing about this smoked fish. No wonder it is the famed ingredient of a kedgeree (my mum's is top-notch). And as with the kedgeree, this union of smoky scents and creamy grains is just awesome. I think it's something to do with the woody – almost bacon-like – scents that come from this meaty fish.

With a risotto (and he makes the best one I've ever tasted), Raf swears by extra dry vermouth rather than wine. So I'm using it here, so he'll stop banging on. It is an Italian wine infused with herbs. It smells quite like a sour aromatic sherry, and gives a much deeper dimension to the risotto (which if in the wrong – criminal – hands, is a tasteless bowl of gruel). He is right, though. Just you wait and see the intense and fragrant results. And it's not bad to have a sip while you are nurturing the risotto too. Just splash a few centimetres over some ice.

Smoked Haddock & Watercress Risotto

2 tablespoons olive oil
50g butter
2 shallots
600ml fish or vegetable
    stock
200g Arborio rice
200ml extra dry
    vermouth
6 spring onions
125g watercress
250g smoked haddock
freshly ground black
    pepper

Find a medium saucepan with a matching lid, and heat the olive oil and half the butter slowly on a low flame. Meanwhile, peel and finely chop the shallots so that they are really small. Locatelli says as small as the rice, so that you can't differentiate one from the other at the end. Now add these to the fats and sweat away for a few minutes. While this is sizzling, boil the kettle and make your stock. Next add the rice to the saucepan and seal it with the oil again for a few minutes. Add a little stock and vermouth, alternating each for 20 minutes, mixing all the time. At this point you should roughly chop the spring onions and add them to the pan. When the rice is plump but still a little al dente, turn the heat off and add the watercress. The risotto will be just hot enough to wilt this. Skin the haddock by positioning a large, very sharp knife at 45 degrees between the skin and meat and slowly easing one from the other, with a firm grip. Slice the haddock now into 2cm cubes, removing any rogue bones if necessary, and again gently fold into the risotto. Now add the rest of the butter and lots of pepper and fit the lid on the saucepan. Let it sit for 5 minutes before giving it a good mix around and serving up. As you can see, the risotto's emanating heat will wilt the watercress and poach the haddock beautifully and prevent anything overcooking.

Griddled Courgettes

Courgettes are best if, when you slice them, they are almost sticky to touch and smooth and buttery to the eye. Though it took me a long time to learn to love these prickly green truncheons. I used to absolutely hate them, but they grew so prolifically in our Suffolk garden that I really had no choice but to get over it. I'm now so glad I did. And here, the lemon with courgettes will perfectly enrich and marry with the fellow fish risotto.

Slice the courgettes diagonally so that you achieve elongated discs a few millimetres wide. (If they are too thick, they'll take ages to cook.) In a griddle pan (one of those great striped heavy-bottomed pans – I got hold of one for £7, so it's not a massive investment), warm the olive oil on a medium heat. Add the courgettes carefully when the oil is really hot. You may need to do this in two batches, depending on the size of the pan. Sizzle away for a few minutes before carefully lifting the courgettes to see that they are charred in beautiful stripes and beginning to turn translucent. Now turn the courgettes, squeeze over the juice from 1½ lemons, and fry the same way on the other side. Turn them four times so that you get a kind of hatching effect. Season enthusiastically with pepper. Gradually the juice should have been absorbed from the pan, with a little smoke rising. Remove to a good flat serving dish, with the remaining lemon chopped into wedges, and serve with the risotto.

3 courgettes
2 tablespoons olive oil
2 lemons
freshly ground black
    pepper

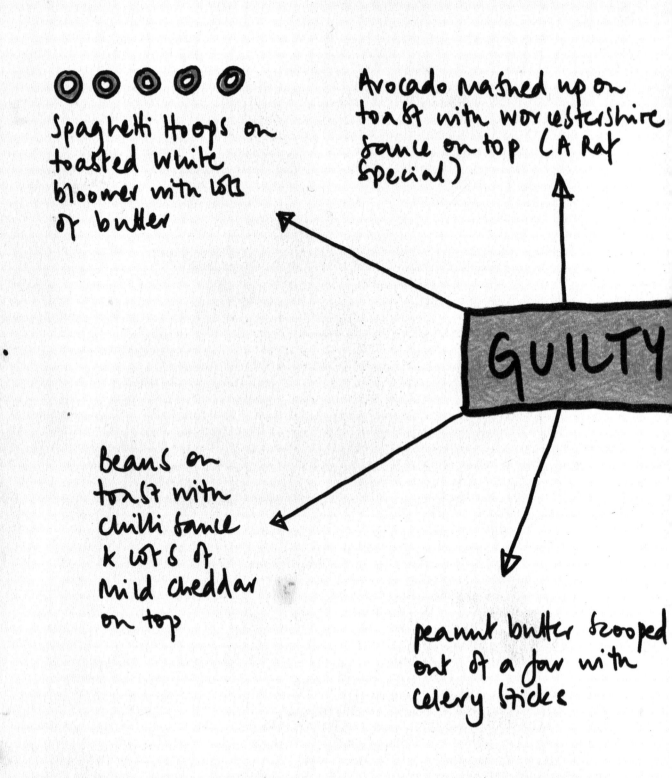

Spaghetti Hoops on toasted white bloomer with lots of butter

Avocado mashed up on toast with worcestershire sauce on top (A Raf Special)

GUILTY

beans on toast with chilli sauce & lots of mild cheddar on top

peanut butter scooped out of a jar with celery sticks

Goat's cheese on toast in the early hours (was once my failed attempt to woo)

FEASTS

Hot wings from the chicken shop downstairs with Lexi

Greek yoghurt & runny honey for a midnight pudding

it reminds me of my Granny Bun, and evenings playing cards

Moules Marinière with Spaghettini

For 3

This dish of mussels with pasta is as old as time, and the soup that is made along with it is out of this world. It has the same effect as a miso soup: cleansing, salty and full of flavour. And of course, these rocky beckoning black shells are full of promise, and look dramatic and beautiful, making them an ideal treat for friends who like to huddle around a steaming pot. There is something so satisfying about rolling up your sleeves and getting up to your elbows to prize out these little creatures, dripping wet. I love the mollusc.

You can buy mussels from any good fishmonger. Berwick Street market in particular has a great fish stall and they do an excellent bag of them inexpensively, so if you are shopping in Soho, then pick some up on the way home.

First of all you need to immerse the mussels in a big sink of freezing cold water. Religiously chuck out any that are beginning to open, as they are wrong 'uns. With a sharp little knife, scrape off any crusty bits and remove the little beards, which are a bit like limbs that they use to hold on to the rocks by, but isn't too pretty. Now moderately heat the oil in a really deep saucepan. Peel and finely chop the shallots into rings and the chilli into tiny pieces the size of grains of rice. Add these to the pot, and sweat for 5 minutes so that the shallots are transparent and wilted. Boil a kettle for the pasta. Now add the carefully prepared mussels, followed by the white wine, and water. Place a lid on the pot and simmer for 5 minutes. Now the mussels should be opening out, about a couple of centimetres. Discard any mussels that haven't opened. Give it all a good mix around with a large wooden spoon, and turn the heat down. Finally add the cream and replace the lid for a further few minutes.

Meanwhile, heat the boiled water in a large saucepan on a high flame with a pinch of salt. It may take 1½ kettles; to cook pasta well you really need lots of water. Add the spaghettini when the water is rumbling, and simmer for about 5 minutes, until al dente. (Or follow the packet instructions.) Drain the pasta, and dish out into really big bowls. Finally chop and fold the parsley into the mussels and, using a ladle, plate up with the pasta. Top with Parmesan and pepper and perhaps salt, if needed.

You may want to put out warm water bowls for your friends to dunk their messy hands into.

2.5kg mussels
2 tablespoons olive oil
4 shallots
1 plump red chilli
300ml white wine
100ml water
100ml single cream
Maldon sea salt
300g spaghettini
100g or 3 good handfuls
    of fresh parsley
150g freshly grated
    Parmesan
freshly ground black
    pepper

Pumpkin & Gorgonzola Lasagne

A wholesome feed for 3

We ate this on one of our many Friday nights in with Jonathan Ross and a catch-up. Those nights when you have a plan to go to a gig, or meet some friends in town, but then it gets to 4 p.m. and your legs just won't carry you any further. Now's the time to turn off your phone, get simmering, and hang with your best friends, a nice bottle, and some homemade lasagne. This one is thick, rich and really tasty.

So this recipe uses the same fresh pasta as the herby pasta sheets mentioned on page 176 but half the quantities. However, if you haven't got time for the fresh rolling, shop-bought is fine, either dry or fresh: I keep some de Cecco white label lasagne packs at the back of the cupboard for when I've run out of energy. Bought fresh lasagne is tasty too.

Preheat the oven to 180°C/Gas 4. Now peel the pumpkin with a sharp long knife, as this is hard on the hands. Then chop it into rough chunks about 5cm wide and place them in a roasting tin. Drizzle with half the olive oil and place in the oven for 35 minutes, or until the pumpkin slips easily off a sharp little knife. Meanwhile start cracking on with the tomato sauce. This is a simple one. Slowly warm the remaining oil in a medium frying pan. Peel and finely slice the onion and add to the pan. Sweat for a few minutes, until the onion is turning transparent, but not brown. Then roughly chop the tomatoes and add these too. Turn the heat down to medium and simmer for 10 minutes, then peel and crush in the garlic cloves and stir in the tomato purée. Simmer for a further 10 minutes with the lid off, then set the sauce aside. When the pumpkin is well roasted, remove from the oven and blend with the mascarpone and thyme (or use a decent potato masher if you don't have a blender).

To prepare the lasagne, find a medium but quite deep baking dish. Preheat the oven again to 180°C/Gas 4 if necessary. Pour in a layer of tomato sauce and then press and line a layer of pasta on top. Now spoon over a layer of the pumpkin purée and put thumb-sized pieces of Gorgonzola over this. Add another layer of pasta and repeat until everything is used up. Bake in the oven for 25 minutes, or until bubbling at the edges and crisp on top. Serve this lasagne with a crisp Cos lettuce salad served with a clean lemon juice and extra virgin olive oil dressing. This will perfectly cut the rich leftfield lasagne.

800g pumpkin
2 tablespoons olive oil
1 onion
10 fresh plum tomatoes, or just salad ones if you can't find plum
2 garlic cloves
1 dessertspoon tomato purée
250g mascarpone
2 teaspoons thyme
about 250g fresh herby lasagne (see recipe, page 177)
100g Gorgonzola

Herby Homemade Pasta Sheets with a Perfect Yellow Tomato Salad

For 2 or 3

I loved getting into making fresh pasta. It's really much easier than you might immediately think, and the difference in texture (like tender meat) and flavour (wonderfully rich in eggs) is amazing. The nature of making something as sophisticated and delicate as fresh pasta is that you won't need to overload it with complicated sauces or rich ingredients. This pasta has herbs rolled into it and is full of flavour and substance, so it only needs a squeeze of lemon, some Maldon sea salt, freshly ground pepper and a glug of superior extra virgin olive oil. In fact, this is when you will appreciate having some good-quality oil, as the bittersweet peppery quality will really come through. I warn you, though, once you've got the hang of it this delicious pasta will be rolling out of your ears, and endless combinations will unfold. Some coarsely ground nutmeg? Pesto? A little chilli? To make it really well you will need to invest in a pasta machine. They are well worth it and fun to play with.

Herby Homemade Pasta Sheets

This makes 500g pasta and feeds 5; or divide into two batches, and either freeze half or save half for the pumpkin lasagne.

Fill a small bowl with water and have it at the ready. Remove the leaves from the herb stems (which you can discard), seriously finely chop and set aside. Measure the flour out and put it into a really big mixing bowl with the salt and herbs. Toss it around a little to combine. Make a big well in the middle of this. Beat the eggs and egg yolks and olive oil together and pour this into the well you have made in the flour. With your index finger, swirl the liquid to gradually combine the wet with the dry. It should become a crumbly mess, so don't worry. In order to draw it together, tentatively dip your fingers into the water and continue to work the pasta. When it is entirely combined into a dense ball, knead it for at least 15 minutes in the bowl, until it is entirely smooth and elastic. If you have a pasta machine, which is not an expensive toy (given the hours of potential fun), then set this up, securing it well to a worktop so that it can't move. (If not, some vigorous rolling pin action will be required.)

Tug off a little ball of pasta about the size of a walnut and begin rolling, on the widest setting on the machine. Roll the sheet about three times on each declining setting, in alternating directions to create a consistent texture. When you are satisfied, at about the fifth notch, lay out the sheet to dry. I use my clotheshorse, which looks pretty funny but does the job fine. When the pasta is almost brittle (after a few hours), remove it from the rack. Bring the stock to the boil and plunge in the pasta. It will take about 2 minutes to cook. When you have drained the sheets, squeeze the lemon over it and add some olive oil, toss it around, and serve with Parmesan and lots of pepper and salt.

a handful of fresh
    parsley
a handful of fresh sage
2 teaspoons thyme
300g '00' flour
a pinch of salt
2 medium free-range
    eggs
2 medium free-range
    egg yolks
1 tablespoon olive oil
a large pan of vegetable
    stock or salted water
1 lemon
2 tablespoons really
    good-quality extra
    virgin olive oil
freshly grated Parmesan
freshly ground black
    pepper
Maldon sea salt

Perfect Yellow Tomato Salad

This yellow tomato salad is a favourite of my flatmate Anna Green-Armytage (or 'dude' as I call her). The sweet yellow tomatoes, salty French olives and sour red onions are a perfect *ménage à trois*, and were our addiction for a while. And you'll just need a little oil on top. Nothing more. So it's a really simple affair. These tomatoes are distinctively different from their red friends and are firm and sweet when at their best. And if you invest in some well marinated lovely wrinkly olives covered in lots of herbs, you'll be in for a treat too.

1 small red onion
500g yellow cherry
   tomatoes
200g pitted marinated
   black olives
½ tablespoon balsamic
   vinegar
2 tablespoons extra
   virgin olive oil
2 teaspoons golden
   caster sugar

Peel and really finely chop the onion so that it is a decorative smattering of white and purple. Place it in a nice but smallish salad bowl. Slice the tomatoes in half and add to the onions. Now do the same with the salty olives, slicing each into about 3 roundels. Drizzle over the balsamic vinegar and olive oil and sprinkle with a little sugar to balance the sharpness of the tomatoes. Toss it all around, and serve up the perfection.

Homely Saffron Chicken

For 6

We used to have this all the time at Yew Tree Cottage, and it was one of my and my brother Olly's favourites: a chicken hotpot with rice and lots of colourful red vegetables. It's warming and yet full of occasion too. The best bit about it is the way that the slow, pot-roasted chicken imbues the rice with a wonderful oily wetness. It's impressively colourful and is surprisingly easy to make. Added to this, it's pretty filling, so if you end up with more than the expected mouth count, everyone will still be well sated and happy.

2 red peppers
1 yellow pepper
1 generous handful of
    pitted black Kalamata
    olives
4 anchovies preserved in
    oil
2 medium onions
8 garlic cloves
1 teaspoon salt
1 teaspoon freshly
    ground black pepper
1 teaspoon dried thyme
a few sprigs of saffron
1 bay leaf
½ teaspoon cayenne
    pepper
1 dessertspoon tomato
    purée
1 tablespoon olive oil
a knob of butter
1 x 1.2kg free-range
    chicken or 8 pieces of
    free-range chicken
250ml chicken stock
1 x 400g tin of chopped
    tomatoes
320g basmati rice

Preheat the oven to 160°C/Gas 2. Prepare all the vegetables and put them into a bowl (you can easily set yourself up in front of the TV for this bit): deseed the peppers and chop into hunks; scatter over the olives and anchovies; peel and roughly chop the onions and garlic; heap in also the salt, pepper, thyme, saffron, bay leaf, cayenne and tomato purée. Set this bowl aside now that all the preparation is done, and you have a mountain of colourful spices and vegetables.

This dish is best cooked in a deep, heavy-bottomed Le Creuset casserole if you are lucky enough to have one. Heat the oil and butter in a large pan until it is just spitting. Brown the chicken in the fats, turning after a few minutes so that the whole bird is tinged and coloured and the skin a little crisp. Remove the chicken briefly from the pan while you add the vegetable mountain. Bring these to the boil with the chicken stock and tinned tomatoes. Throw in the rice, give it a stir and replace the chicken on top, nestling in all this goodness. Put the lid on and place the pan in the oven. Bake for 1¼ hours. Make sure the rice and chicken are cooked thoroughly. Now finally remove the chicken from the pot to rest. Leave the lid off the pan and return it to the oven for another 10 minutes to crisp up and dry out the rice a little. Carve the chicken, dishing it up with this gluttonous colourful rice feast. The best bits of this dish are the burnt stodgy brown bits at the bottom.

Pearl Barley Risotto with Tomato & Ricotta

Cleverness for 2

I love pearl barley. When I was younger I often made and loved a winter Guinness stew, which had this as the final ingredient. But until I went to Ancona, I'd never seen pearl barley used in many other ways. Then I had this risotto, which uses barley instead of rice. I suddenly realised how potentially versatile an ingredient it is too. This dish is totally amazing because of the inherent sweetness and nuttiness in the barley, combined with the fine homemade tomato sauce. The ricotta here really balances each mouthful, so that it is creamy and tangy, crunchy and again creamy. This recipe is also very straightforward, and uses few ingredients, so is a good one for a simple supper party. It won't cost more than a few quid either.

Slice the tomatoes and place in a medium saucepan. Pour in the chicken stock, put the lid on, and bring to the boil on a steady heat, for 15 minutes. Now remove from the heat and thoroughly blend with a hand-held blender, then add the sugar and balsamic vinegar. Using a sieve, strain this fine soup, removing any skins and seeds from the tomatoes, into a measuring jug. Top up this soup with hot water so that you have 1 litre of liquid.

Put the olive oil into a pan over a low heat. Peel and finely chop the garlic cloves and add to the hot oil. Toss them for a minute and then add the barley, to seal it in the oil. Now add the tomato stock and simmer for 40 minutes or until the liquid has been almost entirely absorbed. Taste to make sure that the risotto is springy but juicy and cooked. Now season with salt and pepper and dish up with chunks of ricotta on top and a drizzle of extra virgin olive oil.

500g fresh plump tomatoes
750ml chicken stock
a generous pinch of caster sugar
2 teaspoons balsamic vinegar
2 tablespoons olive oil
4 garlic cloves
200g pearl barley
Maldon sea salt
freshly ground black pepper
100–150g ricotta
2 tablespoons extra virgin olive oil

My Lasagne, with Chestnut, Pancetta & Cabbage

Feeds 4

This is a lasagne I conjured up, as the trinity of chestnut, pancetta and cabbage is so magical. I wanted a way of combining them in a new vein. It came to me in the night, so I made it for Pat's birthday lunch which I was laboriously planning, along with an awesome lemon tart for pudding. We all hung out at his beautiful and meticulously decorated flat up Brixton Hill, and had an urban family gathering. These were really good times. Our heyday consisted of Alice, Pat, me, Doctor Helen and Jules and Bharat sometimes too. I think we were still lunching at sundown as another red was popped open, to the sounds of some classic dusty Dylan records.

I love a creamy lasagne, and that is exactly what this is. The chestnut adds a sweet floury element, the cabbage keeps firm green vibes, and the pancetta adds just the right kick of substance and salt. All in all it's pretty perfect. Just make sure that you make the béchamel sauce runny enough, because you have only one sauce, not the usual two as in a classic red and white meaty lasagne. I make this to feed 4, and then live off any leftovers. It's delicious cold, so I hoof a mouthful each time I pass the kitchen.

1 medium spring
cabbage
50g butter
1 onion
60g plain flour
300ml full-fat milk
300ml vegetable stock
(better still fresh
chicken stock, if you
have made some)
12 slices of pancetta
240g cooked peeled
chestnuts
freshly ground black
pepper
Maldon sea salt
12 leaves of dried
lasagne
some freshly and
coarsely grated
Parmesan for the top

First prepare the cabbage, removing any ropy tougher leaves. Slice off the end of it, in order to unleash the young pale green leaves. Slice down the thicker main vein halfway up the leaf so that it cooks through. Place the cabbage leaves in a large saucepan and cover with water. Bring this to the boil, and then remove from the heat and drain, leaving a little water in the bottom to keep the cabbage moist. Set this aside while you make the sauce and preheat the oven to 180°C/Gas 4.

Melt the butter in a medium saucepan over a medium heat. As it dissolves, peel and dice the onion and add to the pan when it is slightly spitting. Thoroughly coat the onion in the melted butter. Now add the flour and sweat for a few moments in order to cook it. Gradually add the milk and then the stock, using a whisk to make sure that there are no lumps. Turn the heat right down while you roughly chop the pancetta into 2cm pieces and the chestnuts into quarters. Add these to the béchamel sauce. Season and taste to make sure it is really silky and delicious. Remove from the heat.

Using a good ovenproof dish, about 30 x 23cm, layer the wet cabbage leaves followed by the pasta, and then ladle over the chunky béchamel sauce. I like it when the final layer is the béchamel sauce, topped with some good Parmesan, and a little more seasoning. Bake in the oven for about 25 minutes. Serve just as it is.

Super Easy Mushroom & Chicken Korma with Raita

For 3

This really was a total coup. When I was in a six-month recuperation after a brain haemorrhage, I spent a lot of time, no surprises, thinking about food, but also being looked after by Raf. We cooked this together, bickering over whether tomatoes would be a right addition. Being my kitchen vibe master, he was indeed right: the tomatoes really work. It is simple and smooth, and got us both really excited about the January jollies that we were planning to India. With piles of perfect rice, it fed the two of us and Raf's bestest, Jamie. He's nothing short of brilliant, and constantly takes the mickey out of me for being ridiculous.

I had bought a piece of rotisserie chicken and biked it over to his, as these are deliciously moist and flavoursome. Although it is entirely unorthodox to do so, it is easy, and tasty too, so I would highly recommend such cheating, or using some leftover roast chicken, stripped off a carcass. Or you can bone a couple of chicken thighs and add these. It really depends on what's around.

This is not a full-on meat dish. I'm often put off by the massive hunks of meat ever-present in Indian takeaways. So this recipe should have less chook than veg. The meat will be one of a number of elements that make up the dish: either it makes for a much lighter meal, or it means you can eat more of it … whichever way you like to look at it! It's sweet, so is great with the salty sour raita. Oh, and if you've got vegetarians in the house then abstaining from the chicken element would be fine, and you could just add a tin of chickpeas at the same time as the spinach instead.

Mushroom & Chicken Korma

2 handfuls of cooked
    stripped chicken
    meat, or 2 organic
    chicken thighs
2 tablespoons coconut
    oil
1 teaspoon mustard
    seeds
5 whole cardamom pods
1 shard of cinnamon
1 teaspoon cayenne
    pepper
1 teaspoon ground
    ginger
1 teaspoon garam
    masala (Goan if you
    can find it)
1 teaspoon hot chilli
    powder
4 fresh curry leaves or
    8 dried ones
250g chestnut
    mushrooms
1 onion
2 bird's-eye chillies
3 garlic cloves
2 large fresh tomatoes
1 bag/225g spinach
50g ground almonds
200ml natural yoghurt
1 teaspoon caster sugar

First, if you are using fresh chicken thighs, debone by cutting around the bone in order to release it. Then give it a mighty tug to remove the meat. You may need to trim any remaining gristle or fat from these pieces. Slice them into small pieces about the size of a gizzard. Now warm the coconut oil in a large pan on a low heat, and add the chopped fresh chicken (if you are using already-cooked chicken, skip straight to the spices). Fry slowly for 5 minutes, or until it is just cooked. Remove from the pan with a slotted spoon and set aside. Keep the remaining juices in the pan and set aside. In a pestle and mortar, grind up the mustard seeds, cardamom pods and cinnamon. When they have been well worked on, remove the cardamom husks, leaving the black seeds in the mortar. Add the cayenne, ginger, garam masala and chilli powder and give it all another grind. Reheat the pan and add these spices, along with the curry leaves, frying for a few minutes to bring out the awesome flavours.

Clean any dirt off the mushrooms. Now peel and dice the onion, and finely chop the chillies and peeled garlic. Add these to the spice paste in the pan and give it a good shake around. Roughly chop the tomatoes into quarters, and the mushrooms into sixths, and add these to the pan too. Place the lid on the pan and simmer the whole lot on a medium heat for 15 minutes. Now turn the heat right down to low and add the spinach, so that it wilts, again replacing the lid. Turn the heat off and add the ground almonds and lightly cooked chicken (or stripped chicken leftovers), giving a good mix to thoroughly distribute it. Let it cool for half an hour before adding the yoghurt and a little sugar. Return the pan to a low heat in order to warm it through before serving.

Raita

Measure the cumin seeds into a dry frying pan and toast for a few moments. Set them aside on a plate to cool. Now pour out the yoghurt and beat it with a whisk so that it is silky smooth. Peel the cucumber, slice in half and then lengthways into about 6 strands and then finely dice and add to the yoghurt. Peel the garlic cloves, crush through a garlic press and add to the yoghurt, along with the cooled cumin seeds. Add lots of salt and dust the top with cayenne pepper.

2 teaspoons cumin
  seeds
400ml natural yoghurt
1 medium cucumber
2 garlic cloves
Maldon sea salt
1 teaspoon cayenne
  pepper

Coconut & Cardamom Custard

For 4

This was my second childhood pudding triumph, after Biddy's steamed pudding (see opposite). It is truly graceful and light, melts in the mouth, and looks tender and inviting. And it couldn't be easier either. All you will need are four little ramekins. I quite like making these for three, and saving the last for a midnight feast just for me.

1 x 225ml tin of coconut milk
4 cardamom pods
3 medium free-range eggs
110g caster sugar

Preheat the oven to 150°C/Gas 2. Begin by heating the coconut milk and cardamom pods in a small pan on a medium flame. Meanwhile, beat the eggs together, preferably in a lipped bowl, or a wide jug. Add the sugar to this, while continuing to beat. When the milk is beginning to foam at the edge and slightly rise, remove it from the heat and gradually add it to the eggs, through a sieve to catch the pods, being careful to whisk all the time and meticulously combine. Place the ramekins on a baking tray and fill this with water so that the level comes halfway up the pots. Pour the custard equally between the dishes (hence the lipped bowl) and place in the oven for 35 minutes. Remove the custard ramekins from the oven and cool to room temperature, before finally removing them from the warm water.

Biddy's Microwave Steamed Pudding

One of my first ever dishes, and ideal for a coven of 4

My aunt Biddy used to run a natty and rather classy little catering business. When I was little, about eleven, I would go round to her house and help out with the cooking, sitting at her big kitchen table, quietly and contentedly making smoked salmon rolls and filling baby pastry cases. I was always happy and humming. This is her famed steamed pudding. My cousins, Jemma and Pat, who are very grown up now, still rave about it. As everyone loves cake mix as much as the actual baked cake, this is best when it's actually quite undercooked, and the hot gooey sponge collapses around itself like hot magical Vesuvian lava. Serve either with single cream or some ice cream.

Lightly butter a glass pudding basin (a plastic one won't do here), and paste the honey, syrup or marmalade in the bottom (this will become the sugary lava of the pudding). In a big mixing bowl, beat the butter and sugar together into a light paste. Now beat in the eggs so that the mixture is loosened, and then fold in the self-raising flour and vanilla essence with a slotted metal spoon. Spoon the cake mix out into the prepared pudding basin, and place in the microwave for about 3 to 5 minutes, depending on the power of your microwave. If you are unsure of its strength, do it for less time, and you can always return it once you have speared the surface with a toothpick. You really want this just cooked and super-gooey when you turn it out on to a serving plate.

110g softened butter, plus a little more for greasing
2 tablespoons runny honey or golden syrup or marmalade
110g caster sugar
2 medium free-range eggs
110g self-raising flour
a few drops of vanilla extract (this is a kitsch pudding, but if you want it to be more upmarket, scrape out ½ a vanilla pod)

Dark Chocolate & Raspberry Cups

Feeds 3

Everyone loves a chocolate pudding. This one will need to set for a few hours, so make it before starting on the rest of your meal. It's a serious gluttons' pudding, so it's one I have made a few times for Raf and Anna Green-Armytage. They are the best people to cook for because they are so enthusiastic and appreciative. This pud is just the thing for a decadent gas.

100g dark chocolate (I try to get anything above 60%)
1 tablespoon water
2 medium free-range eggs
a knob of butter
150g raspberries (in season during July and August)
a few sprigs of mint

Preheat the oven to 100°C/Gas ¼. Get three coffee cups ready on a tray. Break up the chocolate into a pudding basin along with the water, and place in the oven for 10 minutes to melt. Meanwhile separate the eggs, putting the whites into a big enough bowl for some airy whisking. Set the yolks aside and begin whisking the whites so that they form soft peaks. Check that the chocolate is smooth when beaten, and then add a knob of butter, beating all the time to melt it in. I have a useful little whisk for this, or you could use a fork. Set the chocolate aside to cool for a few minutes and then beat in the yolks, again with vigour. Give the whites another quick whisk, to make sure they are firm, before adding 1 spoonful to the chocolate paste. Fold carefully so that you do not knock the air out of it. Now that it is loosened up, add the rest of the whites, folding in the same way. Just before it is homogenised, add the raspberries, keeping a handful aside, and fold one last time. Spoon the mousse equally between the coffee cups, topping with the leftover raspberries. Place in the fridge to chill for at least 2 hours. If you are feeling really decorative, a sprig of mint in each looks really sweet too.

Sweet Yellow Lentil Dhal

For 4

I was totally blown away by this sweet take on a dhal. I ate it nestling in a valley view of Gokana, a pilgrimage town in Karnataka. It's the wickedest place I've ever been to: juggernauts, monkeys, elephants, crazy plastic-eating cows, and even a little dosa shack we called Rosie's because it was just like my deli. We had a brilliant time there, and were very happy swimming in the bay at Kudli beach and eating amazing deep-fried cauliflower salads. And then these were in turn punctuated by weird Indian beers, and card games (that I always lost). We checked into a delicious spa overlooking the town and sea, with brilliant views and fantastic food: lovely lime pickle, smooth coconut chutney, delicate little palm sugar sweets, shredded cabbage with mustard seeds. It was an awakening in every way. Gokana taught me to relax, and this thick sweet pudding takes me immediately back to that quiet spa, and makes me want to do it all again.

1 mug of yellow lentils
4–5 mugs of water
6 whole cardamom pods
1 teaspoon ground ginger
2 tablespoons golden currants
1 x 400g tin of condensed milk
natural yoghurt, to serve

Place the yellow lentils, water, cardamom pods and ginger in a medium saucepan and bring to a gentle boil. Turn down the heat a little and simmer for 50 minutes with the lid off, until all the water has been absorbed. When the lentils are ready they will be floury and soft to bite. If they dry out too quickly while still nutty, add another half a mug of boiling water at a time, and continue to simmer. Now mash them up a bit, so that you have a half-puréed mixture. Add the golden currants and condensed milk, and warm for a further 10 minutes, on a low heat. The condensed milk burns easily, so keep a close eye on the pan. Serve with a dollop of yoghurt on top to cut the thick sweetness.

Baked Amaretti & Goat's Cheesecake

For 6

This cheesecake is ridiculous. It's totally decadent and rich and the opposite of Doctor Helen's fresh mascarpone one on page 335. I make it at Rosie's when I'm feeling really wanton, so it would be the *pièce de résistance* of any get-together: sticky from the amaretti biscuits, madly creamy on top with just a hint of orange. I make this cheesecake with real goat's cheese, because it seems obvious to actually use a real and tangy cheese. Chèvre log works the best, and gives a wonderful sour edge to the sweetness. This cheesecake is so tasty, and I am so impatient and greedy, that I once blistered the roof of my mouth eating it straight out of the oven.

50g butter, plus a little extra for greasing
200g amaretti biscuits
180g chèvre log
3 medium free-range egg yolks
120g caster sugar
1 orange
284ml double cream

For this recipe you will need a round, loose-bottomed or springform tin about 15cm in diameter. Line the base of this with baking parchment, and grease the sides with a little butter. To make the base, crush up the amaretti biscuits. In the shop I do this with a rolling pin. At home, I have a little blitzer these days. It does the job really well, especially if you pulse it. When the biscuits are like breadcrumbs they are good to go. Measure out the butter into a little saucepan, and heat on a low flame until it is entirely melted. Pour this into the biscuit crumbs and, with a spatula, thoroughly work this so that the butter is binding and making the biscuit dark and damp, but is not oily. Press the base down into the bottom of your lined tin and refrigerate while you work on the top of the cake.

Preheat the oven to 150°C/Gas 2. Trim the goat's cheese, removing only the rind. Place the cheese in a medium measuring jug and, using a whisk, break it up a bit. Add the egg yolks to the cheese. Vigorously beat to remove all lumps. It should gradually become a smooth creamy paste, but will take some serious pep. Now add the sugar, and beat again. Grate the zest off the orange, and add this, along with the double cream. Finally squeeze in the juice from the orange. Taste the mix to see that it is cheesy and yet not salty. Pour it over the chilled biscuit base and place in the oven for an hour. When the top looks quite brown, turn the heat down to 100°C/Gas ¼ and continue cooking for a further half an hour to just set it. Provided the top no longer wobbles, your cheesecake is ready. Release the sides with a palette knife, and remove the base of the tin. Leave it to cool before serving, just like this, or you too will burn your mouth.

Really Easy Brandy & Almond Tiramisù

Feeds 4 or 5, depending on what came before it

This is a mascarpone-based pudding. People say tiramisù is unfashionable. I'd say they had no taste. Fashion doesn't count where this finale is concerned, but I have added to the original tiramisù, by including flaked almonds, which gives a wicked and crunchy twist. This recipe is a really simple version of that classic Italian treat, and it's not at all as fiddly as you may have feared.

I used to be obsessed with tiramisù. It was the only pudding I ever ordered in restaurants, such was my love. I probably could have done a Zagat survey on them, I've tasted so many. The ecstasy of those squidgy wet layers of sponge, the slightly sour creamy duvet and the alcoholic aftertaste, drive me a bit demented. It may also explain my addiction to any spiked coffee.

120ml strongly brewed fresh coffee, made in a cafetière, cooled
50ml French cooking brandy
12 large savoiardi biscuits
2 teaspoons drinking chocolate
2 medium free-range eggs
75g caster sugar
about 300g mascarpone
50g flaked almonds

Mix the coffee and brandy together in a jug, and pour half this liquid into a wide cereal bowl. Dip 6 of the savoiardi biscuits on both sides into this, and arrange in a medium serving bowl (preferably glass, as it looks so brilliantly 1980s). Now do the same with the rest of the coffee-brandy mix and biscuits. They will drink up quite a lot of this nectar, which is why I suggest doing the dipping in halves and rationing. That way you shouldn't suddenly run out of coffee. Sprinkle with the drinking chocolate and set this aside.

Now separate the eggs into two generous bowls, ideally metallic. Add the sugar to the yolks, and beat until it forms a pale yellow creamy mousse. Gradually fold the mascarpone into this with a slotted spoon or spatula. Set this aside while you whisk the egg whites. They should be a little firmer than a soft peak. Finally fold this into the mascarpone mix. Be careful to maintain the lightness that you have created in the whites, as this pudding is delicious when almost foamy. Turn this mixture out, over the biscuit base, smoothing over the top. Place in the fridge for a few hours to set.

For the almond topping all you need to do is toast the flakes. Place the almonds in a dry frying pan on a low heat. Do not move your gaze from the hob, as you will undoubtedly burn the nuts if you do. They are quick to ruin. Toss them from time to time. After a few minutes they should be warmly coloured an orangey pink. Turn them out on to a plate to cool. Add these to the top of the tiramisù at the very last.

Golden Brown Tarte Tatin

Makes 4 to 6 slices

This is a surprisingly easy tart, considering it is one of the most famous and loved sorts. I'd almost go so far as to say it is foolproof. The joy of the dish is in the sweet wetness of the deliciously stodgy pastry, and the near golden and caramelised apples. It looks fantastic straight out of the oven, all gleaming with syrup. Keep this really simple, and serve with just some single cream or smart vanilla ice cream. It's super quick too.

In this case I use shop-bought frozen puff pastry, to lighten the culinary load. If you are doing it for a dinner party, I would recommend preparing the recipe in advance, up to the point that the tart goes into the oven. When you have finished your main course, place the tarte tatin in the preheated oven, and then that gives a half-hour gap, so that everyone will be gagging for your sweet fruity offerings by the time it arrives gleaming and steaming on the table.

a little plain flour for
rolling the pastry
250g puff pastry
(defrosting bought
ready-rolled puff
pastry will take
1½ hours)
6 medium apples
90g golden caster sugar
60g unsalted butter
3 sprigs of mint

You will need a 24cm non-stick frying pan with a metal handle.
Preheat the oven to 180°C/Gas 4. Dust a worktop with some flour
and roll out the defrosted puff pastry so that it is a little larger than
the frying pan. Trim it into a circle and set this aside while you deal
with the fruit and topping.

Peel, quarter and core the apples. Heat the sugar in the pan on a very
low flame, and watch it melt. This looks amazing. Do not stir, only
tip and swirl the pan using the handle as the tool. Be careful not to
scorch it. It should become oily and a dark golden brown. Add a third
of the butter to this, once you have removed it from the heat. Again,
swirl this around to melt and combine with the liquid sugar. Now
return the pan to the heat and add the apples, curved side down,
fanning out in a circle. Heat these for 7 to 10 minutes, with the rest of
the butter dotted around and melting on top and around the apples.
Now remove the pan from the heat and roll the pastry over the top.
Tuck the pastry around the edges, down and into the sides of the pan,
so that it contains and cups the syrupy apples in a snug fit. Pat the
pastry down and place in the oven for 25 minutes. When the top is
coloured and puffed up, remove from the oven and let it sit for a few
minutes. Now, using a cloth to protect your hand from the heat of the
pan handle, place a plate on top of the pan and flip the tart swiftly
over. Lift the pan off and there you have a wet burnished tarte tatin.
Dot the mint leaves over the tart and serve with a little cream.

Mallika's Baked Yoghurts Two Ways

Makes 4 ramekins

Mallika is a new friend of mine, an amazingly skilled Indian cook, and a force to be reckoned with too. She's a gorgeous whirlwind. This is a recipe that I found on her blog, which is really funny and well written. It's a genius 'cheesecake' using only yoghurt and condensed milk, poached in a bain marie to set and become a deliciously thick creamy pot of pudding, like the top layer of an actual cheesecake. Mallika does it very Indian-style, with toasted cardamom in the cheesy bit and saffron-infused milk decorating the top, which is really delicate and looks fantastic. Sometimes, though, I like it really simple, with a layer of jam as the only additional vibe. They are super easy to make, and won't take long either so are ideal for quick entertaining.

Baked Yoghurts with Fig Jam

500g natural yoghurt, plus a little more for serving
1 x 397g tin of condensed milk
4 tablespoons fig or gooseberry jam

Preheat the oven to 180°C/Gas 4. Measure out the yoghurt into a lipped mixing bowl and thoroughly whisk, so that there is no contrast between curd and whey and it is fine and creamy. Now pour in the condensed milk, using a spatula to get as much of it out of the tin as you can. Thoroughly beat these two together so that they are perfectly combined. Pour the mixture equally into 4 ramekins. Place these on a roasting tin and fill the tray up with water so that it comes two-thirds of the way up the little pots to make a bain marie. Place the tray in the oven for 20 to 25 minutes. When the pots are ready and set they will wobble only a little bit at the centre. As they cool they will continue to set.

Remove the pots from the bain marie. Place the jam in a small saucepan on a low heat. As it melts and bubbles it will loosen. When it is quite fluid, remove from the heat and spoon over the 'cheesecakes'. Cool, and serve with an additional dollop of yoghurt to cut the sweetness.

Baked Yoghurts with Frangelico & Hazelnuts

The other way I like doing this pudding is with Frangelico, a hazelnut liqueur made in Canale, Italy. Supposedly it was concocted by Fra Angelico, who knew lots about nature and the secrets of the wild. It certainly does taste fantastically aromatic: I fell in love with it when Stav squeezed lime over lots of ice and added a generous glug of Frangelico, so now it's my new drink of choice. As I've not yet found a bottle shop that sells Frangelico, I get the girls at the Bar & Grill to make me a little takeaway of this sweet treat, to add to the pot. If you can't find Frangelico, Amaretto will work too.

Preheat the oven to 180°C/Gas 4. Measure out the yoghurt into a lipped mixing bowl and thoroughly whisk, so that there is no contrast between curd and whey and it is fine and creamy. Now pour in the condensed milk, using a spatula to get as much of it out of the tin as you can. Thoroughly beat these two together so that they are perfectly combined. Now grate half the zest of the lime into the dairy bowl, along with the Frangelico, and stir. Pour the mixture equally into four ramekins. Due to the extra liquid from the liqueur, there may be more than can fit in four ramekins. If you have a spare one, fill this one up too. Place them on a roasting tin and fill the tray up with water so that it comes two-thirds of the way up the sides of the little pots to make a bain marie. Place the whole tray in the oven for 20 minutes. When the pots are ready and set they will wobble only a little bit at the centre. As they cool they will emulsify.

Roughly crush up the hazelnuts either by pulsing in a blender, or on a chopping board with a long sharp knife. Toast them in a dry frying pan on a medium flame, tossing the pan from time to time so that the nuts don't burn. When they are turning golden, remove from the pan to a plate to cool. When the ramekins have been removed from the bain marie, sprinkle these toasted hazelnuts over them so that your puddings are encrusted with the dark nuts. Devour at room temperature.

500g natural yoghurt
1 x 397g tin of
    condensed milk
1 small lime
100ml Frangelico liqueur
3 handfuls of hazelnuts

BONITO DEL NORTE
en Aciete de Oliva

SOULFUL GRUB

When you have a sore head or a broken heart (and these two often come together) and need to share a bottle of wine with a close friend, soothing food is required. Some lolling on the sofa with soul food and comfort: red wine, *EastEnders* and the ones you love. The recipes in this chapter are individual dishes for simple nurturing. The only thing you will need afterwards is a big mug of tea, a bag of Maltesers and the knowledge that next time, you'll mix some water with your wine.

Of course these recipes also suit some weekend soothing. I love a Sunday afternoon when some long cooking and lazy kotching is the only thing required. Watching all the omnibuses, locking out the rain and taking refuge in some winter fodder. Hearty food to allay the inevitable Sunday blues. I sometimes spend a winter Sunday cooking just for the comfort of the process. Get a few friends over for a late, late lunch, and enjoy the dwindling weekend.

Menu

Soups

Meals

Soups

The joy of soups is that they keep for a couple of days, which is ideal if you are also a few days short of payday and feeling the financial pinch. And by their very nature they are warming and wet and full of comfort, whether that is rejuvenation or solace. I used to make a daily soup for my dad's lunch, as he got so cold making furniture in his workshop that it was the ideal lunch for us all – cheap and yet tasty and warming, often with a few vegetables from our garden. They are really addictive once you realise how easy the process is. Most of these soup recipes make a big saucepan's worth, which will be enough to feed about six people. If you aren't going to sup it all in one go, you can freeze the rest for another even more rainy day.

These days I also make a daily soup in the shop, so have probably combined every possible vegetable, herb and cheese together, to console my customers. It is a very satisfying process, so I hope you enjoy it too. Unless I have stated otherwise, the stocks for all my soups are Marigold Swiss vegetable bouillon powder. This is what I use when making vats in the shop, but if you are at home with a little time on your hands, a proper homemade chicken or vegetable stock will really make the difference here.

Stav B's Pumpkin & Red Lentil Soup

For 8 to 10

Stav is one of the wonderful waifs and strays of Brixton. She served her time at Rosie's when I was ill and off work for a few months, and was a total life-saver (even if she did bake vegan muffins!). I stamped those out, but her delicious pumpkin and red lentil soup survives. It's got a wonderful texture that is further thickened by the little fluffy lentils, making it almost reminiscent of a light dhal. And the pumpkin is sweetness itself. It's a real winter warmer and easy to create. It's mostly about simmering and sensitively seasoning.

Skin the onions and roughly chop them. Warm the olive oil in a big saucepan over a medium heat, add the onions and gently fry until browning and sweet at the edges. Meanwhile deseed and remove the waxy skin from the pumpkin. This will take some gusto. Chop this into 2cm-ish chunks along with the courgette and add to the sizzling pan. It should be caramelising now. Add the sprigs of mint, and give it all a good mix around. Add the tomatoes and sweat all the vegetables together for 5 minutes. After that, you should add the red lentils and water. Place a lid on the saucepan and let it simmer for 30 minutes, on a low heat. The reason you add water is that stock is too salty, and would prevent the lentils from cooking. Now, mix up a vegetable stock and add to this the smoked paprika. Pour this into the soup after it has cooked down and the lentils are floury and well cooked. Blend to form a smooth silky soup. Taste and season accordingly. And as Stav would say, 'Kiss the peace.'

3 little onions
2 tablespoons olive oil
1kg pumpkin
1 courgette
3 sprigs of fresh mint
1 x 400g tin of chopped tomatoes or 5 large fresh tomatoes
280g red lentils
1.2 litres water
500ml vegetable stock
½ teaspoon smoked mild paprika
Maldon sea salt
lots of freshly ground black pepper

Raf's Lettuce Soup

For 3 or 4

I first ate this soup in Raf's tumbling garden. We'd had little sleep, after careering around the now defunct Astoria, with The View. And typically, I had a big bruise on the bum to show for it. This soup provided the perfect rejuvenation, as it's full of verdantness, and the feta crumbled on top will offer you all the salt you need on a day like this! It's a quick thing to make too, so you will be satisfied within minutes. Eat this with soft Portuguese aniseed bread, and long iced lime sodas with the Sunday papers, and your world will be complete. It's food baptism, and will wash away the sins of the weekend.

I have a clever way here for giving the chilli kick, but with a more subtle angle: by piercing the strong Scotch bonnet chilli and letting this infuse the soup you get all the heat, but none of the pain. You then remove the chilli from the soup before blending. The kick is most definitely there, but more of an infusion. And in Jamaica recently, this method was confirmed by the lovely Miss Anne. She runs the kitchen where I was lucky enough to be staying and offered up lots of great cooking tips to me.

1 shallot
1 large knob of butter
1 Scotch bonnet chilli
2 Little Gem lettuces
1 litre vegetable stock
200g frozen petits pois
3 or 4 sprigs of fresh
    mint
200g feta
freshly ground black
    pepper

Peel the shallot and slice into roundels. Heat the butter in a medium pan, on a medium heat, and fry the shallot, stirring to break it up a bit. Pierce the chilli with a sharp knife in a few places and add this to the pan. Roughly chop the lettuces into hunks about 2cm wide and add these, opening them up a bit. Then place a lid on the pan to let the lettuce wilt down for a few minutes. Meanwhile, make up the vegetable stock. Add this to the pan and simmer for 5 minutes with the lid on, until the lettuce stalks are transparent and the leaves soft and darkly wilted. Now add the sweet little petits pois and mint, and simmer until the peas are just cooked, but still sweet. Sift out the chilli before blending the soup with a hand-held blender, and dishing out. This should feed about 4 people, each with a chunk of crumbled feta scattered over the top of the soup along with some black pepper.

Gascon Soup made with Wild Mushrooms, Tomatoes & Sherry Vinegar

For 6 to 8

I went to the Gers with Pat, a brief but significant boyfriend, a Francophile, a chronically stylish man and now a good old friend. His parents have a house in the Gers, and so we went for a long weekend, to coincide with the annual tradition of killing the pig. We all mucked in and made *pâté de tête* and *saucisson*, and all kinds of foreign cuts of meat. The barn we worked away in was icy cold, and wonderfully falling down and draughty. I had a gastronomic awakening, and came back a little porky myself with a reaffirmed interest in good French fare.

This soup is one I started making on my return from this trip to France, as the deep rich flavours conjure up the food that we ate, the smells and, well, the whole rural adventure. Regarding the ingredients, if you can get hold of sherry vinegar you will be really pleased with the results here. It gives a dry but also a sweet shock to the soup. If not, then some immature balsamic vinegar will do the trick. And also, the use of bread here is a good one, if you have some stale lying around, that you are loath to waste.

1kg tomatoes, the riper
   the better
3 little red onions
2 tablespoons olive oil
20g dried cèpes or
   morel mushrooms
6 garlic cloves
1.5 litres vegetable stock
1 tablespoon sherry
   vinegar
130g stale bread
2 good handfuls of fresh
   parsley
2 teaspoons golden
   caster sugar
lots of freshly ground
   black pepper
Maldon sea salt

Slice the tomatoes into 4 pieces each and peel and finely dice the red onions. Heat the olive oil in a large pan on a medium flame and add the chopped tomatoes and onions. Mix around and fry for 10 minutes. Meanwhile pour enough hot water over the wild mushrooms to cover and let them sit and rehydrate. When they have plumped up, scoop them out of the water, squeeze and finely chop, along with the garlic that you should have peeled. Add the vegetable stock, mushroom water, vinegar and sliced stale bread, and place the lid on the pan. Simmer for 15 minutes, really quite energetically on a high flame. Meanwhile finely chop the parsley, and then fold this into the soup, along with the sugar, freshly ground pepper and salt. Thoroughly blend this soup for a creamy heady brew, or lightly pulse for a more rustic affair.

Onion & Butter Bean Soup

Feeds 3 or 4

My old school friend Chloe, or Das Klo as she's known to us Wycombe girls, is the source of inspiration for this recipe. We've always had a thriving food relationship: in our last few years at school, we would sign out for the weekend, head to London to her mum's wonderfully bohemian flat in Bayswater (it was here that I first discovered the genius of halloumi, the only cheese that doesn't melt), and cook delicious dinners with Em and Haz before going out in Chelsea to scout for boys. We no longer hunt in quite the same areas, but we do still frequently exchange food ideas. This is great and warming and very simple. The soup can be done either as a blended soup as Chloe recommended or it can be left with wonderful buttery sweet chunks floating in a clean broth. It's up to you and very much depends on your mood. Do experiment.

The ingredients are amazing – about as easy as you can get. Do you have a little open jar of anchovies lurking in the back of the fridge? A few old onions hiding in the salad bowl? And a rogue tin of butter beans that you've never known what to do with? You're off … and soon you will be eating the most smoothly knitted flavoursome soup ever. The sweet onions and salty anchovies, homogenised by creamy butter beans, are sheer brilliance and smooth comfort.

3 bog standard onions
2 garlic cloves
2 tablespoons olive oil
a knob of butter
3 anchovies preserved in oil
1 x 400g tin of butter beans
700ml good homemade chicken stock
1 teaspoon fresh or dried thyme, depending on what's around

Peel the onions and roughly slice each one into quarters. Peel the garlic too, chop it up quite finely, and set aside. Warm the olive oil and butter in a medium-sized pan on a medium heat. When they have melted together, add the onions and sweat, lowering the heat. When the onions are softening and beginning to look shiny and delicious, add the anchovies and thoroughly mix around. The anchovies will begin to dissolve and colour the onions as they heat through. Now add the garlic and sweat for a further few minutes while you drain and rinse the butter beans. Add these to the pan, along with the chicken stock and thyme. Bring to a moderate simmer and continue to cook for 20 minutes. You can either serve it now, just as it is, all chunky and floaty, or vigorously blend to create a flavourful creamy soup. It depends so much on your mood. This dish doesn't need salt, as you will be gleaning all of that from the anchovies. You can add pepper, but I like it naked. It's perfect just as it is.

Courgette, Chickpea & Mint Soup

For 4

This is a really simple and fresh-tasting soup. So it's ideal for some replenishing goodness or indeed happiness. I love mint in soup, as it makes you feel like spring is coming. 'A sliver of light in an otherwise bleak world', as my old school friend Haz says. It only struck me after making this soup many times in the shop – where it has a very enthusiastic reception – that it's pretty healthy too. So all the bases are covered.

Trim the courgettes, slice them lengthways in half, then roughly chop them into chunks. Heat the olive oil in a large saucepan, on a medium flame, and add the courgettes. Peel the garlic cloves and roughly chop these too. Add after the courgettes have been sweating for about 5 minutes. Continue to fry for another few minutes. Now pour over the vegetable stock and bring to a simmer. Rinse the chickpeas and add too, along with the mint leaves. You don't need to chop these, just remove them from their stems. They will be pulverised later by the blending. Simmer for half an hour. Remove from the heat to cool for a moment before blending. I like it not quite perfectly smooth, but with green flashes of courgette and mint, and a little nuttiness from the chickpeas. Finally, season with coarsely ground pepper, and squeeze in the lemon juice. This really brings out and lifts the flavours.

4 large fresh courgettes
2 tablespoons olive oil
3 garlic cloves
1 litre vegetable stock
1 x 400g tin of chickpeas
a handful of mint leaves
freshly ground black
    pepper
½ lemon

Spiced Carrot Soup

For 6 to 8

Good for a cold, these sweet spices really give zing to a load of crunchy carrots. It's a cheap pick-me-up too, as carrots tend to be a bargain. And if you fancy a variation on this theme, you could substitute the carrots with parsnips here. This sort of soup takes quite an English approach to spices, rather like the currying of a Coronation chicken. But if you get the blend right, it really does work wonderfully to create a smooth, powerfully sweet and explosive meal. The cardamom seeds smell near medicinal.

Lelah Peach, a little angelic urchin who used to work at Rosie's, taught me to make spiced soups. She ran away to Brighton last summer, and Brixton misses her badly, so I like to cook her soups in her absent honour, to remind me of her lovely and wily ways.

Peel and roughly chop the onion. Now peel away the skin of the ginger and finely slice into little cubes. Warm the olive oil in a large saucepan on a low heat. When it's hot, add the onion and ginger and sweat for a moment. Measure out each spice, the cinnamon, masala, cardamom (split the husks of the cardamom, and release the little dark tasty seeds), nutmeg and caraway seeds, and add in turn to the pot. Coat the onion in the spices and continue to sweat for a few minutes while you peel and chop the carrots into about 6 pieces each. Do the same with the apple, peeling and cutting into 8 pieces. You may need to remove the pan from the heat for a moment so as not to burn the onion during this time. Now add these two to the pot and again coat in the spices. Fry for a few moments, then add the vegetable stock. Place a lid on the pan and turn the heat up to medium. Simmer for 45 minutes. When the carrots slip easily off a small sharp knife you are ready to remove the soup from the heat. Let it sit for a moment, and now, with a blender, thoroughly break down the carrots to form a silky smooth sweet soup. Season, and squeeze in the lemon juice if the flavours need a lift.

To serve, ladle a few spoons of the soup into a big bowl, add a dollop of natural yoghurt in the middle, and grate over a little more nutmeg (my friend Flora's tip).

1 onion
15g fresh ginger, about a thumb
2 tablespoons olive oil
1 teaspoon ground cinnamon
1 teaspoon garam masala
4 whole cardamom pods
¼ of a nutmeg, plus extra at the end, on top of the soup
1 teaspoon caraway seeds
1.5kg carrots
1 medium English apple
1.5 litres vegetable stock
freshly ground black pepper
Maldon sea salt
¼ lemon
250ml natural yoghurt

Beetroot & Pear Soup

For 8 to 10

I have only recently discovered beetroot. I had always had an aversion to it. It struck me as messy, with all that staining on my plate. I would almost go so far as to say it annoyed me. However, I've come to understand that it has a flavour quite unlike anything else. Sweet, but not sickly; clean but not too far from the muddy earth, and obviously a wonderfully loud and deep colour. Beetroot is in season all the way from July to January, so there's a lot of scope in the year for making this soup. It's super in risotto too. The pears in this recipe add a wicked grainy texture too.

When I make this soup in the deli, I cook double quantities and pour it into a massive salad bowl from which to ladle. Everyone wants a piece of the action. But it's the tarragon vinegar that really gives this soup a song, and lifts the flavours so that the whole thing really pings out at you. I think I love this tarragon intervention because it reminds me of home, and my mum making delicious hollandaise sauces with this vinegar. It really clears your face and head and heart.

Place the beetroots in a bowl of body-temperature water. With a scrubbing brush, give them a really good once-over, to remove all the mud, as you will be keeping the skins intact. When they are clean of earth, dice into 2cm pieces, trimming any gnarly bits. Warm the olive oil in a large deep saucepan on a medium heat. When it's hot, add the cubed beetroot and sweat. Meanwhile peel and finely slice the onions and garlic, and add to the pan. Fry the vegetables for 5 minutes. Pour over the vegetable stock and place the lid on the pan. Simmer for 30 minutes, or until the beetroot slips off a sharp knife. Now core the pears and roughly chop. Also, discard any frumpy leaves from the spring onions and chop these into rounds. Add the pear and spring onions to the pan, and continue to simmer for a further 5 or 10 minutes to blanch these latecomers. Now remove the soup from the heat and add the vinegar. Let it cool for 15 minutes, then add the cream. Thoroughly blend and season the soup, so that it is a delicious fuchsia whirlpool. To serve, bowl it up and add more pepper on top, and a drizzle of extra virgin olive oil.

1kg muddy beetroots
3 tablespoons olive oil
2 red onions
4 garlic cloves
1.5 litres vegetable stock
2 pears
1 bunch of spring onions
2 tablespoons tarragon
 vinegar
100ml single cream
freshly ground black
 pepper
Maldon sea salt
extra virgin olive oil,
 to serve

Munching Maps

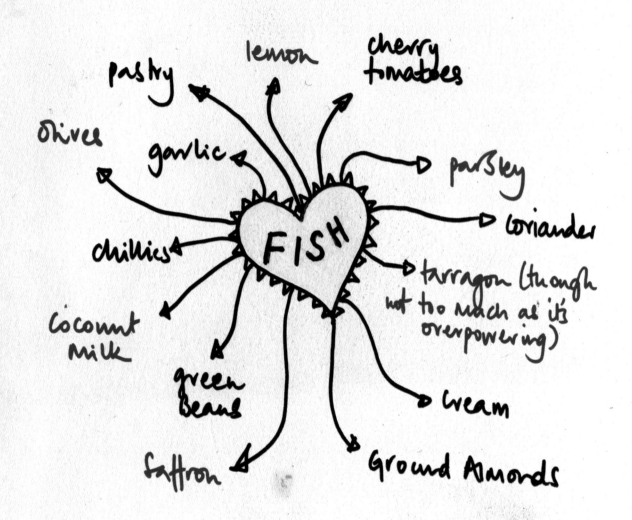

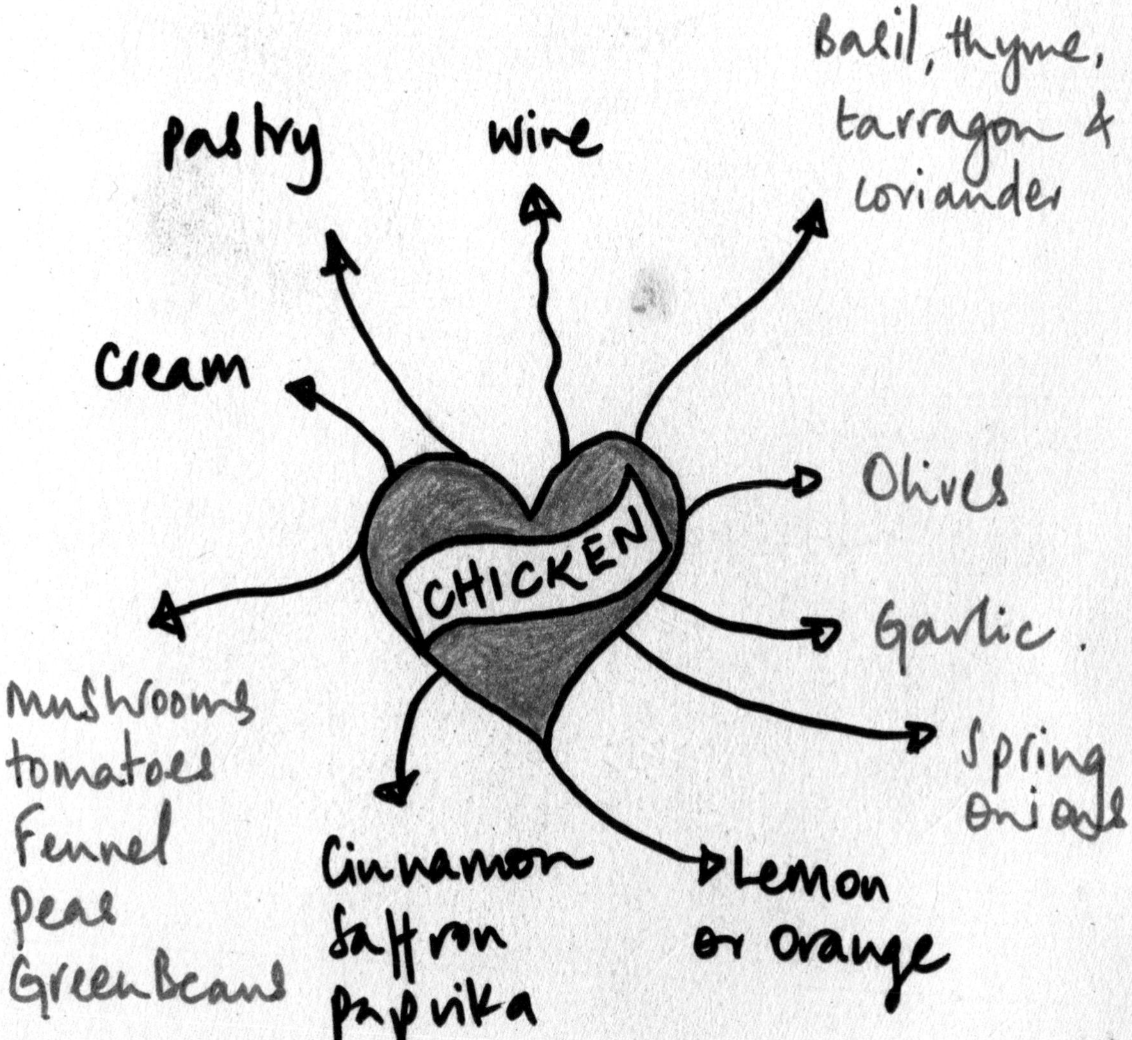

pastry

wine

Basil, thyme, tarragon & coriander

cream

CHICKEN

Olives

Garlic.

Spring onions

mushrooms
tomatoes
Fennel
Peas
GreenBeans

Cinnamon
Saffron
paprika

Lemon
or Orange

Munching Maps

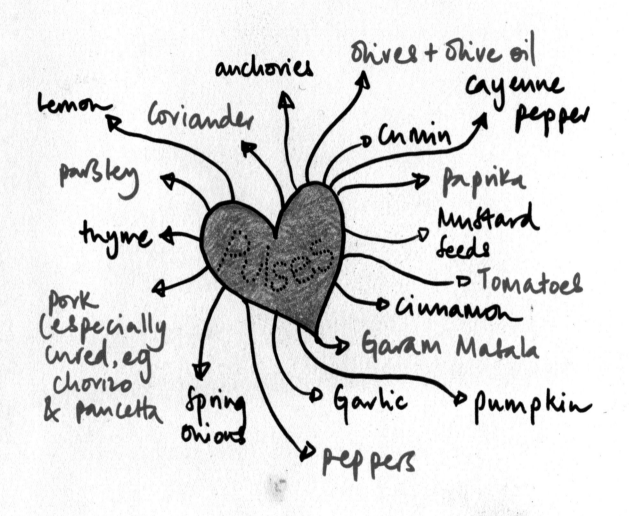

NEVER COOK DRIED PULSES WITH SALT OR STOCK. THEY WILL NEVER SOFTEN ~ ADD LATER ON. ♡

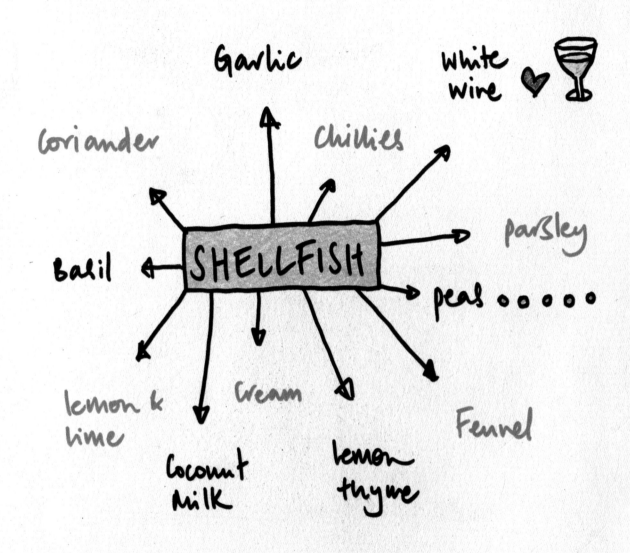

Munching Maps

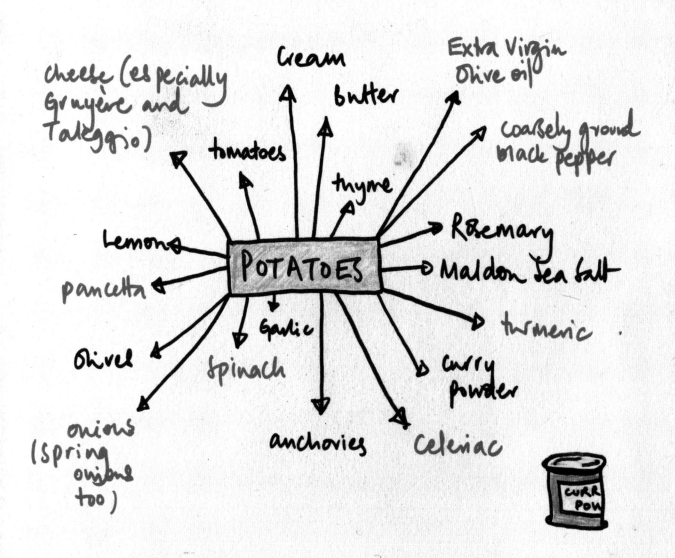

Munching Maps

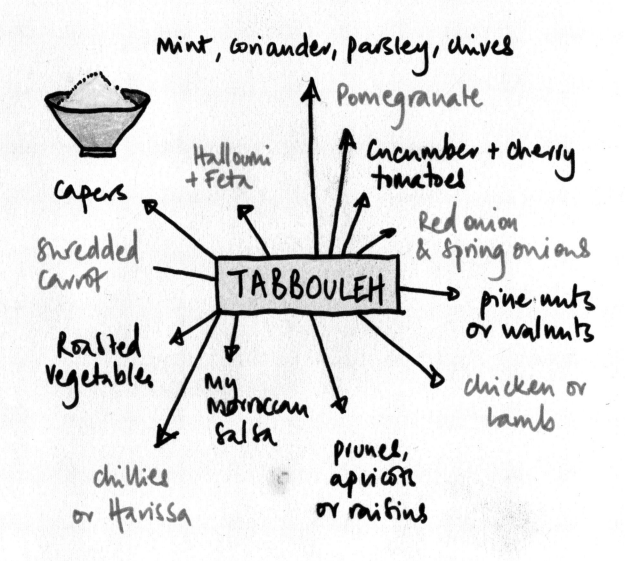

Mint, coriander, parsley, chives

Pomegranate

Cucumber + cherry tomatoes

Halloumi + Feta

Capers

Red onion & spring onions

Shredded carrot

TABBOULEH

pine nuts or walnuts

Roasted vegetables

My Moroccan salsa

chicken or lamb

chillies or Harissa

prunes, apricots or raisins

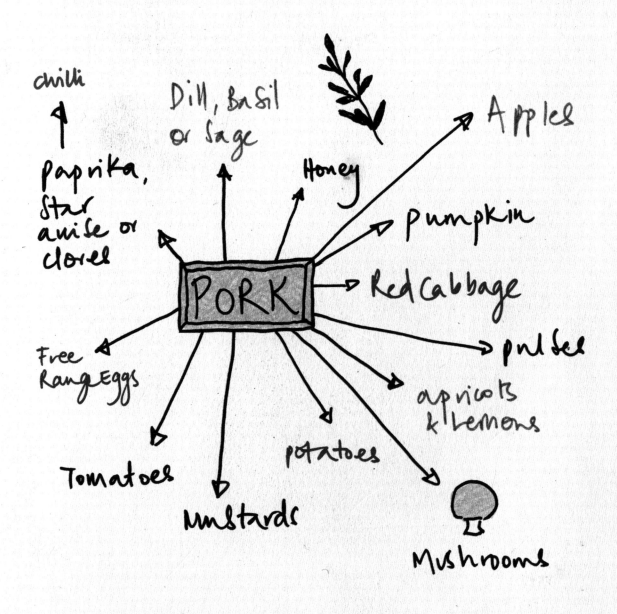

chilli

Dill, Basil or Sage

Apples

paprika, Star anise or cloves

Honey

Pumpkin

PORK

Red Cabbage

pulses

Free Range Eggs

apricots & Lemons

Tomatoes

potatoes

mustards

Mushrooms

Warming Orecchiette with Sausage & Sage

For 3

I really associate creamy foods with a kind of decadent comfort. It's my favourite way of eating that ambrosial gift to the kitchen, pasta. This is a rich and wonderful dish full of tang, from the wine and sage, and love, from the pasta and cream. It's swift and simple to make, full of instant gratification, which is ideal if you are feeling blue and need a rich injection.

I get sausagemeat from my local butcher, Michael, in Brixton Market, as he makes all different kinds on location: leek, apple, sage. If you can't find proper sausagemeat, by weight, then buying some good-quality sausages and skinning them is just fine. Make sure that whichever kind of sausagemeat you plump for, you meticulously break it up as it fries. It should end up almost as fine as mince, which requires a little bit of elbow stamina. Sometimes I substitute the usual orecchiette with a smaller narrower shell called gnocchetti sardi too.

Heat the olive oil in a wide frying pan on a low heat. Slice the spring onions into finger-width rounds and add to the warm oil. As they sizzle, break the sausagemeat into the pan, and then with a flat-ended wooden spoon go about thoroughly breaking this meat up. After about 5 minutes, it will begin to brown and stick. At this point very finely chop the sage leaves and add, along with the white wine. This will deglaze the browned tasty meat on the base of the pan. You may need to give it a bit of a scrape with your spoon. Simmer for 5 minutes on a low heat before removing from the heat and adding the spinach in order for it to wilt, and for the sauce to cool enough in anticipation of the cream (which may curdle if the sauce is too hot).

Put a pan of salted water on a high heat to bring it to the boil. When it's rumbling, add the pasta and give it a good stir to stop it sticking to the bottom of the pan. Meanwhile, return the sauce to a low heat and add the single cream and mustard. Stir to combine it fully with the sausage and wine. The pasta will be cooked after about 8 minutes, depending on the brand that you are using. Drain, and spoon over the sage and sausage. Season each plate with lots of coarse black pepper.

2 tablespoons olive oil
3 spring onions or
    1 small onion
350g good-quality pork
    sausagemeat
1 handful of fresh sage
1 large glass of white
    wine (about 200ml)
4 handfuls of spinach
300g orecchiette (my
    favourite is chunky
    and porous and
    made by Rustichella
    d'Abruzzo)
80ml single cream
2 teaspoons grainy Dijon
    mustard
freshly ground black
    pepper

Raf Daddy's Groundnut Curry

For at least 3, but that depends on your greed

When I'm really blue, this is what I make for myself. It is Raf's comforting and filling signature dish. I remember the first time being totally blown away by this African curry. The peanut magnificently thickens and gives body to the sauce. He eats it with rice because he's a greedy thing, but really it'll suffice on its own, or with a little bread for some good mopping at the end. Eating this is like receiving one of Raf's back-crackingly asphyxiating hugs. Just the thing when you are feeling the effects of a late night or the sudden onset of despondency.

I do, however, bastardise this recipe, sometimes using Raf's sweet potatoes, sometimes chickpeas, and as here, with pumpkin (my favourite, and abundant Brixton vegetable): when cooking we absorb from all around us, and inherit from those close to us, which means that recipes are always evolving and changing. I miss out the ginger that Raf describes and use a big juicy red chilli from the freezer. And I prefer the added surprise of bits of peanut, enabled by using a crunchy rather than a smooth peanut butter … take your pick, and play around with it. Here's what he has to say:

hey darlin,
sweat onions, garlic, ground ginger, then put in two cubed sweet
potatoes and fry em a bit with a good dusting of cayenne and a tbsp of
hot curry powder. two cans chopped toms hubble bubble for a bit add a
little water if you need it then ladle out a bit of the sauce into a bowl
and stir in a good load of peanut butter depending on how fat you're
feeling. stir the thinned peanut butter into the pot and chuck in a bag of
spinach. once it's all wilted then voila! enjoy.

500g pumpkin
1 large onion
2 garlic cloves
1 juicy chilli
2 tablespoons olive oil
1 teaspoon hot curry
   powder
1 teaspoon cayenne
   pepper
2 x 400g tins of chopped
   tomatoes
3 generous tablespoons
   crunchy peanut
   butter
1 bag/225g baby
   spinach
100ml water
a generous pinch of
   white granulated
   sugar
lots of freshly ground
   black pepper

First prepare the pumpkin, onion, garlic and chilli: deseed and peel the pumpkin using a sharp knife and cut into 2cm hunks; peel and dice the onion; peel the garlic cloves and finely chop; slice the chilli in half, then remove half of the seeds and discard. Very finely chop the chilli so that it becomes like grains of rice.

Warm the olive oil in a large saucepan on a low heat. When the oil is shimmering and hot, add the pumpkin and onion. Let them sweat a little before adding the finely chopped garlic and chilli. Give it all a good mix around and let it cook for a few minutes. Now measure out and add to the pan the curry powder and cayenne pepper. Coat the vegetables well and sweat away for a few minutes. Add the 2 tins of chopped tomatoes and place a lid on top. Simmer on a medium flame for 15 minutes, or until the pumpkin is tender but certainly cooked. Stir from time to time so that it doesn't stick to the bottom of the pan too.

Skim a ladle of the sauce off the top of the pan, and place in a measuring jug along with the peanut butter. Blend this together with a fork and then return the whole sauce to the pan and mix with the curry. Finally pile on the spinach and fold it in, along with the water if it needs loosening, and also the sugar. Replace the lid of the pan for a further 3 to 5 minutes, just long enough to let the dark green leaves wilt. It should now have a silky but thick texture, and be ready to heap into bowls. Shower with freshly ground pepper.

Polenta & Vegetable Bake for Dani

Feeds 4

Like many of my kitchen incarnations, I'm not really sure where this dish hails from. It first came to light when I was chatting with my mum's best friend, Clare Newbolt, coming from a sort of soul food angle. But it also has an Italian vibe. That's because polenta, or cornmeal, as it's also called, is so diverse in its origins. There's something really, really comforting about this nutty and wet grain, which in this recipe has added crunch from the baking process too. And combined here with sweet rich Italianate vegetables, it is the perfect combination. This would be a good thing to cook and carry on grazing on the next day. Make a batch and you will be sorted for a few more nights during the week.

I made it for an evening with Dani Siciliano, a super cool lady who sports svelt clothes and sings like a diva. At the time she was staying with me frequently, both individually nursing our hearts, and sharing my room. We were both blue to say the least, and needed this, along with some heady red wine. It's the stuff for temporary medication.

The Vegetables

1 aubergine
2 tablespoons olive oil
1 red onion
1 chilli
3 garlic cloves
1 yellow pepper
1 red pepper
2 courgettes
1 x 400g tin of cherry
  tomatoes
2 teaspoons dried thyme
  or oregano
2 fresh sage leaves
1 bay leaf
3 pinches of demerara
  sugar
a handful of fresh basil

First of all slice up the aubergine, dividing it lengthways and then slicing it into semi-circles of half a finger's width. Layer these in a colander over a draining board, salting each layer. This will draw out excess liquid while you get on with the first stages of the dish, though if you are in a rush you can cut the salting stage out.

Warm the olive oil in a large heavy-bottomed pan, on a low heat. As it warms, peel and slice the red onion into about 8 pieces and add to the pan to gently fry. Now also chop, but very finely, the chilli and peeled garlic cloves and add these to the pan. Toss all of this around in the pan and then start preparing the other vegetables: deseed the peppers and roughly chop into about 16 pieces each; slice the courgettes into roundels about 1cm wide. Add these to the pan, and sweat for 10 minutes, stirring frequently. Return to the aubergines. Under a running tap squeeze out a handful at a time. This will remove the salt, and some of the moisture. Add these to the pan and sweat for another few minutes, stirring from time to time. Now add the tin of tomatoes with the thyme and finely chopped fresh sage leaves, and bay leaf. Add the sugar and place a lid on the pan. Simmer for 30 minutes and then rip and fold the basil into the sauce.

The Polenta

300g medium-ground
polenta, but not the
easy-cook kind
1.2 litres water
a knob of butter
1 tablespoon olive oil
200g Provolone or
Taleggio
lots of freshly ground
black pepper
1 teaspoon Maldon sea
salt

Preheat the oven to 180°C/Gas 4. While the vegetables are melging, prepare the polenta. Measure the polenta and the water into a medium saucepan with the butter and olive oil. Simmer this on a low flame until it begins to emulsify and thicken. It's best to use a sturdy whisk. It should be gently bubbling, and will require constant stirring. Add more water if it looks like cement. Now grate the strong Provolone and mix it into the polenta along with the pepper and salt. When the vegetables are tender and a little reduced turn them out into a large ovenproof dish. Spoon the polenta on top, and place in the preheated oven for 30 minutes. When this soulful pie is ready, it will be firm and golden on top and bubbling red at the edges.

Ebi Chilli Men for Tom & Olly

Feeds 2 or 3, depending on the hunger of your soul

I first made this for Tom Punch and Oliver Danger, two of my favourite boys from university. Tom and I lived together for a year in my cranky flat in Brixton, and we three got up to all sorts of mischief, from Friday through to Monday. We would eat intermittently to keep our dancing alive, and this was one of the dishes that most soothed our collectively empty souls at the end of yet another fun-fuelled weekend. The general pattern was that I would leave them dancing at 6 a.m. in a shameful club, make my way home on the first tube, do some sofa snoozing, then cook something to allay our broken bodies. When they got back at midday, we would devour whatever I'd mustered up.

The reason·I wanted to recreate this dish was that it is my most ordered meal at Fujiyama (Brixton's Japanese noodle bar), whether getting takeaway on a Sunday, or stopping off there before heading to the Ritzy for a film. The colours are fantastic, full of punchy red, orange and green from the peppers and carrots. It's worth being bold with the barely cooked chillies and garlic, as this will really blow your mind and clear your head. I make it two ways, depending on my bank balance. Really it should come with six juicy king prawns on each pile of noodles, but when I'm feeling poor, as I frequently was with those boys after a weekend blow-out, it's just as good with simply the fiery vegetables.

First prepare the prawns by shelling them. You may imagine this to be a bit fiddly, but really all you do is simply twist the head to remove it and in doing so pull the legs off too. Then, hold the tail and lift the shell upwards and away from the body. (You can keep these shells for making stock for a fish-based soup.) Alternatively, you can cook them with the shells on. Although this is more messy when you come to eating ebi chilli men, it adds extra flavour to do so. Whichever you decide, the prawns will need a rinse under a cold tap.

Heat the sesame oil in a flat frying pan, or a wok if you have one. Deseed the green pepper and cut into hunks about 2cm square. Add these to the oil when it is hot. Fry for about 8 minutes on a medium flame while you finely slice the Romano pepper. It should be as small as you can get it, almost a wet paste, if you can manage it. Add it to the green pepper, and give the pan a good shake. Continue frying while you peel and finely slice the carrot into similar sized pieces (I use my mandolin slicer). Now add these to the pan too. Finely chop the peeled garlic and the chilli, but do not deseed this, as you want all the heat you can get. Add the garlic and chilli at the same time as the sweet chilli sauce. Bring to the boil for a few minutes. If you are using king prawns, this is the moment to add them. They only need to cook long enough for them to turn from that wonderful translucent stone grey to an orangey white.

During these last few minutes of boiling the ebi chilli men, bring a medium pan of salted water to the boil and add the noodles. Give them a good swirl with a fork to break them apart. Simmer for 6 minutes, or according to the packet instructions, as they will definitely vary. Drain, and serve up on wide plates with your hot and sweet zinging prawn sauce.

12 king prawns, weighing about 400g
1 tablespoon toasted sesame oil (vegetable oil will suffice)
1 big green pepper
1 red Romano pepper
1 carrot
4 garlic cloves
1 plump red chilli
7 or 8 tablespoons sweet chilli sauce
300g medium rice or udon noodles

Doctor Helen's Signature Butternut Squash Pasta with Chilli Flakes & Chorizo

Feeds 4

Doctor Helen, my oldest friend, frequently cooks this, as it incorporates all her favourite ingredients. She's spent a lot of time in Spanish-speaking countries, has a weakness for slick Latin dance moves and therefore loves a meaty pimento-based dish. We usually cook it together to the sounds of Mara Carlyle's songs, and accompany it with a good old rant on our family politics and the state of today's boys. I call her my oxygen, which makes her wince.

This is an easy-peasy one-dish meal, combining the pasta with the roasted butternut squash and cherry tomatoes. So it's the kind of thing that is great to decant into a big salad bowl and plonk in the middle of the table for your friends to have a good dig around and help themselves to. And because the method of cooking is almost entirely roasting, it is pretty easy to conjure up so you won't have a coronary over it either. All you will need is the time – just over an hour – for the magic of the roasting.

I use a formidable chorizo here, mostly for fear of the tales of donkey meat that Pat's father, Doc Bill, used to frequently regale us with. Brindisa sells a particularly good one that I also stock in the shop – Chorizo Magno Alejandro – which has the texture, frankly, of spicy butter melting in your mouth. Heaven. So it's worth forking out a bit more for a good one. And the genius of chorizo is that it is filled with wonderful smoky paprika and spices, so it will be your all-encompassing cheat's seasoning.

Preheat the oven to 140°C/Gas 1. First of all get the butternut squash out on a large wooden chopping board, and peel off the hard waxy skin. I use a long, very sharp knife but you can also use a tough potato peeler. Chop the squash into 2cm cubes, and place on a baking tray. Pour over the olive oil and cook on the top shelf of the oven for 35 minutes. Now remove from the oven and chuck in the cherry tomatoes, whole, along with the peperoncino. Return to the oven for a further roasting for 20 minutes. When you remove the tray again, the squash should be soft when pierced with a knife, and the tomatoes should be bursting open and burnt in places. Set this aside while you slice the chorizo into 0.5cm roundels, removing the skin. Add the chorizo to the vegetable tray and give it all a good mix around. Set this aside while you bring some salted water to a rumbling boil and add the pasta. Refer to the packet instructions, but it should take about 9 minutes.

When the pasta is al dente, drain the water into a colander in the sink and give it a good shake, as rigatoni can hold a fair bit of water inside. Now, return the same empty pasta saucepan to the hob on a low heat. Add the roasted pumpkin and tomato to the pot, and now spoon in the crème fraiche, water and vinegar. Give it all a good mix and allow to melt into a light but creamy sauce. Don't be shy: it doesn't matter if the tomatoes or pumpkin break up a little, as you are heading towards a thick sweet creamy sauce anyway. Remove the basil leaves from the stems, and add these to the sauce. Now lastly pile the pasta tubes in as well. If you have a spatula, this would be ideal for giving a thorough mix and coating the pasta well. Decant the creamy vivacious pasta into a big old salad bowl, season thoroughly with coarse pepper and Maldon sea salt, and help yourselves. Grate Parmesan over each plate and you are at Helen's inviting kitchen table.

600g butternut squash or pumpkin
2 tablespoons olive oil
300g cherry tomatoes
2 teaspoons peperoncino (chilli flakes)
200g superior chorizo
350g rigatoni
150g crème fraîche
2 tablespoons water
1 tablespoon balsamic vinegar
25g fresh basil
freshly and coarsely ground black pepper
Maldon sea salt
150g Parmesan

Korean Beef Salad

For 2

When I've really been burning the candle at both ends, or working my socks off, I yearn for freshest vibrant ingredients that will bring me back to life. Eating a crunchy salad makes me feel like I'm in some way replacing the spent goodness. This salad, which uses beef, gives an added injection of robust iron. When I returned from Glastonbury, deranged and bruised after a mud-and-fun-filled weekend, all I wanted was steak and carrots. And so, inspired by one of my favourite Korean restaurants, Ran, I thought of this perfect and pinging beef salad, based on their house salad with chilli and surprising apple. The best place to get the ingredients is around Centre Point, as there's loads of Korean and Japanese supermarkets there.

The sweet crunch of carrot and apple here works wonderfully with the salty and funky soya paste. You can find this relative of peanut butter in Korean and Japanese supermarkets. It's strong smelling and acts as an emulsifier for the dressing. The unusually potent chilli powder, which comes in dinky little sachets, can also be found at these shops (see My Favourite Places to Eat, Drink & Shop, page 338). It will purge you of your sins. Adding strips of rare beef on top of these powerful and loud noises is the culmination. I cannot tell you how good you will feel after this reviving salad.

Peel the carrots and then, using a mandolin slicer, shred them. Peel and halve the onion, then really finely slice into hair-like strips. Divide the Chinese pear into 4 pieces and core. Really finely slice these segments lengthways. Thoroughly combine the carrots, onion and pear in a salad bowl.

For the strong dressing, measure out the soya paste into a little mixing jug. Pour the fish sauce over this and, using a fork, blend and loosen the paste. Now add the rice wine vinegar, sesame oil, sugar and Korean chilli powder. With gusto, beat this until it is thick. Taste to check that it makes your saliva glands ache with tang. Pour over the salad with the sesame seeds and mix it up with your hands or some tongs. Let this melge while you get on with the steaks.

Using a griddle pan, heat the oil on a medium heat for a few minutes so that it is hot hot. Now turn the heat down and add the steaks. They should gently sizzle but not go mental: you want to maintain the inherent tenderness of the flesh. Fry each side for about 3 minutes, or until a little blood is releasing and they are striped with colour. How well you cook the beef depends on your taste. I like it pretty rare. Now remove the steaks to a chopping board, and, using a fork and serrated knife, finely slice them into strips. Toss the salad one more time and then divide between two plates, making sure you pour out all the pungent dressing. Pile the delicate strips of beef on top and enjoy your medicine.

3 large carrots
½ white onion
1 large Chinese pear
2 teaspoons soya paste, more if you are bold
1 teaspoon fish sauce
1 tablespoon rice wine vinegar
2 teaspoons toasted sesame oil
1 teaspoon caster sugar
½ teaspoon Korean chilli powder
2 tablespoons toasted sesame seeds
2 tablespoons groundnut or vegetable oil
2 small fillet or sirloin beef steaks

Broccoli & Cauliflower Cheese

For 3 or 4, depending on what it comes with

This is a great all-encompassing dish, either for a cosy night in, or a cheap Sunday lunch with friends. Cauliflower cheese is easy nursery food and really only depends on making a delicious béchamel sauce. Once you have the knack of this sauce it will come in very handy: spinach in white sauce with a bit of nutmeg, the base of any soufflé, cheesy leeks, a main component of a lasagne, or the lubrication in a sturdy winter pie. And the good thing about a white sauce is that you can season it to lean in different national directions, as it's key in French, Italian and British food.

If at all possible, buying your broccoli and cauliflower from a good market would be best. These are British seasonal vegetables, so you might as well make the most of what's grown on our doorstep. And the bonus of adding broccoli is that it looks much more colourful and enticing than its more demure and sometimes insipid old relative. Using this delicious Lancashire, Mrs Kirkham's, gives a strong cheesy element which is inexpensive too. But if you can't find it, another crumbly British cheese will do fine.

1 cauliflower, weighing about 700g
2 small heads of broccoli, weighing in total about 600g
60g butter
65g plain flour
700ml full-fat milk
220g Mrs Kirkham's Lancashire
1 generous teaspoon grainy Dijon mustard, or English if you want more fire
freshly ground black pepper
Maldon sea salt

First prepare the vegetables. Hack off the florets of the cauliflower – these have a natural definition dividing each branch, so follow the flow of the plant. I use the stalk too, cut into cubes. ('Waste not, want not, darling,' as my Granny Bunty says.) Add the cauliflower to a large pan of salted water and bring to the boil. Meanwhile, chop the broccoli the same way, dividing it into a pile of little trees. When the water is simmering again, add the broccoli to the pan. Continue to cook for 5 minutes, or until the stalks are tender, even al dente, just slipping off a sharp knife. Do not over-boil at this stage, because the whole dish, remember, is going to go into the oven later for another blast. Drain the vegetables and set them aside.

Preheat the oven to 180°C/Gas 4. To make the béchamel sauce, melt the butter on a low flame in a medium pan. When it is totally melted, add the flour and mix to a deep yellow paste, using a whisk or wooden spoon. It should begin to look crumbly, and as it sweats it should become slightly paler. After a few minutes, gradually add the milk, thoroughly whisking all the time to prevent lumps developing. When it is silky, turn the heat down a little and let it cook for a few minutes. Then take it off the heat. Grate two-thirds of the cheese into the sauce, along with the mustard and lots of seasoning. Taste to make sure it is really flavoursome with cheese. Pour this sauce over the vegetables, and then, with a good spatula, mix to entirely coat. When they are wrapped in cheesy goodness, turn the whole pan out into a baking dish and distribute evenly. Grate over the rest of the cheese and place in the oven, on the top shelf, for half an hour, or until the top is golden and crisp, and some of the moisture has evaporated.

Simplest Red Spaghetti with Thyme, Straight From Urbisaglia

For 3

Sometimes you taste something, and, even though you have eaten it a thousand times before, this time it is a new-fangled experience, and the best thing ever. About once a year, for instance, I have a particularly delicious cup of tea and it strikes me like a bolt. This dish, just garlic, tomato and spaghetti, is pretty familiar territory. And yet when I ate it in Urbisaglia, I thought I'd died and gone to heaven. The puréed tomato that makes up passata is the most wonderful and simple pure coating on good spaghetti. With this dish it's all about having courage with generous amounts of loud garlic. The strong flavours of fresh herbs and garlic should really knock you for six and make you reel. Sometimes the simple things are the best.

It may, however, have been something to do with the whole package. I was being swept away by a little whirlwind spring-time affair, with the best-looking man I've ever met. He was like a grown-up angel, complete with dreamy eyes. Exhausted after a great party the night before, under a veranda in spring-shine, drinking wine, we were served this, literally, by Il Postino. My heart had been a little rare in the darkness of the winter, and this meal and holiday was the perfect tonic. I recommend both the affair and the food. The icing on the hill-side-cake was that Mara, who I was staying with, literally reached down behind her and pulled up some fresh thyme out of the garden. We all shredded it on top of the pasta, and the experience was just a little bit more perfect, if that's even possible.

12 garlic cloves
4 tablespoons olive oil
600g passata
1 teaspoon dried
   oregano
1 teaspoon dried thyme
1 teaspoon golden
   caster sugar
freshly ground black
   pepper
Maldon sea salt
400g really good-quality
   spaghetti
1 tablespoon really
   good extra virgin
   olive oil
a bunch of fresh thyme
150g really freshly
   grated Parmesan or
   mature Pecorino, to
   serve

Peel the garlic and seriously finely chop it so that it is like coarse salt. Heat the olive oil on a high flame in a wide, flat frying pan. It seems like a lot of oil but the reason is that you almost want to deep-fry the delicate garlic. Sweep the garlic into the pan when the oil is really hot and quivering. Turn the heat down to low straight away, and watch it jiggle and dance in the oil, shaking the pan from time to time. After a few minutes, when the smaller pieces of garlic are just turning a golden colour, add the passata and mix thoroughly. Add the dried oregano and thyme, sugar, pepper and salt and simmer slowly for 20 minutes. It will pop a little and spit with red dollops. Stir occasionally to make sure it is not sticking.

When the sauce has been simmering for 10 minutes, start to cook the spaghetti by adding it to a large pan of boiling salted water. Simmer on a medium flame until al dente. This should take about 8 minutes, but do check the packet instructions too, as they vary. Drain the pasta, and coat in the extra virgin olive oil. Dish out equally on to four plates and top with the reduced passata sauce. Strip the fresh thyme from the stalks and sprinkle on top, along with a generous grating of Parmesan.

Alice's Cottage Pie

For 4 hungry ones

This was Alice's delicious staple offering at university if ever I went on a kitchen strike (which was not very often). It's so properly old-fashioned that I would never normally have thought of cooking it, but Alice made it so well that I now love it. I have expanded on her original ingredients. The addition of ox heart is wonderfully rich and you feel like it's really doing you good, as it's full of iron. However, if you are not game for this hard-core bonus, just double up the quantities of mince and follow the method as normal. The carrot adds a sweetness that is perfectly timed here too, to offset the richness of the lean mince. There are lots of different textures going on here, that all weave together very well. It is really an old-fashioned, hearty, homely, all-encompassing meal and it's surprisingly easy. I'd be astounded if there were any leftovers. Serve this up with some tender little peas.

2 tablespoons olive oil
1 super big onion
400g lean Scottish
    minced beef
500g diced ox heart
2 young bay leaves
2 carrots
2 tablespoons plain flour
400ml red wine (about
    2 large glasses)
1 tablespoon tomato
    purée
1 dessertspoon
    Worcestershire sauce
1kg firm Maris Piper
    potatoes
a knob of butter
100ml double cream
100ml warm full-fat milk
freshly ground black
    pepper
Maldon sea salt

Preheat the oven to 150°C/Gas 2. Heat the olive oil in a big pan on a medium flame. Peel and finely dice the onion and add to the pan. Sweat this for a few minutes before adding the minced beef. With a flat-ended spoon, thoroughly break the meat up as it cooks. This requires some careful attention and love. It should form a mess of succulent strands, and not have any of those monstrous solid grey lumps that occur in an unloved mince. Now add the diced ox heart and bay leaves and continue turning with your big spoon. Cook and stir nearly constantly for 5 minutes. Peel the carrots and slice into the pot with a mandolin slicer set on the finest shredding blade (if you don't have a mandolin, coarsely grate them and add just before the meat goes in the casserole dish). Now, in a measuring jug, mix the flour with a little of the wine, to form a paste. Gradually add the rest of the wine to amalgamate it, with no lumps, along with the tomato purée and Worcestershire sauce. Add this concoction to the meats, while gradually stirring. Simmer for 10 minutes on the hob. Decant the meat to a casserole dish and place in the oven for 20 minutes, uncovered. This will dry it out a little. During this time, you can make the mash for the top.

Peel the potatoes and chop into about 4 pieces each. Remove any dark spots or stray roots. Place them in a big saucepan, and cover with salted water. Bring to the boil, then maintain the heat for about 20 minutes. When the potatoes slip off a small sharp knife quickly and easily they are ready. Drain them now, and add a generous knob of butter, the double cream, and the warm milk. Vigorously mash so that you have a creamy inviting potato cloud. Season to taste. Now take the casserole dish out of the oven and spoon the mash on top. Run a fork over the mash to make risen stripes. Return the cottage pie to the oven for a further half an hour. It should be brown and bubbling at the edges with wine-enriched mince, and the mash should be flecked brown and beginning to crisp in the middle of the casserole dish.

Sweet Laksa with Udon Noodles

Makes 3 steaming bowls

This is a vegan meal, but mostly by accident. I cooked it for a simple Sunday night dinner with Zezi and Zahra. They are both beautiful fun African queens, and it provided pure comfort for us all. Perfect after our heavy weekend. The sweet pumpkin, puréed with coconut milk, forms a silky base for the chunky vegetables and slippy meaty udon noodles. The method is very simple. You just need to understand that you are making a blended soup base with the pumpkin and coconut, and then simmering everything else in this. It really was followed by a few rounds of tea, lots of Maltesers, and a dumb dude movie, which is the ideal way to finish off the weekend.

I've also made this for dinner parties, as it looks really fantastic, with loads of colours and textures swimming around in the bowl. One of these impromptu dinner parties was with a bunch of the DJs from the Horse Meat Disco. We supped on this delicious spiced noodle soup, went off to our friend Severino's party, and then returned in the early hours to finish off what little was left. The remnants were just as good cold, scooped out of the saucepan with spoons.

First skin the pumpkin with a long sharp knife, then cut it into 2cm pieces. Place it in a medium pan with water and bring to the boil. Simmer for 5 minutes. When the pumpkin slips off a sharp knife, remove from the heat and drain. Place back in the saucepan, along with the coconut milk (which may need mixing a little with a fork, as it sometimes separates). With a hand-held blender, work this into a smooth silky soup base adding the water to loosen if necessary. Return the pan to the heat, but on a very low flame.

Tail the woody base of the pak choi. Remove the gleaming white stalks, cutting them into 2cm pieces. Add these to the warming soup, as they will take the longest to poach. Meanwhile, set aside the green darker leaves and prepare the rest of the vegetables. Finely slice the chillies, along with their seeds. Remove any frumpy leaves from the spring onions and then chop them up into little rounds. Drain and rinse the shiitake mushrooms and cut into quarters. After the pak choi stalks have been simmering for 15 minutes, add the rest of the vegetables that you have prepared, along with the soy sauce, sweet chilli sauce and fish sauce. Continue to simmer for a further 15 minutes, stirring from time to time.

Now, finally, remove the udon noodles from their packs and immerse them in the soup. They will take roughly 2 minutes to cook. You may need to gently release them from their tangle with a fork. Just before serving, squeeze in the lime juice, stir, and serve up this steaming spicy laksa in deep little bowls. Decorate each bowl with toasted sesame seeds and some ripped-up Thai basil leaves.

400g pumpkin
1 x 400ml tin of coconut milk
120ml water
5 pak choi
2 large red chillies
3 spring onions
1 x 280g tin of shiitake mushrooms
3 tablespoons dark soy sauce
1 tablespoon sweet chilli sauce
1 teaspoon fish sauce
400g udon noodles (they are available vacuum-packed in the chill counter of a Chinese supermarket)
1 juicy lime
3 teaspoons toasted sesame seeds
a small handful of Thai basil

Cabbage & Sausage Hotpot

For 4

I was brought up just outside Newmarket, the home of the famed Musk's Newmarket Sausage (though this is also a term my father uses to describe those men who sleep with their secretaries… 'He's a Newmarket Sausage, you know'). The sausages are truly amazing and the pride of the place. My brother eats them like they are going out of fashion, so I truly recommend hunting them down. I'm told, amazingly, that Harrods food hall stocks them and Waitrose too. The reason I have included quite so many sausages in this recipe is that when Olly is at home, he demands at least four. You too may find that you have a giant stomach when it comes to this amazing homely meal.

This recipe is wonderfully easy, and requires few ingredients, making it ideal for a rainy day or a grey mood. The spices give an extra kick to the dish and the pear a grainy sweetness too. I always remember my mum steaming into the sitting room from the kitchen, armed with a huge saucepan of this simple goodness, and sitting it right in front of the fire, where we would all kneel around and help ourselves. It is best served up with some well crispy baked potatoes, stuffed with butter and lots of pepper and salt.

Heat the olive oil in a large saucepan, preferably something like a Le Creuset with a heavy bottom, on a medium flame. Add the sausages (do not prick them as you will lose the flavour – keeping the juice in the sausage also means that the meat is more succulent) for a few minutes with the fennel and mustard seeds and the cayenne pepper or chilli powder. The sausages should get a little browned and then be removed with some tongs on to a plate. Set them aside while you finely slice the cabbage with a sharp knife. You could also use a mandolin slicer here if you have one. Now add the cabbage and wine to the saucepan while you core and roughly chop the pear and add this in its turn. Place the lid on the saucepan and simmer for 10 minutes, removing the lid occasionally to stir and witness the wilting of the firm leaves of cabbage. Now turn down to a low flame and return the tinged sausages to the pot, along with the pepper, salt and granulated sugar. Simmer with the lid on for a further 20 minutes. The cabbage should be delicate and have a transparent sheen to it by the time the hotpot is ready. Wash down with an accompanying cider or white wine.

2 tablespoons olive oil
12 sausages, which is about 770g
2 teaspoons fennel seeds
1 teaspoon mustard seeds
½ teaspoon cayenne pepper or mild chilli powder
1 white cabbage, weighing about 1.5kg
1 large glass of white wine (about 200ml)
1 large pear
freshly ground black pepper
Maldon sea salt
1 teaspoon granulated brown sugar

Penne with Creamy Tomato & Tuna

For 2

When I was a teenager I used to baby-sit for the Smiths. They took me under their wing, and I loved their children so much: Arabella was the eldest, and feisty too (which I love in a small girl); Milo, the middle child, was full of little beans and brains; Lettie was beautiful and newborn and I used to sing her to sleep and tell her my secrets. I must be getting old, because they are now thriving teenagers. Their mother, Sophie, became my confidante too. When they went out for dinner she would always leave me an amazing ready-made tomato sauce, good tuna, cream and fresh pasta, for the ultimate night in. I still cook this when I'm in need of some creamy comfort.

I've used Ortiz tuna here, from Rosie's. It comes in beautiful tins and is wonderfully meaty, unlike most floury, flaky tinned tuna. It's also line-caught, therefore your conscience will be clear and you will only need a little tin, so it's worth investing. The better the ingredient, the less you need. You can get this from good delis and it is imported by the wonderful Brindisa (see My Favourite Places to Eat, Drink & Shop, page 338).

BONITO DEL NORTE
en Aciete de Oliva

Heat 2 tablespoons of the olive oil in a large frying pan. Peel and finely slice the onion and add to the pan. Sweat for a few minutes on a low heat, until the onion becomes transparent. Now add the chopped tomatoes and simmer for about 15 minutes, until the tomato is breaking down and the sauce is thickening. Drain the tuna and flake it into the pan. Give it a thorough mix around to distribute the meat. Heat for a further few minutes, then take it off the heat to cool down a bit.

Bring a medium pan of salted water to the boil and add the penne. Gently boil for about 8 minutes, or according to the packet instructions. While it is cooking, return to the sauce. Add the cream and return the sauce to a low flame. Season to taste with salt, pepper and sugar. When the pasta is cooked, drain it and pour over the remaining olive oil. Serve up in bowls, with the creamy sauce, and decorate with a few basil leaves.

3 tablespoons olive oil
1 large onion
1 x 400g tin of chopped
    tomatoes
1 x 112g tin of Ortiz tuna
200g penne
100ml single cream
Maldon sea salt
freshly ground black
    pepper
a good pinch of sugar
a few fresh basil leaves

Lamb & Aubergine Pilaf

For 4

This pilaf works wonderfully with lightly cooked crunchy French beans on the side. It is full of colour, boasting varied textures with the soft comforting aubergine and flaky crumbling lamb and Eastern cumin. I love making this meal because there are lots of different processes involved, so it's ideal if you fancy an afternoon pottering in the kitchen (my favourite thing ever). There's the salting of the aubergine, simmering the soft lamb, toasting the pine nuts (buttery and delicious) and spicing the rice. Enjoy the ride.

This is a meal I've made for a cosy afternoon's entertainment, but I'd equally serve it for a fine feast. It really depends on your whim. I cooked it the other day for Raf and Jamie, who couldn't get enough of it, which made me, and them, super happy. That's the whole point of cooking.

Preheat the oven to 130°C/Gas ½. Slice the aubergines lengthways in half and then finely slice into semi-circles. Layer these in a colander, with a smattering of salt on each level of aubergine. Leave for at least half an hour. When beads of water are appearing on the aubergine slices, rinse them under a running tap to remove the salt, squeezing with vigour to remove any surplus water. Set the aubergine aside.

Warm the olive oil in a large saucepan on a medium flame. Peel and dice the onion and add to the pan when the oil is hot. Coat and fry for a few minutes, then add the dehydrated aubergine and cook for a few more minutes. Meanwhile, trim any excess hard fat from the lamb. You may need to further dice the meat. I like it quite small, as hunks of intimidating meat stress me out. I cut the pieces about the size of my thumbnail. Now add the lamb to the pan, and after 5 minutes add the chopped tomatoes too, along with the star anise, cinnamon and sugar. Now give everything a good mix and place the whole pan in the oven with the lid on for 1½ hours. Remove from the oven and give it another good mix, then return the pan to the oven for 1 hour and 20 minutes with the lid off. During this last oven stretch, rinse the rice in a sieve under a cold running tap. Then sit the sieve in a bowl of water for half an hour. This will remove some of the starchiness that makes it too sticky in this instance.

For the final leg of the pilaf journey, place the rice in a large saucepan with the water. Grind the cumin seeds and cardamom pods in a pestle and mortar. This will remove the husks from the cardamom, leaving the black seeds. Add the spices to the rice, along with the knob of butter. Bring to the boil, then place the lid on top and simmer on a very low heat for 10 minutes. Now take off the heat, fluff up the rice with a fork, replace the lid and let it sit for a further 10 minutes, adding a handful of golden currants.

2 large aubergines, plus salt for pulling out the moisture
5 tablespoons olive oil
1 large onion
600g diced leg of best lamb (my butcher does a wonderful job preparing this for me, so just ask yours to do the same)
2 x 400g tins of chopped tomatoes
5 whole star anise
1 cinnamon stick
a generous pinch of sugar
400g basmati rice
700ml water
2 teaspoons cumin seeds
10 cardamom pods
a knob of butter
2 tablespoons golden currants
100g pine nuts
a handful of fresh flat-leaf parsley
3 sprigs of fresh mint
freshly ground black pepper
Maldon sea salt

Meanwhile, in a dry frying pan, toast the pine nuts on a low heat, tossing from time to time until the nuts are tinged with golden brown. Finally, chop the parsley and mint and fold into the rice, along with the lamb and aubergine, and the pine nuts. Season a little before dishing up in bowls.

If you choose to serve this with French beans, you will need about 300g, simmered for a few minutes so that they are crunchy and brilliantly green.

Tuscan Bean Stew with Riso Pasta

For 4 or 5

I cooked this dish the first night we arrived in Urbisaglia, and it is inspired by the wholesome soups of Tuscany that I discovered when I lived in Florence, after leaving school. When we got to the farmhouse it was pretty late, and freezing cold, due to the flagstone floors, and howling a gale outside so much that all the shutters were banging madly as if it was a haunted house. So I set to making this big pot of warming vegetables, with pasta plunged in at the last for extra filling value. I've also made this for the odd winter dinner party too. One notably with Will and Charlotte. They are a brilliantly erudite and excellently hedonistic pair.

I love the type of pasta in this recipe. It's tiny, like rice, and cooks quite quickly, absorbing a little of the liquid in the pot. It really brings the whole dish together and makes for a silky and yet wonderfully stodgy plate of steaming vegetables. And the pork really gives some flavour and texture to the whole affair. Grate over Parmesan at the end, as you would with any other pasta dish, and relish some economical comfort.

Prepare the vegetables by peeling and finely dicing the onion, along with the carrots and celery. The pieces should be a little smaller than your smallest fingernail. Heat the olive oil in a very large saucepan on a medium heat. When the oil is shaking, add all the diced vegetables. While these sweat a little, peel and very finely chop the garlic and add to the pot. Continue to fry for about 10 minutes, stirring from time to time with a wide flat-ended wooden spoon. Now slice the bacon into strips a couple of millimetres wide, making lardons, and add to the pan. Fry for a further 5 minutes, until the bacon has infused the vegetables and the streaks of fat are just beginning to brown. Add the tomatoes, bay leaf and the wine and simmer with the lid on for half an hour.

Meanwhile drain and rinse the borlotti beans. Add these to the pan, along with the pasta, and simmer for a further 5 minutes. It should become thicker and wonderfully glutinous, in a buttery way. At the last moment, fold in the parsley and season. When serving, grate over a healthy amount of Parmesan, then tuck in. Mop up any leftovers with some crusty ciabatta.

1 large onion
4 carrots
300g celery (which is about 1 medium celery plant, including the leaves)
3 tablespoons olive oil
4 garlic cloves
200g streaky bacon or pancetta, depending on what's available
2 x 400g tins of chopped tomatoes
1 young bay leaf
1 large glass of red wine (about 200ml)
1 x 400g tin of brown borlotti beans
100–150g riso pasta, or any other tiny type
2 generous handfuls of well-chopped freshest parsley
Maldon sea salt
freshly ground black pepper
150g Parmesan

Grease 2 pint earthenware dish removed bay leaves from marinade → bottom of dish with pepper corns. lay bacon around dish at a ... Spoon meat into dish. cover with foil & put in a pan of water (bain marie). Oven bake @ 6 mark & for 1½ hrs (until it ... away from dish sides) ... for an hour or two with ... weights on top to press it.

Rosie'...
14c Market Row, SW...
www.rosiesdelicafe...

balmy bites

◦ Serve this with a chickpea salad

Heap salsa on top of a piece of chicken. Place in a rectangle of foil, fold into a sealed pillow & bake

Substitute chicken with cod, but cook for less time

MOROCCAN SALSA ♡ SERVE WITH:

FETA, SPINACH SALAD

◦ As a dip

◦ with griddle fried Halloumi as a starter

◦ SANDWICH: Feta, Spinach in toasted Ciabatta

BALMY BITES

Recipes to bring sunshine into your life, good times to accompany a barbecue or garden picnic. These fresh, zesty foods come soaked in the flavours of my travels, from an Italian fling to a Spanish festival. I like to make a couple of the dishes described below and serve them together with additional deli fare like a crusty campaillou and spicy olives, or some fine slices of fennel salami and a wedge of Hereford Hop, and you could bake a quick soda bread too. This way, you get to buy some serious high-end produce, which is always a treat, and pump it up with some well-conceived dishes of your own.

We used to have picnics in our garden in Suffolk all the time, so this kind of easy and informal entertaining is comforting second nature to me. All you need are some nice big salad bowls, a few beers and a sturdy rug, and you'll feel like you are on holiday. Each summer I have a deli anniversary party in my yard, and barbecue all afternoon with an array of these balmy bites for customers, friends and family. This year we made an ace rum punch to get everyone in the mood to carry on up at The Windmill for a gig.

Menu

Bites

Pea & Mint Dip

For 5 or 6

This is a really fresh dip, ideal to serve up along with some good grilled pitta, as a help-yourself starter or as part of a whole feast. I was alerted to the idea by Eddie Temple Morris (he's a DJ who champions the indie remix) on a long, mostly food-related car journey. We (Eddie, Alice, me and Sarah B) were all on our way to the first festival of the summer, Gatecrasher, which was an absolute smasher. Pea and mint is a brilliantly well-worn marriage. The last time I made this was for an early evening dinner, and the bowl was being licked clean by the time I returned from the kitchen, not a scrap left for me!

250g frozen petits pois
1 tablespoon olive oil
juice of ½ lemon
a handful of fresh mint
1 generous tablespoon yoghurt
1 garlic clove
100g feta
a little extra virgin olive oil
freshly ground black pepper

Place the frozen peas and olive oil in a small saucepan over a low heat. Stir from time to time. This will gradually defrost and lightly cook the peas. It will take about 5 minutes. Taste them to make sure that they are juicy and sweet and al dente. Decant the peas and residual oil into a blender or a jug (depending whether you are using a blender or a hand-held blitzer). Add the lemon juice, mint and yoghurt. Peel and slice the garlic clove and blitz, along with the salty feta. Add a little more olive oil if it needs loosening. It should be creamy and homogenous, with the texture of humous. Taste, and add as much freshly ground pepper as you like. Decant the purée into a small bowl, and drizzle over more olive oil and another grind of pepper.

Aubergine & Salami Stacks

Feeds 3 or 4

These are rich and intoxicating high-rise blocks. Raf's favourite and unerring choice of ciabatta at Rosie's is with grilled aubergine, Milano salami and baby spinach. His fascination got me to thinking about alternative ways of combining this perfect marriage. And so these wicked stacks came to pass. It works really well as a starter, with an accompanying handful of fresh balsamic-dressed baby salad leaves, or you can make a whole batch of the towers and add them to a table of summer salads and bits to munch on.

Preheat the oven to 160°C/Gas 2. Slice the aubergines into thin roundels and arrange in a colander in layers, with table salt scattered over each level to extract the moisture. Leave this to sit for about an hour, until little beads of water are appearing on the surface of the aubergine. Under a running tap, rinse the aubergine pieces and thoroughly squeeze handfuls like a sponge so that they are limp rather than rubbery. Swipe each piece with a little pesto and set aside while you finely slice the tomato. Season the tomato with some pepper and salt. Now alternate the aubergine, tomato and salami in layers so that they form towers. Harpoon each with a toothpick, and place them on a baking dish, which then goes in the oven for 30 to 35 minutes. Make sure the aubergine is well cooked and soft before removing from the oven to cool a little.

1 aubergine, plus some salt for extracting the moisture
some Genovese pesto
1 to 2 large ripe tomatoes
freshly ground black pepper
Maldon sea salt
12 fine slices of Milano salami
2 toothpicks

Pat's Green Beans with Goat's Cheese

For 3 or 4

Pat is the most fantastic and thoughtful cook. He goes to extreme lengths to get his friends' tastebuds going. He once even brought his homegrown radishes to the Effra pub, in order for us all to try them specifically with pints of Guinness. He was hooked on combining flavours and was desperate for us to share his crunchy vs. malty delight. I remember when he first devised this green bean recipe; he was so excited I thought he would burst. So he made it for one of Helen's epic summer barbecues that would go on all night, and involved lots of beers and a fair amount of dancing in the kitchen.

And he was right. This salad is great. The combination of green beans and goat's cheese is a good one, and the addition of toasted sesame seeds and little lardons really clinches the deal. I quite often eat his warm salad for supper during the summer, piled on top of a mountain of rocket and baby spinach. It really satisfies an urge.

40g sesame seeds
1 tablespoon olive oil
4 medium rashers of
   pancetta
350g fine green beans
150g quite ripe chèvre
   log complete with
   rind
2 tablespoons extra
   virgin olive oil
1 tablespoon white wine
   vinegar
freshly ground black
   pepper
Maldon sea salt

Preheat the grill so that it's really hot. In a dry frying pan, toast the sesame seeds on a low heat. Keep tossing them so that they don't burn. After a few minutes they will begin to turn golden and start clumping together. Remove them from the pan to a plate to cool. Now, using the same frying pan, warm the olive oil on a medium heat. Using some kitchen scissors, finely chop the pancetta into the frying pan and cook until the lardons are becoming crisp and golden. Remove from the pan and also set aside.

Top and tail the beans and place them in a medium saucepan of water, on a high heat. Bring to the boil, then gently simmer for 4 or 5 minutes, so that they are still crunchy. Drain the beans into a colander and decant them to an ovenproof dish. Scatter the lardons over and then crumble the goat's cheese on top. Place the whole salad under the grill for a few minutes, until the cheese is beginning to melt and become a little caramelised on the top. Dress the salad by drizzling over the oil and vinegar and then scatter over the toasted seeds. Season with pepper and salt and then serve up this Patrician delight.

White Alubias with Anchovies & Herbs

For 3

This salad is great. You can actually use almost any pulse. I sometimes use flageolet or cannellini beans, but mostly I use these wonderful round pure-looking beans that are really soft and almost sticky. Brindisa do a good jar of these alubias. And anchovies are a brilliant addition to a salad dressing. They give a delicious and subtle saltiness and are a wonder ingredient. Add them to a pasta sauce and they will dissolve, giving a subtle salty texture. Or drape them over some roasting peppers and you will get a magic scent.

First drain the beans and thoroughly rinse them under a running tap. Be careful not to break them up too much in this process, as they are quite delicate. To make the dressing you can either use a little blender, pile everything in and pulse it, or really finely chop everything by hand. If you do the latter, take the handfuls of herbs and chop within an inch of their lives. (Think of how the basil in pesto looks, and work towards that.) Place the herbs in a medium salad bowl and pour over the olive oil and lemon juice. Using a large wooden spoon, bruise the herbs into the liquid. Peel and finely chop the onion so that you have pieces the size of grains of rice. Add this to the salad bowl. Break up the anchovies, and cream these into the dressing. Pour in the beans and coat really well with the dressing, using a spatula, though they are delicate so don't overwork them. Taste and season accordingly.

1.2kg white alubias beans
1 handful of fresh coriander
1 handful of fresh mint
1 handful of fresh parsley
2 tablespoons extra virgin olive oil
juice of 1 lemon
1 small red onion
3 anchovies preserved in oil
freshly ground black pepper

Sonar Lentil Salad

For 4

Alice and I ate this delicious salad perched on bar stools at a tapas joint right in the thick of La Boqueria. She's my raving best: it was our last meal after a marathon few days at Sonar, an electronic music festival that boasts some pretty far-out haircuts, and lots of piercings. As we sat on our cheap flight back to London, pondering on the good times (Matthew Herbert, Miss Kittin and Laurent Garnier to the rising sun), I swiftly penned this salad because it was so striking and such a high note to leave this city on. Perhaps it was the place, the friends or Barcelona's amazing food market, but it felt sent from the heavens. Every time I make it, I feel a little trip – back – to this hot party city.

The raw red peppers give a good crunch and colour injection to the tender little lentils, and the herbs are brilliantly summery. It's really good quite soaked in oil with the tang of spring onions coming through as an afterthought. Using dried lentils instead of tinned ones also makes for a super economical salad.

Pour the lentils out into a large saucepan and cover with water so that it comes at least 8cm above them. Bring to the boil on a medium heat. Simmer for about 20 minutes, or until the lentils are definitely cooked and tender but not floury. Drain them into a sieve and run them under a cold tap for a moment to cool and clean them. Set aside to further cool.

To prepare the rest of the salad, deseed the peppers, finely slice lengthways and then dice them as you would an onion. Finely chop all of the parsley and mint with a large knife so that they become deep green sparks. Chop the spring onions into little roundels and then slice these again so that they too are small pieces of lighter green. Add these to the cold lentils and mix with a wooden spoon. Pour over the olive oil and vinegar, and season with lots of salt and pepper to really bring out the pinging flavours.

500g dried Puy or small brown lentils
4 red peppers
3 handfuls of fresh parsley
1 handful of fresh mint
6 spring onions
3 tablespoons extra virgin olive oil
3 tablespoons red wine vinegar
Maldon sea salt
freshly ground black pepper

Herby Spare Ribs, Porchetta-style

For 4

Porchetta is a stuffed whole suckling pig. It's amazing, and totally moreish. When I went to Italy last year, it was Mara's brother's birthday, and in celebration, on top of dressing up and having a smashing party, he ordered one of these classic Italian pigs. The animal is unzipped, and filled with wild dill and wild garlic and all sorts of other hillside delights. It was a beautiful feast and lasted us for days, and is one of those amazing foods that you get to tax a piece of, each time you pass by. I was never far from another hunk of piglet.

In an attempt to recreate this dish at home, I marinate spare ribs in dill, garlic, honey and olive oil. It isn't the same of course, like any holiday romance, but it comes pretty close. The ribs become sticky and aromatic as they are slowly roasted. It's an ideal thing to get mucky over on a summer's day, and the added lemon juice makes it all fresh too. Eat this with a few salads and some crusty bread, and you'll feel like you are on an Italian hilltop. I get my spare ribs either from one of the Chinatown supermarkets, or from my local butcher in Brixton Market, and they are not expensive either, so you can invite loads of friends over. These are also delicious done slowly over a barbecue, and went down very well with the Endeacott kids just the other day at the deli's fourth birthday party.

1–1.2kg pork spare ribs
a bunch of fresh chives
    (about 50g)
a big handful of fresh
    dill (about 60g)
6 garlic cloves
juice of 1 lemon
2 tablespoons extra
    virgin olive oil
3 tablespoons runny
    honey (*Millefiori* if
    possible, to add to
    the Italian hill vibes,
    though it is quite
    steep)
3 good pinches of
    Maldon sea salt

If the butcher hasn't done it already, divide the ribs between the bones with a sharp knife, so that they form tails of firm flesh. Keep them in the bag from which they have come. To make the marinade, finely chop the chives, dill and peeled garlic cloves and decant into a sturdy bowl. Squeeze over the lemon juice, olive oil and honey. Give it all a good mix around to really bruise the flavours out of the herbs. You could do this in a pestle and mortar, or in a blender, too. Now, taste it, and then season with sea salt. Pour the marinade into the bag containing the spare ribs and give it a good squelch around to entirely drench the pork. Tightly tie a knot in the bag, removing as much air as you can. Let it melge for an hour at room temperature to really infuse the flavours. During this time, preheat the oven to 140°C/Gas 1.

Pile the spare ribs into a large baking tray, getting as much of the marinade out with them as you can. Place on the top shelf of the oven for 1½ hours, turning twice during this time, to continue coating the ribs all over. They are ready when they are slightly burnt on the bottom of the pan and sticky all over. When decanting from the baking tray, try to scrape off as much of the sticky marinade as you can, and lather this over the crisp ribs. You can either eat them hot out of the oven or leave them to cool a little before getting messy.

Moroccan Salsa

For 6, as a side dish

This recipe came about because of that holiday to Marrakesh with Tom Punch and the Golding girls. I'm not sure it's really Moroccan but it conjures up the smells and colours that invigorated us so much there. When I got back from our jollies, I put my mind to re-creating the vibes of this intoxicating city. It was cumin that really made it.

This is a brilliant recipe because you can use it with lots of different foods. I make it in the shop to go in a ciabatta with feta, roasted peppers and spinach. But you could equally lather it into a cold chicken sandwich to take to work. This salsa would be great with some of these barbecued little fishes (very Portuguese) or a fillet of grilled salmon. How you combine this salsa is up to your mood really. I've also heaped it over chicken pieces in winter and baked it all in the oven.

view from cafe des Epices

If you are using a little blender, pour in the olive oil first. Deseed the pepper and tomatoes and chop into cubes. Peel and finely chop the red onion and add all the vegetables to the blender, along with the cumin. Roughly chop the coriander and add to the mix. Pulse the salsa to combine the ingredients. Taste to see what it needs. The added sugar will add depth to the tomatoes

If you are doing the salsa by hand, you need to really finely chop the vegetables and coriander with a long sharp knife until it is almost a paste of colours. In a bowl, paste in the olive oil and cumin and season to your taste. Lather this salsa on almost anything.

1 tablespoon extra virgin olive oil
1 pepper, either red or yellow
2 ripe tomatoes
1 small red onion
2 teaspoons ground cumin
a handful of fresh coriander
2 teaspoons golden caster sugar
1 teaspoon Maldon sea salt

Dom's Marital Potato Salad

For 4 or 5

Dom and I were inseparable for years. I met him temping at the Country Landowners' Association when I was eighteen, and he took it upon himself to educate me in 1980s pop music, and almost everything else too. Every day he would come in with a different mix tape, and talk me through every minute synth, while we smoked Silk Cuts and read *Heat* magazine in the basement of Belgrave Square. And so when I went to university he often came up to stay, and would fill up all the boys with his 'Marital' potato salad. So called because apparently it has frequently prompted marriage proposals. It must be all the delicious cream he puts in it. It's a rich and velvety version of a classic.

However, Maggie Rundell wowed me with her totally different potato salad full of lardons and delicious anchovies. Everyone was pretty tired after a weekend of festival fun, and it provided the best respite along with a cold roasted chicken on a warm Kentish evening. And in turn, my mother makes hers by cutting the mayonnaise with some yoghurt, to lighten the whole dish. There are so many ways of making a potato salad, so I combine Maggie and my mum's recipes for fresh summer salad. Below I've offered up both Dom's and my cloned potato salads. Which you cook, will depend on your yearnings.

Dom's Marital Potato Salad

Dice (but do not peel) the potatoes into 2cm blocks. Place them in a large saucepan with lots of salted water and bring to the boil. Cook for about 20 minutes, or until they are really soft and slip immediately off a knife. While the potatoes are cooking, beat together in a large salad bowl the mayonnaise and double cream. Finely chop the chives and add these to the dressing, and season with pepper and salt. When the potatoes are perfectly soft, drain and then return them to the pan. Replace the lid and give them a really good shake, to fluff them up and make them more porous, then add the thick dressing. Leave it to cool for an hour or so, with clingfilm or a lid sealing the pan. This will slowly melt the cream into the pots, and make a wonderfully gooey mess.

1kg potatoes
4 tablespoons mayonnaise
4 tablespoons double cream
a handful of fresh chives
freshly ground black pepper
Maldon sea salt

A Melged Potato Salad

Slice the potatoes into quarters or so that they are all about the same size. Place these in a pan of salted water and bring to the boil. Simmer the potatoes for about 20 minutes – or until they slip easily off a small sharp knife – then drain and thoroughly cool.

For the dressing, beat together the mayonnaise and yoghurt in a salad bowl so that it is smooth and light and quite thin. Now peel the garlic cloves, and crush them into the mix. Very finely slice the anchovies and herbs with a large sharp knife and then paste them together with the side of the knife. Add this to the dressing and give it another good beating. Grind in the pepper and finally add the cool potatoes. Thoroughly coat the potatoes by mixing them really well with a spatula, digging into the bottom of the bowl to scoop up all the goodness. Grind over a little more pepper before serving up.

800g new potatoes
3 tablespoons mayonnaise
2 tablespoons natural yoghurt
2 garlic cloves
3 anchovies preserved in oil
some sprigs of fresh thyme, mint and parsley
lots of coarsely ground black pepper

Mum's Lemon Garden Vegetables

For 3 or 4

This is a real Suffolk classic, fresh and flavoursome, either warm or cold. My mum made this almost every day during one summer holiday. We'd eat it outside, with humous and salads. The taste brings back rambling bike rides, walks in the wood, horses and jumping naked through sprinklers. The herbs – marjoram, dill, parsley, tarragon, mint and basil – are key here. Back then, my mum would send me out with scissors to squat over the plants, and I would pick them all from our raggedy garden. Few people are this fortunate. I strongly recommend planting a few window boxes with herbs and rocket, as an alternative. That's what I have on my balcony in Brixton. By doing this, you get to live in the metropolis, but still make nostalgic fresh food. If you grow a few herbs (it's really not hard), you'll also save a good deal of money and depression on buying packets of supermarket herbs that you then watch wilt in plastic bags.

3 tablespoons olive oil
500g new potatoes
2 green courgettes
1 yellow courgette
1 medium onion
2 garlic cloves
juice of 3 lemons
small handfuls each of
  fresh tarragon, dill,
  basil, mint, parsley
  and marjoram
lots of Maldon sea salt
lots of freshly ground
  black pepper

Heat the olive oil in a considerably large non-stick frying pan on a low heat. While this is warming, slice up the new potatoes, getting about 6 pieces from each. Add these to the pan. Now slice the courgettes lengthways into quarters and then into triangular nuggets. After the potatoes have been sizzling for about 15 minutes, add the courgettes to the pan. Peel and roughly chop the onion, then peel and finely chop the garlic. Now add these and fry for a further 10 minutes, giving everything a good shake around. Make sure you frequently turn and mix the vegetables. Squeeze over the lemon juice and continue frying for another 15 minutes. When the potatoes are really soft and have absorbed most of the lemon juice you are ready for the final fling: finely chop the array of garden herbs and fold them into the pan, coating the vegetables entirely and seasoning with lots of salt and pepper. Now you are ready to spoon this dish out straight from the frying pan into the plates. Smell the summer.

Summer of Love Salad

Makes a big bowl for 6

When I worked in the deli in Rotherhithe, Lulu and I would frequently make this salad. We had such fun giggling together over our saucy stories and older lovers. The salad is sort of New York deli inspired, and was designed by the owner of the deli Dazzler, a gorgeous stubbly but gentle bruiser. It's bursting with pasta, and fresh spinach, and kicking red onion. The Caesar dressing gives it a real gluttonous edge too. It's become one of those stock recipes that I pull out for deli catering jobs, and also for summer picnics. The colours look wonderful, dripping in Parmesan and deep yellow egg yolk.

Caesar Dressing

To make the rich Caesar dressing, separate the eggs, keeping the whites aside for something else, like meringues. Beat the yolks together in a lipped bowl with a whisk, gradually adding the olive oil and lemon juice. It will become thick, almost like proper mayonnaise. Now finely chop the anchovy fillets so that they are almost a paste. Add these to the thick dressing. Peel and crush the garlic cloves into the dressing too. Grate in the Parmesan, using a fine blade, and season with pepper. Taste the dressing and add salt if necessary. Set this aside.

6 medium free-range eggs
100ml extra virgin olive oil
juice of 1½ lemons
2 anchovy fillets preserved in oil
4 garlic cloves
100g freshly grated Parmesan
freshly ground black pepper
Maldon sea salt

The Salad

300g penne
2 generous handfuls of
    baby spinach
1 red onion
400g ripest cherry
    tomatoes

For the actual salad, bring a large pan of salted water to a rumbling boil and add the penne. Simmer for about 8 minutes, or according to the packet instructions. When the pasta is cooked and quite soft, not al dente, drain, and rinse under a running cold tap to cool. When it is cold throughout, empty into a large salad bowl. Roughly chop the baby spinach and fold this into the pasta. Peel and very finely dice the red onion, halve the cherry tomatoes, and finally add these to the bowl, thoroughly mixing. Dress the salad with the Caesar dressing just before serving. If you combine it too soon, the pasta will absorb a lot of the moisture. It's best when unctuous and dripping.

Nutty Brown Rice & Bean Salad

For 4 or 5

Brown rice is intrinsically not my scene. I've always been put off by the healthy 1970s hippiness of it. And yet I was totally proved wrong last year. I became obsessed with this husky rice and also with watermelon, another food I was irrationally against. But after the brain haemorrhage, my tastebuds couldn't handle much. Because of this, other things I'd never liked became my bread and butter. Brown rice is actually really nutty and delicious, and works wonderfully as my mum does it, with kidney beans, soaked in an oily dressing.

Place the brown rice in a medium saucepan and fill it with water so that it comes a few centimetres above the rice. Bring to the boil on a medium flame, simmering the rice for about half an hour. Taste to check that it is still nutty, but tender. Drain any excess water from the pan, and set the rice aside to cool. To speed up this process you may want to rinse it under cold running water. Drain the kidney beans into a colander and rinse them too under a running tap until the water runs clear of the dark red thick liquid. When the rice is cool, combine it with the beans in a medium salad bowl.

To make the dressing, put the olive oil into a mixing jug, squeeze in the lemon juice, and whisk these together. Peel and crush the garlic and finely chop the parsley and add these to the dressing. Season accordingly and pour the dressing over the salad. Give it a thorough toss before serving up.

300g brown rice
2 x 400g tins of kidney beans
6 tablespoons extra virgin olive oil, or more
1 lemon
2 garlic cloves
a big handful of fresh curly parsley
a generous pinch of Maldon sea salt
freshly ground black pepper

Mr Dan's Bulgar Wheat Salad

For 5

Mr Dan and his superwife, Jane, live a bike ride away from me up Brixton Hill. He has a studio where he produces lots of amazing musicians, including my dear friend Mara, and throws ridiculously fun all-night parties. When Mara was recording her album last year with Mr Dan, I happened to be off work and whimsically biking around, dropping into charity shops to buy china. They are ever-welcoming, and invited me over for a studio lunch. Mr Dan made his favourite tabbouleh. It's full of coriander and parsley, and came with his contagious cherubic enthusiasm. It was a brilliant afternoon. This mountainous salad is super easy to construct and is full of Eastern flavours, so is ideal for a bunch of your friends to dig into in the garden.

500g bulgar wheat
1 litre hot vegetable stock
4 lemons
2 large red onions
a large bunch of fresh coriander (2 bunches if supermarket-bought)
a large bunch of fresh parsley (4 bunches if supermarket-bought)
300g feta
4 tablespoons extra virgin olive oil
lots of freshly ground black pepper
2 teaspoons Maldon sea salt

Place the bulgar wheat in a really large saucepan. Pour on the hot vegetable stock and heat on a medium to high flame, with the lid on, for 10 minutes, or until it is nutty to bite into, really juicy and with the liquid almost entirely absorbed. Now squeeze over the lemons, getting all the juice out. Give it a thorough mix through with a large fork. Now peel and really, really finely dice the red onions and mix these into the hot grains. Replace the lid and let it sit for about an hour. All the flavours will melge wonderfully.

Now finely chop the coriander and parsley. You may need to do this in a few batches if there is too much for your board. Fork the herbs into the bulgar wheat, distributing well. Crumble in the feta, and add lots of extra virgin olive oil and lots of seasoning. Taste to make sure it is fresh and light and full of summer smells. You may want to spoon the salad out into a large salad bowl before serving.

Radicchio & Pancetta Salad

For 3

This radicchio and pancetta salad is a dish I picked up when out for a big dinner with lots of Italians in Ancona. We had a great time, savouring every morsel on the menu. There it is done with lard, which I have only found in a few delis here, so I suggest pancetta, which gives a wonderful sweet and sour element to the dish. This recipe would be equally good as a starter, decorating individual plates with the green leaves and nestling radicchio piglets.

Preheat the oven to 180°C/Gas 4. Break away any frumpy leaves from the radicchio. For each little piglet, you need one leaf and one strip of meat. Curl the leaf up and wrap the sheet of pancetta around it, tucking in the soft top of the leaf. Arrange the parcels in a baking dish, drizzle with olive oil and sprinkle with a little sugar. Place in the oven for 15 minutes, then remove to cool to a warm room temperature. To serve, scatter the rocket and spinach leaves on a large flat serving dish, and place the radicchio parcels among them, finally splashing with balsamic vinegar and any excess oil from the baking dish.

1 small radicchio
12 slices of really thin
   pancetta or lard
a drizzle of olive oil
½ teaspoon sugar
2 handfuls of fresh
   rocket
2 handfuls of baby
   spinach
2 teaspoons balsamic
   vinegar

Gillie's Chicory & Orange Salad with Two Different Dressings

For 4

This chicory salad is a staple dish at Alice's house. Her mother, Gillie, is amazing, an icon in maternity and career success all at the same time. Lunches at their house in leafy Richmond are bountiful and generous and everyone is welcome. There are babies and grandmothers and everyone in between. That's what I want my home to be like when I'm a grown-up. Chicory has a bitterness that is really well balanced by some juicy sweet oranges. It couldn't be simpler to make this salad. And the ratios of one chicory to one orange (which feeds two) means if you've got a handful of friends round for lunch it's easy to do the maths.

The Salad

Roughly chop the chicory into 2cm roundels, widthways. Pulling these apart, scatter in a large salad bowl. Now, using a serrated knife, peel the oranges, making sure there is no pith left. Slice each fruit in half, and then each half into 3 segments. Dice these into small chunks and add to the salad bowl.

2 chicory bulbs
2 lush oranges

The Dressings

To make the dressings (not both, but whichever one you are choosing to use), beat all the ingredients together in a measuring jug. Alternatively you can decant all the ingredients into an old jar, and give it a good shake. Pour the dressing over the salad when you are ready to serve up.

2 tablespoons extra virgin olive oil
1 tablespoon white wine vinegar
3 teaspoons grainy Dijon mustard
1½ teaspoons caster sugar

or

1 tablespoon extra virgin olive oil
1 tablespoon crème fraîche
3 teaspoons grainy mustard
1 teaspoon caster sugar

Rosemary-roasted Sweet Potatoes

For 4

Sweet potatoes are delicious, and all over Brixton market, being a classic Jamaican ingredient. They are wonderfully long and knobbly and have rough and dark pink skins. They are really versatile, and can be made into a delicate mash, with lamb, or added to Raf's groundnut curry (see page 231), or, as here, roasted. They are indeed sweet, and softer than an average potato. Roasting these with rosemary is an ideal way to fill up your friends on the cheap with something pungent and out of the ordinary. They take little work, so you can make a few more dishes with your time while these are roasting in the oven.

800g sweet potatoes
3 big twigs of fresh
    rosemary
3 tablespoons olive oil
lots of Maldon sea salt

Preheat the oven to 180°C/Gas 4. Well wash the sweet potatoes and slice them into 2cm cubes. Scatter the rosemary twigs over a roasting tin and put the potato chunks on top. Pour over the olive oil and sprinkle with salt. Bake in the oven for 35 to 45 minutes. When they are ready they will be soft and smell wonderful. Either eat straight out of the oven or leave to cool and eat cold in your fingers. Both ways they are delicious.

Fruit Brûlée

For 6

As the title suggests, this is one of my mum's classic summer puddings. It's super simple, consisting purely of sliced-up fruit (whatever you want really), whipped cream and a volcanic layer of caramel. As a child, I remember this being the finale of most of our dinner parties during the Suffolk summer evenings. This pudding is great the next day too: if I wasn't allowed to the parental dinner, the consolation prize would be devouring the leftovers of this brûlée for breakfast the next day. I still do this with what's left after a dinner at my flat. I recently made it for some girlfriends on a Sunday night, and scooped up the rest on Monday morning on my way to work.

If you have a big dish made of glass the stripes of colour will look particularly fantastic, as you'll be able to see the cross-section. You can also mix and match the fruit that you use. I've used mangoes and passion fruit before. It really depends on what you are feeling like, and what you can get hold of.

4 oranges

4 bananas

3 Braeburn apples

2 handfuls of seedless green grapes

2 handfuls of strawberries

½ lemon

a few sprigs of fresh mint

250ml double cream

150g caster sugar

50ml water

Get yourself a large – preferably glass – serving dish about 5cm deep. The kind you might use to make a potato gratin, about 15 x 30cm. Prepare the fruit by first peeling the oranges and slicing them into pieces about 1cm cubed. Then peel and slice the bananas. Core the apples, and chop into equal-sized pieces. Wash the grapes and strawberries and slice these in half. Place all of these fruits in a mixing bowl, and squeeze the juice from the lemon over them. Finely slice the mint and give everything a good mix around with your hands to evenly distribute, then tip out into the serving dish. Whisk the double cream in a mixing bowl until it is stiff. The consistency should be such that it requires a knife to spread it on top of the fruit. Roughly paste all the cream over the fruit, right up to the edges of the dish. Set aside.

Measure out the sugar into a small saucepan, along with the water. Place on a low heat until the sugar has dissolved and it is bubbling gently. Swirl this syrup around the pan from time to time, but do not use a spoon. When it begins to turn golden, remove it from the heat. It will continue to turn a deeper tan. After a few minutes, pour it over the cream lid. Allow the caramel to cool before serving just as it is.

Apple Purée with Syllabub

For 4

This pudding is insane in its goodness. Apple purée was always bubbling away on my mother's Raeburn in late summer, full of cinnamon and ready to be drowned in double cream or piled on some cereal in the morning. So it's a pudding always to the fore in my mind, and is very economical if you find a box of apples on the turn. And then I discovered syllabub, which is a classic, again very English pudding made by sweetening cream, with the added kick of wine, marsala, or sherry or really anything fortified. For some reason, it feels much more Eastern than English though, so works really well with the addition of rose or orange blossom water. By making this purée and then heaping the gentle cloud-like rolls of whipped scented cream on top, you will have a pudding so elegant in aesthetics and flavour that your friends will be quite lost for words. It's one to really savour, and is pretty simple to construct too.

The Purée

10 apples, whatever is crunchy and on the market
1 lemon
200ml water
1 cinnamon stick

First you need to core and peel the apples, roughly chopping them into thumb-sized pieces. This will take about 20 minutes, so can be done in front of the TV or while having a good chat, rather like shelling peas. Place the apples in a large saucepan with the juice of the lemon, the water and the cinnamon. With the lid on, simmer on a medium heat for about 40 minutes, stirring from time to time. When the water has mostly gone, and you are left with a pulpy purée, turn off the heat and leave it to cool right down. This will take a couple of hours.

The Syllabub

3 tablespoons medium sweet oloroso sherry
1 tablespoon dry vermouth
2 teaspoons rose water
3 tablespoons caster sugar
a little orange zest
200ml double cream
freshly grated nutmeg

While the apple purée is cooling, measure the sherry, vermouth, rose water and sugar out into a small mixing bowl, followed by the orange zest. Thoroughly mix this all together and let it sit to dissolve the sugar, and really infuse the scents. When the apple purée is room temperature, you are ready to assemble. So, first decant the purée into four ramekins, coffee cups or small French tumblers, and set these aside. Measure out the double cream into a medium mixing bowl, and add the alcoholic syrup. Using a whisk, lightly beat for a few minutes. When the cream is softly forming peaks and is delicate to the touch, but not too stiff, your syllabub is perfect. Spoon this over the potted-up purée, and grate a little nutmeg over. Place in the fridge for half an hour, until you are ready to serve up and enjoy the most wonderfully English sweet.

Orange Blossom Custards

For 5, washed down with green tea

I've made this recipe for five because I like keeping one aside for a treat. Also, you may plan on having four friends over for lunch, but it frequently turns into five. These are absolutely perfect. The double whammy of orange blossom water and the orange syrup at the bottom really hits home. And by using so many egg yolks, the texture of these custards is utterly delicate. All the flavours are intoxicating and mysterious and Eastern. And for some unknown reason, these are heightened and made even more of a delight by being washed down with little cups of green tea. It just really works.

You should be able to get orange blossom water in any Middle Eastern shop, or delicatessens. It's a wonderfully distinctive ingredient, full of scent and exotic aromas, so it's worth finding a really good one.

Preheat the oven to 150°C/Gas 2 and find 5 ramekins. Mix together the juice from the orange, and 75g of the caster sugar, in a small saucepan. Heat this on a low flame until it starts bubbling and frothing and is thick and caramel-coloured. Dish out the syrup among the ramekins, swirling to level it out. Let it set. Meanwhile, beat together the egg yolks, egg and remaining 150g of sugar so that it forms a smooth paste. Set this aside while, in a medium saucepan, you warm the milk, cream, cardamom pods and the orange blossom water. Do this on a low heat until the flavours are really infused, but don't let the mixture boil. Take it off the heat when it begins to release steam after a few minutes. Now with a sieve, strain this rich milk into a jug. Using a whisk, beat this milk into the egg mix. When it is totally mixed together, pour into the ramekins. Place these on a metal roasting tin, which you should then fill with water so that it comes about two-thirds of the way up the sides of the little pots. Place the whole tray in the oven for about an hour, or until the custards no longer wobble too much. Toast the flaked almonds in a dry frying pan until they are golden and brown. Sprinkle them over the custards and then let the whole lot cool.

1 plump orange
225g caster sugar
5 medium free-range egg yolks
1 medium free-range egg
285ml full-fat milk
285ml single cream
8 whole cardamom pods
1 tablespoon orange blossom water
50g flaked almonds

Semolina & Syrup Cakes

Makes lots of little squares to share around like sweets

Semolina flour has a wonderful texture, slightly nutty, but smoother than polenta. These little cakes are deliciously Moorish in origin, drenched in an orange syrup. They vaguely come from a Turkish recipe that I found when pondering on baklava, one of my – many – guilty pleasures. Sliced into little squares, these make a perfect sweet at the end of a summer lunch, with short coffees or fresh mint tea. And they are super easy and quick to make, so are a good choice if you have been labouring on the other dishes. Lovely Jasmine, one of my beautiful helpers, gives me a hand making them in the shop, and they sell in a flash along with a perfect cappuccino.

Preheat the oven to 180°C/Gas 4 and line a baking tray about 15 x 25cm (something like a brownie tray) with greaseproof paper. In a large mixing bowl, mix together the semolina flour and 120g of the sugar with a fork. Beat 3 of the eggs together in a bowl with 3 of the yolks from the other eggs (therefore separating 3 out of 6). Add the beaten eggs to the dry ingredients, mixing thoroughly to form a paste. Leave aside the 3 remaining egg whites in a very clean metal mixing bowl. Grate the zest from the orange on the finest panel of a grater and add to the cake mix, keeping the rest of the orange aside. Now whisk the egg whites thoroughly so that they are really stiff. Fold these into the cake mix with a slotted metal spoon. Be careful not to knock the air out of the whites, but make sure that everything is thoroughly combined to form a foamy batter. Turn out into the baking tray and place in the oven for about 20 to 30 minutes. When cooked the cake should be soft to the touch, like supple young flesh, and a toothpick should emerge clean from the centre.

Leave in the baking tray to cool a little while you make the syrup: first squeeze the juice of the orange into a small saucepan. Add the remaining 170g of sugar and the water and place on a low heat. Allow to bubble away until it is a little thicker. This will take about 5 minutes of simmering. Now pour this syrup over the baked cake. It will seem like a lot at first, but much of the syrup will be absorbed into the sponge, so that it becomes sticky and sodden. Leave to sit for about half an hour before slicing into squares and removing to a serving dish or cake-stand. Pour over any leftover syrup in the bottom of the baking tray.

180g fine semolina flour
290g caster sugar
6 medium free-range
    eggs
1 orange
100ml water

Far Out Eton Mess

Feeds 6 to 8

My good friends Kylie and Bharat reminded me of Eton Mess. They had a lovely Sunday lunch for our Brixton family, culminating in Eton Mess with strawberries. Kylie's Australian, so makes a mean meringue, and Bharat made the most brilliant and tender lamb tagine. They are a dream team. So, they got me to thinking about this old-fashioned dish. Apparently it is traditionally served for the Fourth of June, Eton's sports day. Given that I have frequented this occasion on the lookout for boys (a long time ago), I thought it fitting to add it to my repertoire.

Brixton market is not full of strawberries, however. Instead we have a wealth of exotic and other-worldly fruits. So I've devised a Far Out Eton Mess, with Brixton's prolific supply of mint and mangoes. It works a treat. The proof in this pudding, therefore, is that you can really use any well-ripened fruit and be a little creative, so long as you've got whipped cream and a pile of meringue. Try grapes and bananas, lychees, or those wonderful waxy lantern-protected Chinese gooseberries.

If you are short of time, you can always buy the meringues and then all you will be required to do is the final messy assemblance. Though I usually have excess whites from other bits of cooking, just begging to be made into meringues.

Preheat the oven to 150°C/Gas 2. First you need to make the meringues, which will take a couple of hours from start to finish. Using a whisk, beat the egg whites until really firm. This is arm-breaking, so if you have a mixer, that would be preferable, and it would need to be on a slow setting. I don't, so have to just push on through. When you have weighed out the caster sugar, gradually add it to the whites, whisking all the time. As you combine the sugar, the mix will become more and more heavy and gloopy. If you are using a Magimix, at this point you can turn the power up to a more powerful setting so that it becomes really glossy. Turn the mixture out on to a baking tray lined with greaseproof paper. It doesn't really matter what shape it is, as the whole meringue will be broken up later on. Place in the oven for 1½ hours, or until it is quite firm to the touch, then remove from the oven and leave to cool.

Crush up the hazelnuts, using a rolling pin or a long sharp knife so that they are about quartered. Warm a dry frying pan on a medium heat and add the hazelnuts to toast them. This will take about 5 minutes and may require a little tossing. Remove them from the pan to a plate to cool.

Now prepare the mangoes by slicing off discs. With the skin on a chopping board, score the discs so that you have a grid of scoring on the sticky flesh. Push the fruit down so that the cubes of fruit pop up. Slice between the fruit and the skin, releasing these little pieces. Work your way around the mango like this, decanting each harvest into a bowl. Squeeze the lemon over the fruit, and give it all a good mix around. Finely chop most of the mint and add this too. Let this infuse for about 20 minutes.

To construct the whole pudding, all you now need to do is whip the double cream with a whisk. When this is nicely firm and forming peaks, but not cheesy, fold in the meringues and fruit. Decant this to a large serving dish or a nice bowl. Finally scatter the hazelnuts over the pudding, along with the remaining mint. Enjoy the Far Out Mess.

6 medium free-range
  egg whites
350g caster sugar
60g hazelnuts
4 large ripe mangoes
½ lemon or 1 lime
a handful of fresh mint
450ml double cream

Rhubarb & Whiskey Fool

For 4

This amazing combination of knife-edge-sharp fruit, whipped cream, and grainy booze makes for flavours that are buttery and tart all at once. The whiskey tingles with the sweet acidity of this mad fruit. It's a proper taste sensation, an ideal sharpener after a summer lunch in the garden. Rhubarb is in season from June to September in Britain, but stay away from the leaves as these are pretty toxic.

400g colourful rhubarb stems
550ml water
100g caster sugar
1 tablespoon runny honey
284ml double cream
3 tablespoons Irish whiskey

Chop the rhubarb into 2cm pieces and place in a medium saucepan with the water, sugar and honey. Bring to the boil and maintain for 10 minutes. Then reduce the heat and simmer the fruit for 1 hour or until thick with strands of broken-down rhubarb. Leave to cool, preferably overnight.

Whip the cream until it is really stiff and doesn't move when wobbled. Mix the whiskey into the rhubarb and, finally, fold this into the whipped cream. Don't overdo the mixing. It's lovely when each spoonful is full of varied textures of foamy cream and silky sharp alcoholic fruit.

Essentials

The following essential information will mean that you can rustle up almost anything at short notice, solve a few domestic dilemmas, and make a mighty fine meal for whoever drops by. With a few tins of lentils you can make a Barcelona lentil salad; knowing you've got chillies in the freezer means you can make a dish with some added kick; if you've some spare chickpeas you can pad out almost anything for that extra mouth to feed; and with pastry in the freezer you will always be dressed to impress.

Equipment

I think you can have a go at creating anything in the kitchen, so long as you have …

a good sharp knife
a mandolin slicer
a hand-held blender
a whisk

None of these gadgets will set you back a great deal, and good food doesn't depend on an endless array of grills, toasters, mixers and blenders, which will most likely just clutter up your kitchen. Whipped egg whites are all the more satisfying if your arm is in agony by the end (it makes me feel like a wartime domestess), and most vegetables will look dead sophisticated once under the blade of a mandolin slicer. If you have a hand-held blender, each and every fine soup and dip can be yours. But most of all, a good knife will make your job a lot easier. My fuzzy-haired friend Don Livione bought me a beautiful Sabatier knife for my twenty-first birthday, and it's been with me ever since, one of the best presents I've ever received.

Shopping

When I'm shopping I always pick up a few extra storecupboard essentials, be it some tinned tomatoes or a jar of anchovies. You won't notice the difference to your bill, and it will mean that come the end of the month when you are broke, you've got some food to play with. Life will be a little less heavy then.

And if you want to plump up a simple meal, buying just a few extra special ingredients will really turn it around. A good example of this is those lovely but rather expensive dried Italian mushrooms. By combining simple chestnut mushrooms with a handful of wild porcini you will suddenly achieve economical sophistication, as if from nowhere.

And then there's padding out a meal. If you can't afford lots of meat, then adding a couple of tins of chickpeas will be equally satisfying. Also, if you find that there are some unexpected extras around your kitchen table, then again this pulse-padding trick usually stretches a meal. If it's a pasta bake, with tomatoes and fusilli, then by adding some tinned borlotti or cannellini beans you could satisfy at least two more friends. And I'd much rather have more friends around my table than send anyone away unloved.

Ethics

It's really difficult to know which bandwagon to jump on regarding food ethics. There's the carbon footprint of food miles; supporting British produce; free-range, organic and Fair Trade, to name just a few. Being very much part of a small local community, my allegiance usually lies with the independent business, and supporting my lovely Brixton market. If I'm – rarely – shopping in a supermarket I try not to buy beans from Kenya, but if I'm in the market, then whatever I buy I'm supporting my local community, just as they do by shopping at Rosie's. It gets pretty complicated if you try to satisfy everyone, so if I were you, I'd shop in whatever way feels right at the time.

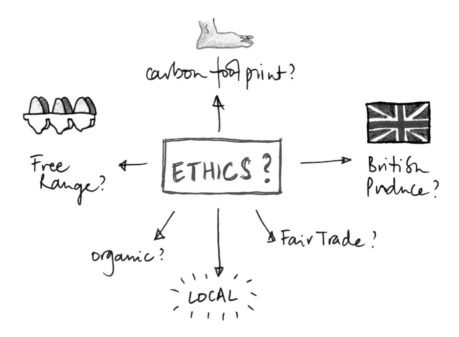

Gardening

I highly recommend planting a few bits and bobs on your window ledge. Plant a little bay tree on your balcony in a good deep pot. You don't need to have a yard the size of Kew Gardens. It's just about planting from seed a few fresh herbs and some rocket. I've even grown radishes in old coffee tins on my balcony. And I love the tending and watering that comes with this pastime too.

You can get seeds in supermarkets, hardware stores and even some delis (Valvona & Crolla in Edinburgh, and Lina Stores in Soho). The usual sowing time for rocket and other salad leaves is February through to September, so you can harvest all summer. Do this by picking the outside leaves first, always plucking from the outer and bottom part of the plant, leaving the young ones to carry on maturing. Home-grown rocket is usually much more peppery too, so really adds some oomph to a bowl of dressed greens.

Fridge Essentials

tomato purée

capers in brine

good pesto

free-range eggs

grainy Dijon mustard

smooth Dijon mustard

unsalted butter

halloumi and feta (both keep unopened for a long time in the fridge)

anchovies in oil (add to a tomato pasta sauce instead of salt – just one way of using this magic ingredient)

top-notch mayonnaise

creamed horseradish or shredded wild horseradish, if you can find it

Freezer Essentials

puff pastry

broad beans

brown bananas

petits pois (A note on peas: you don't need to cook them in water.
Just pour out the frozen peas into a pan, add a little butter or oil and
gently heat through. They are coated in frozen water and this way you
won't drain away any of the sweet flavour.)

You can also freeze

fresh chillies

sage leaves

berries

Storecupboard Essentials

tinned chickpeas

olive oil for cooking

extra virgin olive oil for fresh use

balsamic vinegar

white wine or cider vinegar

tinned white and green haricots

tinned lentils

baked beans

tinned cherry tomatoes

miso soup

superior saffron

cinnamon (ground and sticks)

smoked paprika, hot or sweet

peperoncino (chilli flakes)

caraway seeds

mild curry powder

ground ginger

cayenne pepper

lots of pasta

whole nutmeg

bay leaves

whole cloves

bouillon (I like Marigold – check the labels, because many have MSG)

fresh garlic

soy sauce

fish sauce

rice wine vinegar

coconut milk

coconut oil

peanut oil

fresh ginger

toasted sesame seed oil

peanut butter

Rosie's
www.rosiesdelicafe.com

ORGANIC BREAD
CHARCUTERIE
ARTISAN CHEESE
ANTI PASTI
SANDWICHES
COFFEE & CAKES
Classic Victoria
Sponge ♡

Rosie's Deli Cafe

COFFEE, TEA OR ME?

Tea was a big thing in Suffolk. Off the school run, we'd dash in to see what Mum had conjured up. It was always a glorious array, on a pretty old tablecloth, with homemade jams and colourful jugs. Baking is such a delicious way of passing a Sunday, especially when the weather is bleak and I'm at a loose end. So here are some therapy ideas which will bring back childhood.

Of course at Rosie's I do a lot of baking and am so lucky to able to start the day with the smells of soft butter and sweet flour. We have a long cake shelf, which is always full of iced delights for grown-ups to pore over and children to drool over. The spiced apple cake and the orange and almond cake are particular sellers, and it's all made in my tiny little Baby Belling bed-sit oven.

Pay attention when baking, though. It's not an art that should be experimented with. If you are precise, the results will be perfect: I always find Delia good for advice in this department. But if you improvise, you are heading for trouble. Many of these recipes can also be used as a pudding if you've got some friends over, especially Helen's mascarpone cheesecake and the orange shortbread.

Menu

Baking

Drop Scones, Mum's Way

Makes 20 small and sturdy little treats

These are gorgeous little raised pancakes that seem wonderfully old-fashioned. They crisp up and become golden at the edges and have a really comforting stodginess to the centre. We would quite often have these for tea when I was little, and I'd have friends round too because teatime was such an awesome occasion. There must still be a bit of a child in me, as I find teatime pretty exciting even now. These drop scones are best with some good butter and a smudge of raspberry jam.

Place the egg, flour, milk, nutmeg and butter in a jug and thoroughly combine, using a hand-held blender, so that there is not a lump in sight. It should be a little thicker than an average pancake mix. Set the batter aside to rest for at least an hour.

1 large free-range egg
225g self-raising flour
280ml full-fat milk
½ teaspoon freshly grated nutmeg
50g butter
2 tablespoons vegetable oil

Warm the oven to 100°C/Gas ¼ and put in a heatproof dish lined with a tea towel, which can then also be lined with some kitchen paper. Pour about a teaspoon of the oil into a large frying pan and get it super hot and quivering. Add about a tablespoon's worth of the mix, dropping it on to the oiled pan. You should be able to get 2 or even 4 drop scones into the pan at a time. Flip them over after about a minute and do the other side. The second side will require a little less frying. Remove the drop scones to the warmed dish and return each batch to the oven. Continue to fry batches until there is no batter left. Serve the warm pancakes with butter and good jam.

Yoghurt Cake

Makes 12 mega slices

This was one of my first real solo challenges in the kitchen. My mum would set me up with all the ingredients, and leave me to it. By the time *The Antiques Roadshow* was on, this delicious Eastern cake was coming out of the oven. It became a Sunday institution. As I made the cake in the privacy of the kitchen, while everyone else was pottering in the drawing room, I would pretend I was hosting a cookery show. I would explain each part of the method to my imaginary camera, hoping for each moment that I was a mini Delia, loving my fantastical limelight.

I like making a bigger version of the cake these days, as it goes so well in the shop. It's moist and is a great one to munch on over a few days. I've formulated a mascarpone icing too. If you prefer, though, a jar of good lemon curd (I use Ada May's homemade curd) is wonderful drenched over the top.

Preheat the oven to 180°C/Gas 4 and generously butter a 28cm loose-bottomed cake tin. Grate the zest off the lemons and add to a large mixing bowl. To make the most of the rind, use a fork to remove as much from the grater as you can. Beat together the butter and sugar with the rind until it is light and pale and smooth, like creamy snow. Having separated the eggs, beat the yolks into this cream. Measure out the flour and yoghurt and alternately add these to the mix along with the salt. In a super clean bowl, beat the egg whites until they form quite stiff peaks. Now, with a slotted metal spoon, fold the egg whites into the thick cake mix. It will gradually loosen. Turn the cake mix out into the greased tin, and place in the oven for 1½ hours, or until it is firm to the touch and golden on the top and cracking open. If you are in doubt, slip a toothpick directly into the centre of the cake. If it comes out smooth, you are good to go. Remove the cake from the tin to a cooling rack and let it cool entirely.

260g softened butter, plus some for buttering the tin
1½ lemons
375g golden caster sugar
6 medium free-range eggs
450g self-raising flour
180ml natural yoghurt
a pinch of salt

Mascarpone Icing

This is soft and delicious, and a good twist on a butter icing. Generally I prefer it for the lightness, and it can be used on many other cakes. I use it on my apple cake too, adding a little cinnamon. You can make it in advance and pop it into the fridge for when the cake has fully cooled. Beware, though – if you don't let the cake cool properly the icing will melt and slither down the sides like your tears.

First loosen the mascarpone by beating it with a strong whisk. Now grate in the lemon zest. Finally, beat in the icing sugar thoroughly, making sure there are no lumps. To apply the icing, ideally use a palette knife and create soft peaks with it, like foamy waves. This is best achieved with a loose wrist.

350g mascarpone
1 lemon
350g icing sugar

Simplest Orange & Almond Cake

Makes 12 shallow slices

This cake is wonderfully light and nutty and follows almost exactly the same formula as the semolina and syrup cakes (see page 298). It uses entirely ground almonds, and it's almost like an Eastern drizzle cake because you will soak it in an orange syrup at the end. The first time I made this cake, it disappeared in an afternoon: Doctor Helen and Bharat were killing an afternoon dancing in my shop and liked it so much they bought the whole lot. And in honour of Bharat's liking, I made it again for his wedding cake. It was a heart-warming afternoon in the shop, his bride Kylie glowing and everyone washing this delicate cake down with champagne out of tea cups.

It's very simple in all respects: it's a cake that I come back to time and time again when either my cupboard is looking bare (because it only needs four ingredients), or my inspiration is waning (because I know I can rely on it and won't have to think). So really it's a trusty friend you can depend on. I've also made it with grapefruit. Incidentally, it's gluten-free – good if you are ever trying to veer away from wheat, or have intolerance under your roof.

6 medium free-range
    eggs
300g golden caster
    sugar
200g ground almonds
1 large juicy orange
2 tablespoons water

To make this I use a long rectangular cake tin or a 25cm loose-bottomed tin, lined with baking paper. Preheat the oven to 160°C/Gas 2. Separate 3 of the eggs, putting the whites aside in a large clean metal mixing bowl. Now, beat together the egg yolks with the remaining 3 whole eggs in a large bowl. Add 200g of the caster sugar and all the ground almonds. Thoroughly mix, using a fork. Grate the orange zest and add this too, keeping the rest of the orange for later. Now beat the egg whites until they form soft peaks. Using a slotted metal spoon, fold the beaten egg whites into the thick cake mix, a spoonful at a time. Be careful not to knock the air out of the whites (as there is no other raising agent in the cake). Now pour this foamy cake mix into the lined tin and place in the oven for 50 minutes to an hour.

When the cake is ready a toothpick will come out clean, without any cake mix on it. Leave the cake to cool in the tin while you make the syrup. Measure out the remaining caster sugar into a small saucepan and add the juice from the orange and a few tablespoons of water. Place this on a really low heat in order to dissolve the sugar and slightly reduce the syrup. Using a toothpick, plant holes all over the cake and pour over the orange syrup. Allow the cake to fully cool and absorb the syrup before removing from the tin.

Edna's Chocolate & Hazelnut Cookies

Makes about 15 treats

These were one of our favourite treats. My brother Olly and I would plead with our mother to make these choc chip biscuits (you would too if lentil rissoles were the alternative!). The recipe originally comes from my great-grandfather's housekeeper, Edna. My mother adored Edna and learned a lot at her apron strings. I love the fact that we are still championing her sweets.

And now that I have baked these so many times, I've developed my own version, with cranberries and white chocolate, purely because that's what I had in the shop at the moment of my cookie yearning. They are totally different but just as delicious. The cranberry is deep and tart and the white chocolate really creamy. So here I'm showing the original formula, and my contemporary twist. Both keep for about a week.

75g butter
1 medium free-range
  egg
140g self-raising flour
150g golden caster
  sugar
1 teaspoon baking
  powder
1 teaspoon vanilla
  essence or some
  scraped-out vanilla
  seeds if you are
  feeling extravagant
60g hazelnuts/60g
  cranberries
50g plain chocolate/50g
  white chocolate

Preheat the oven to 180°C/Gas 4 and line a large baking tray with greaseproof paper. Chop up the butter and place in a medium mixing bowl. Leave to soften to room temperature. Now beat the egg and add this to the bowl, along with the flour, sugar, baking powder and vanilla essence. Thoroughly beat these ingredients into the softened butter until it is a light smooth paste. If you haven't the stamina for this, it can be done in a Magimix. Set aside while you roughly chop the hazelnuts into quarters (or the cranberries in half). Chop the chocolate with a long sharp knife, holding down the tip and working across in all directions until you've got chips the same size as the chopped nuts. Add the chocolate and nuts to the biscuit mix and combine really well. The mix may be quite hard to work, but persevere, and don't be tempted to water it down.

Now, using a teaspoon, make little bundles of the mix and place on the lined baking tray, about 5cm apart (as they will spread considerably). You'll need to do two or so batches. Bake for 7 to 8 minutes – the biscuits should be browning around the edges and still a little soft to the touch in the centre. Once they have been removed from the oven, allow them to set on the baking tray for a further 5 minutes before easing off with a palette knife and placing on a cooling rack.

Classic Cricket Tea: Victoria Sponge with Strawberries & Cream

You will get 12 really generous slices out of this old friend

This is a real vintage summer cake, verging on the kitsch. I wouldn't usually think of making a Victoria sponge, but then I was roped into cricket tea for Grenfell CC. This is Raf's cricket team, and they all take it in turns to offer up a good half-time spread. It's such a serious matter, there's even a prize for the best tea at the end of the season. Needless to say I was ecstatic at the opportunity to do something so wonderfully old-fashioned, and couldn't wait to try my hand at the old classics.

We made mayonnaise-heavy potato salad, a really simple cheese and onion flan, loads of white bread sandwiches (those particularly English fillings like ham and tomato, cheese and pickle, tuna and cucumber), and this elegant cake filled with English strawberries and sweetened whipped cream. It's absolutely perfect in lightness, creaminess and sweetness. The Metros, hungry and roguish boys in a band from Peckham, came down to watch too, and polished off what little was left of the cricket tea. The second over was swift, which must have been my divine reward for such dutiful efforts.

If you are going to get really genuine, it's best to hunt down British strawberries: those that are imported are often picked before they are ripe, and as these fruits don't continue to ripen once plucked, they are likely to be hard and not nearly as tasty as your memory would have them. Check out www.eattheseasons.co.uk for mountains of useful information about seasonal foods.

Preheat the oven to 180°C/Gas 4. You will need a loose-bottomed cake tin measuring about 26cm across, the base lined with greaseproof paper and the sides lightly buttered. Cut up the butter into a large mixing bowl and let it sit out for half an hour so that it is malleable and soft. Now measure in the caster sugar and beat these to within an inch of their lives. The mixture should be light, creamy, pale and fluffy. Now, in a separate bowl, beat the 6 eggs thoroughly together and add to the butter along with the vanilla essence. Using a whisk, beat thoroughly. It may look a little curdled but that will soon be remedied. Gently fold in the flour until the batter is smooth but quite thick. Turn this out into the lined cake tin and, using a palette knife, spread evenly to the edges, smoothing the top. Place the cake in the oven for 50 minutes. Then turn down the oven to 100°C/Gas ¼ and cook for an additional 15 to 20 minutes. Remove, and check that it is cooked by piercing the centre with a toothpick. If the toothpick comes out clean then it is ready. Release the sides with a palette knife, and remove the cake from the tin by pushing up the base. Leave it to cool overnight, or at least a few hours, until it is properly cold.

For the filling, remove the crown of leaves from each strawberry and finely slice from the narrowest point to the fat base. Set the prepared strawberries aside. Pour the cream into a large bowl and whisk until it is forming firm peaks. Now beat in 1 tablespoon of icing sugar. Very carefully slice the cake in half, using a long bread knife. Open it out like a sandwich, and lather the sweetened whipped cream on both sides of the cake. Now arrange the strawberries all over the creamed base, so that they peek out all around the circumference of the cake like jewels. Steadily return the top to the cake. Dust the top with the remaining icing sugar.

330g butter, plus some for buttering the tin
330g caster sugar
6 medium free-range eggs
1 teaspoon vanilla essence or scraped-out vanilla seeds if you are feeling rich
330g self-raising flour
300g plump ripe British strawberries (in season end of May until end of July)
284ml double cream
2 tablespoons icing sugar

My Spiced Apple Cake with Buckwheat

Makes 12 ample slices

This cake really reminds me of childhood, not because I ever made it, but because it just smells so old-fashioned and nostalgic, like it belongs to a great-grandmother. You can either glaze it traditionally with apricot jam or use the more modern mascarpone icing from the yoghurt cake on page 319 (but instead of adding lemon, add a few teaspoons of ground cinnamon).

I was prompted to bake a spiced apple cake after going to the wonderful café at the back of Books for Cooks on Blenheim Crescent with my mum. We were having a lovely day poring over jewellery and clothes in Notting Hill. The rows of cakes on perfect white stands in the back kitchen of this great shop look like a perfect still-life painting. In fact, everything in this place is absolutely beautiful. The menu is simple and thoughtful, and the atmosphere of ladies lunching makes me almost feel like one myself.

Preheat the oven to 180°C/Gas 4, and grease a large loose-bottomed 25cm cake tin. Make a strongly brewed short tea. Allow this to sit while you get on with the cake.

Chop up the butter into a large mixing bowl. Leave to soften to room temperature for about half an hour (in winter this may take a little longer, depending on how tight you are with the heating!). Measure out the sugar and beat it into the butter. I use a strong whisk. Make sure that it is a really light and creamy ball. This will require some elbow grease. Beat the eggs thoroughly, then beat these into the creamed butter and sugar. It may look a little curdled, but don't worry. Measure out the flours, baking powder and spices into a bowl and, bit by bit, beat them into the cake mix using a wooden spoon. Set this aside while you core and peel the apples. Slice them into thumb-sized nuggets and fold into the cake mix, along with the nuts and 4 tablespoons of tea. This will loosen the mix and add some teatime scents.

Spoon this all out into the greased cake tin and place in the oven for 1 hour. Then turn off the heat and leave the cake to sit for a further 20 minutes in the hot oven. Remove to a cooling rack. When the cake is totally cold, loosen the apricot jam in a small saucepan by heating slowly, adding a little water if you need to. Paint this on to the cake with a pastry brush.

220g butter, plus some for buttering the tin
4 tablespoons strongly brewed tea
350g demerara sugar
4 medium free-range eggs
330g plain flour
110g buckwheat flour (or bran for a sweet malty feel)
2½ teaspoons baking powder
3 teaspoons ground cinnamon
½ teaspoon freshly grated nutmeg
8 small firm apples
3 handfuls of flaked almonds or walnuts
a handful of hazelnuts
5 tablespoons apricot jam and a little water to loosen it

Orange Shortbread

Makes 20 biscuits

These are delicious bundles of joy and it's an easy recipe too. Think of it like pastry and it becomes a familiar and manageable task: all you do is rub the dry ingredients with the butter, then bind it, as with pastry, with a little moisture. I usually make a batch of it, but freeze half, which leaves you with about ten biscuits per stint and a spare block to pull out for an emergency, when you haven't the energy to make a pudding.

Obviously with orange zest this is really good as a Christmas treat, but it does work all year round too. Don't feel constricted. Once you have mastered the shortbread method, substituting ingredients is very tempting. It rather depends on what's in the cupboard. I've done them plain, and then bound the mix together with rose water. This variety of scented ball is perfect if you are having an Eastern evening, to eat along with fresh mint teas. And then the other day I felt like nuts, so I made the mix with just cinnamon and fresh grated ginger, and pressed a walnut into the top of each biscuit. These were really fine too. I also make these in the shop when the mood grabs me. They go down well alongside a coffee, the perfect accompanying nugget.

Preheat the oven to 170°C/Gas 3 and line a large baking sheet with baking parchment. In a large mixing bowl, cut up the butter, and measure over this the self-raising flour, sugar, cinnamon, cloves and nutmeg. Now grate the zest off the orange and add this to the bowl too. Using the tips of your fingers, lightly work the dry ingredients into the butter. The lighter and quicker you do this the better. When you have a mixture that looks like breadcrumbs, juice the orange into the mixing bowl and, using a knife, work the dough together so that it forms a ball. You may need to add a little cold water too, if it's not coming completely together.

If you are saving half the mix, now is the time to divide it up. Place half in the freezer, tightly wrapped in clingfilm and a plastic bag, and start working on the remaining half. Take a small apricot-sized clump of the dough and roll it thoroughly in the palm of your hand. Slightly flatten the ball and press the top of it into a plate of flaked almonds. Repeat this process until no mix is left, and position the shortbread balls on the baking tray so that there is about 2cm between them, as they will expand and rise a little. Place in your preheated oven for 15 to 20 minutes or until the almonds are looking touched with gold. Remove the shortbreads to a cooling rack before serving for tea.

200g softened butter
350g self-raising flour
100g golden caster
    sugar
2 teaspoons ground
    cinnamon
1 teaspoon ground
    cloves
2 teaspoons freshly
    ground nutmeg
1 orange
50g flaked almonds

Baby Banana Cakes

Makes about 14 treats

These little cakes are wonderfully light and delicate in flavour. I made them for a special tea party I had planned in the shop. They looked absolutely delicious on a cake-stand, laden with a creamy syrup and with crushed walnuts clustered on top. Although they are perfect for a tea party, they'd be just as good for a little pudding, served with some ice cream full of vanilla seeds. I have brilliant vibrantly coloured silicone cases, which can be washed and reused. If you can't find these, paper ones will do.

What's great about this recipe, like a banana loaf, is that the more brown the bananas the better. Perfect for the 'mature' bananas lurking in your fruit bowl. Here's a tip: if you see that your bananas are on the turn, you can freeze them. Then at exactly the moment you feel like these little cakes you've got the main ingredient on standby. Once the bananas are defrosted, they'll slip out of their skins super easily.

65g softened butter
200g caster sugar
1 medium free-range
 egg
2 bananas
½ teaspoon ground
 cinnamon
1 teaspoon baking
 powder
60g plain flour
65g wholemeal flour
40ml water
2 tablespoons double
 cream
a generous handful of
 walnuts

Preheat the oven to 150°C/Gas 2 and either lay out silicone cases on a baking tray or line a muffin tray with paper cases. Cream the butter and 120g of the sugar together really well so that it is a light paste. In a separate bowl beat the egg, then fork in the bananas. Mash thoroughly so the mixture is well homogenised. Mix the creamed banana with the butter and sugar, and beat with a whisk so that it is thin and consistent. Finally measure in the cinnamon, baking powder and flours. Fold these dry ingredients swiftly into the wet batter, but don't over-mix. It needs to be only just combined. Divide the cake mix equally between the cake cases, leaving a little space for the cakes to rise. Place them in the oven for 15 to 20 minutes.

When the baby banana cakes are perfectly baked, remove them to a cooling rack while you make the creamy syrup. Place the remaining 80g of caster sugar in a small saucepan with the water. Heat on a low flame until fully dissolved and syrupy and reduced, and beginning to turn a little golden. Hold the handle and swirl the pan while adding the cream. Gently twirl until combined. Take the syrup off the heat and let it sit until it is beginning to coagulate. Meanwhile roughly chop the walnuts. Place the banana cakes on a cake-stand or serving plate and spoon the thick syrup over them, following quickly with a pinch of walnut pieces.

Doctor Helen's Mascarpone Mojito Cheesecake

For 4 or 6

This is a bestseller in the deli, and comes from my oldest friend Doctor Helen, who is a brilliant cook. When we were little we would spend whole weekends constructing Delia's mountainous pan-fried pizza. Noshing has always bonded us and I love her like a sister. This cheesecake is really easy to make, as it's quick to prepare and doesn't require the baking of a traditional cheesecake (which cuts out a lot of the time). The mascarpone makes a light snowy pillow that on a tired morning I wish I could dive into and sneak a nap. And it can have various flavourings – I've done it with lemons too. You will need a loose-bottomed cake tin about 18cm in diameter.

Crush the biscuits either in a plastic bag with a rolling pin, or, if you are clever enough to have a Magimix, by pulsing them in that. Melt the butter, either on a low heat in a small saucepan or for a minute in the microwave. Thoroughly mix into the biscuits with a spatula. Turn this mix out into the cake tin and press down with the spatula or even your hands. Chill briefly while you make the top layer.

Turn the mascarpone out into a big mixing bowl and whisk in the double cream so that it is smooth, shiny and creamy. Gradually whisk in the icing sugar. Grate in the zest of the limes, then squeeze in the juice of the limes one by one, whisking all the time. Taste in between so that you get the right tart balance (limes are of various sourness and tang – you may need all of them, or only 2, depending). Lastly, finely chop the mint and whisk it in. Spoon this amazing, speckled cream over the biscuit base and place in the fridge to chill. It is best the next day, but a couple of hours in the fridge will suffice.

300g ginger nut biscuits
75g butter
500g mascarpone
50ml double cream
110g icing sugar
4 limes
a handful of fresh mint

Honey Flapjacks

Makes 8 slices

These are just so easy, and another classic from my childhood kitchen. You can also razz them up with various additions. Beautiful Jasmine, who helps out on a Saturday in the shop, put me on to adding freshly grated ginger, which gives a really spicy edge. You can also add a few handfuls of raisins or chocolate chips. Below is the formula from which you can prosper. Flapjacks are pretty versatile. You can crumble them over yoghurt or ice cream too. My mum rang me the other day to tell me that if these go wrong, you can always break them up and add them to a jar of muesli.

120g butter
4 tablespoons flower honey (I use an upmarket Italian one when I'm feeling extravagant)
75g golden caster sugar
240g Quaker oats
½ teaspoon Maldon sea salt

Preheat the oven to 200°C/Gas 6 and line a small baking tray with greaseproof paper. In a large saucepan, melt the butter, honey and sugar so that it is just beginning to melt and amalgamate, bubbling in a fizzing way. Now, take the pan off the heat and add the oats and salt. Using a spatula, carefully work it all together so that the oats are entirely coated in the syrup. Turn out into the baking tray and press down with a bendy palette knife or the spatula. You want it to be pretty dense and tightly packed. Place the tray in the oven for 15 minutes, or until the edges are just beginning to turn golden and the main surface is slightly rising and throbbing. Remove from the oven and slice immediately with a large knife while it is still soft and malleable. If you leave the slicing until the flapjacks are cool, it is much harder to separate them. When the jacks are cold, slice again in the previously trodden tracks, and remove from the baking tray.

My Favourite Places to Eat, Drink & Shop

LONDON

Rosie's Deli Café
14e Market Row
London SW9 8LD
www.rosiesdelicafe.com
It's mine so of course I love it.

Andrew Edmunds
46 Lexington Street
London W1R 3LH
This is my favourite restaurant and is opposite Fernandez & Wells. It's discreet and always has lovely flowers decorating each table. Helen and I go for special treats. It makes you feel happy to be alive, as the food is so simple and beautifully thought out.

Asakusa
265 Eversholt Street
London NW1 1BA
Raf and I have taken each other here for treats. It's mind-blowing, and worth the wait. The sashimi is like melting butter, but the sea urchin was one step too far for us!

Barrafina
54 Frith Street
London W1D 4SL
www.barrafina.co.uk
This amazing tapas bar run by the Hart brothers is as close as you will get to tip-top authentic Spanish tapas. It's a real treat.

Black's
67 Dean Street
London W1D 4QH
If you know anyone who's a member, bribe them, whichever way you can, to take you here. It's wonderfully Dickensian and is perfect for a late-night squeeze. The food is brilliantly unfussy, and it's my favourite treat.

Brindisa
The Floral Hall
Borough Market
London SE1
www.brindisa.com
This amazing shop sells pretty much every Spanish delicacy. It's all top of the range, and I sell a few of their products in the deli.

Candy Cakes
36 Monmouth Street
London WC2H 9HB
www.candycakes.eu
The cakes in this little shop are ridiculous, so before you eat them, take a picture. They are encrusted and heavy with eye-popping decorations and icing, like cartoon cakes.

Centre Point Food Store
20–21 St Giles High Street
London WC2H 8LN
www.cpfs.co.uk
This shop has everything you could wish for from an Asian vendor. Even funky-looking aged eggs. I've still to pluck up the courage to eat them.

Como y Punto
94–5 Granville Arcade
Brixton Market
London SW9 8PS
For a spicy egg breakfast and really lovely service.

Dombey's Wholesale Butchers
19 Market Row
London SW9 8LB
This lot sell loads of great meat, and even make their own delicious sausages. Really sunny service.

Don Zoko
19 Kingly Street
London W1B 5PY
One of my best ever sushi experiences.

Duke of Cambridge
30 St Peter's Street
London N1 8JT
www.sloeberry.co.uk/duke.html
This organic pub can be pretty expensive, but Alice and I sometimes go there for a Sunday afternoon meltdown. They do a good bloody Mary, and it's a good hangout spot.

Esme's Organics
16 Market Row
London SW9 8LB
Esme is a gem. She's truly kind and will often treat me with little tinctures and oils when I'm looking blue. She sells blooming organic vegetables and her lettuces are amazing.

Fernandez & Wells
43 Lexington Street
London W1F 9AL
www.fernandezandwells.com/lexington
This is the best place to go and share a cheese or charcuterie board, washed down with amazing wines. You can hang out outside too, so there's lots of street watching to be had.

Franco Manca
4 Market Row
London SW9 8LD
Giuseppe and his crew make sourdough pizza and this place is always bursting at the seams with people clamouring for these simple and wild ingredients. The wine and homemade lemonade are good to wash down these fabulous thin tasty pizzas.

Funchal Bakery
141–3 Stockwell Road
London SW9 9TN
This place does a day café with an attaching deli, where you can get some of the best coffee in London. And then next door is the extraordinarily weird and wonderful restaurant where Raf once had a many-meated sandwich swimming in special sauce. I love the family feel.

Ganapati
38 Holly Grove
London SE15 5DF
www.ganapatirestaurant.com
This lovely little restaurant does wicked south Indian dosas and a moreish beetroot curry. It makes me feel like I'm back in Gokana, surrounded by dosas and pickle.

Lina Stores Ltd
18 Brewer Street
London W1F 0SH
This really old-fashioned continental deli in the heart of Soho has everything, including beautiful tiling on the façade. And they make their own ravioli on marble slabs.

M. Moen & Sons
24 The Pavement
London SW4 0JA
They make an awesome pork pie.

Mr Lawrence
389 Brockley Road
London SE4 2PH
This bar has an amazing selection of wines and delicious beers, so is an ideal stop-off point on a Sunday bike ride. It feels more in the south of France than south London here.

O Talho
13 Atlantic Road
London SW9 8HX
This Portuguese-run deli is my absolute favourite on my way home. Open late, and with wonderful and cheery staff, this shop sells every Mediterranean biscuit, sauce and pasta you'll ever want. And wonderful vegetables and delicious Brazilian beef.

Que Viet
104 Kingsland Road
London E2 8DP

I went to this restaurant for my friend Jason the amazing photographer's birthday dinner one time. The rare beef salad was ridiculously good, with finely sliced red onions.

Ran Restaurant
58–9 Great Marlborough Street
London W1F 7JY
www.ranrestaurant.com

Awesome Korean barbecues and wonderful and funny staff. The house salad is particularly good.

The Rock and Sole Plaice
47 Endell Street
London WC2H 9AJ
www.rockandsoleplaice.co.uk

How many puns can you have in a name? I ate rock with chips and coleslaw here, and my good friend Emma Fox ate really delicate skate with mushy peas. The batter in this 'plaice' is particularly crispy and you can eat outside on the street when it's hot.

Ryo Japanese Noodle & Sushi Bar
84 Brewer Street
London W1F 9UB

Emma Fox also took me here, and it's now a regular stop-off as it's cheap and excellent. They do great kimchi, and eels, which are two of my favourites.

Sevilla Mia
22 Hanway Street
London W1P 4DD

To get downstairs to Sevilla, you have to squeeze through a secret-looking and therefore enticing doorway. Downstairs you'll find beer and fellow dive-bar lovers. It's our place, Alice and me, as we often pop in, before and after a gig.

Smiles Thai Café
106 Foxberry Road
London SE4 2SH

This is a favourite joint for Jamie and Raf and the third part of their unholy trinity, Toby. It's cleansing and spicy and feels nothing like a regular stodgy takeout. The atmosphere is really homely, almost like you are in their front room, and you wouldn't expect it on this residential street either.

Tava
17 Stoke Newington Road
London N16 8BH

This is a great new find. The pide are excellent, coming straight out of a wood-burning stove, and the staff gentle and kind. We stopped off here and hoofed down their delights on a Sunday drive. I was ecstatic.

Trisha's New Evaristo Club
57 Greek Street
London W1D 3DX
This is the best place ever. It's how you imagine Soho was in the 1970s. There's always somewhere to sit, and on occasion good live music. Trisha is wonderfully welcoming, and you'll want to go back night after night once you've felt the addictive dive vibe.

The Troubadour
263–7 Old Brompton Road
London SW5 9JA
www.troubadour.co.uk
Laura Huston and I used to go for long mornings here with great eggs Benedict, when I had a broken foot (in five places!). We were inseparable at the time and this was our place.

Unpackaged
42 Amwell Street
London EC1R 1XT
www.beunpackaged.com
This innovative shop, all about bringing your own packing and refilling rather than wasting the world, is run by the lovely Cath, who I met at a Greco-Roman rave. She's bold and is doing something really cool here. The shop's pretty beautiful too.

BARCELONA

Cal Pep
Placa de les Olles 8
Barcelona 08003
www.calpep.com
This is the best tapas ever, and the chefs are really funny too. Helen and I had a really spoiling meal here. Our expressive culinary squeals were hilarious to these chefs, which meant they kept on plying us with more and more little plates of joy.

Oviso
Placa Trippy
Carrer d'Arai 5
Barcelona 08002
A great place for a beer and a hangout. I'm told you can pick up hot boys there too.

CAMBRIDGE

Clowns
54 King Street
Cambridge CB1 1LN
Clowns is a cosy family business, where coffee and sickly cakes overflow, a stream of Italian daughters serve and students prop up every table. It was better when they could freely smoke in true student style, but it's still brilliant. As children, my brother Olly and I got to stop off there at the end of shopping trips. Mine was always a tiramisù.

EDINBURGH

Harvey Nichols 4th Floor Brasserie
30–4 St Andrews Square
Edinburgh EH2 2AD
www.harveynichols.com
This was one of my favourite and very guilty pleasures at university. The view from the top-floor restaurant would take anyone's breath away, because Edinburgh is such an awe-inspiring and soaring city of spires. It's the place to go for tea and be waited on and spoilt.

Nile Valley
6 Chapel Street
Edinburgh EH8 9AY
This is a Sudanese restaurant, which makes spicy flatbread sandwiches. It's great, and it was always Thomas Punch's favourite lunch.

Valvona & Crolla
19 Elm Row (just off Leith Walk)
Edinburgh EH7 4AA
This immense deli, stacked to the ceilings, is an inspiration. When we had forgotten we were students, we'd go to Valvona on our lunch break and order outrageously decadent ciabattas filled with hams and antipasti.

FLORENCE

Art Bar
Antico Caffe del Moro
Via del Moro 4r
Florence 50123
They do delicious cocktails, so my travelling History of Art partner Tash and I were very happy scouting for boys here.

Capocaccia
Lungarno Corsini 12–14
Florence 50123
Amazing eggs Benedict, great free canapés and the place where I discovered massive caperberries on stalks. We whiled away many a day in Capocaccia, looking over the Arno, and I thought myself very grown-up.

ISLE OF WIGHT

The Spyglass Inn
Esplanade
Ventnor
Isle of Wight PO38 1JX
www.thespyglass.com
I spent one of the nicest days in the history of man outside this funny old pub. We ate ploughman's with the Draytones, and laughed away the afternoon. It's what the sea front is all about. They have rooms to stay in too.

NEW YORK

Florent
69 Gansevoort Street
New York NY 10014
This diner is super cool and just how you might imagine New York, full of chrome with efficient all-American waiters. I had a delicious breakfast here with my friend Caspar, and heard all about the delights of living in this wicked city where everything makes you smile.

The Gershwin Hotel
7 East 27th Street
New York NY 10016
www.gershwinhotel.com
The Gershwin feels really cranky and has massive paintings everywhere, and really makes you feel like you are in a film.

Ottomanelli & Sons
285 Bleecker Street
New York NY 10014
When I was in New York in 2006, I sniffed this deli each time I passed through Bleecker Street on my way to meet Thomas Punch and Emily London. The piles of meat and olives are so particularly New York; I fell in love with it. It's a feast not only on the eyes but the tastebuds too.

PARIS

Le Marché des Enfants Rouge
39 Rue de Bretagne
3rd Arrondisement
Paris
I spent a few lovely days here with Dani. There's Japanese, Italian, Moroccan, French and loads of other stuff, and a variety of cafés and stalls. But it's small and perfectly formed too, so it won't overwhelm you. I came away feeling much more chic.

ACKNOWLEDGEMENTS

To Nigel Slater, my absolute food hero.

To Jenny McVeigh for her total faith in me.

To Fourth Estate for all of their unerring work and especially to Louise Haines for taking a chance on me.

To my parents for their continual and constant support and my super gran.

To all my girlfriends Helen, Alice, Zahra and Zezi for their tear mopping, tasting and tolerance and Dani and Mara for their lady wisdom.

To all of my customers at Rosie's, who returned even when I'd curdled the milk and burnt the bread.

To Tom and Olly, my Asian inspirations and most loyal boys.

To kind Stav, for stepping into my shoes and taking the helm of Rosie's when I was ill.

To Guy and Jamie, who each independently make me see the silly in myself.

To Rose, Jaz, Peach and all those who've dipped their hands in the deli washing-up bowl.

INDEX